RIVER OF PROMISE, RIVER OF PERIL

DEVELOPMENT OF WESTERN RESOURCES

The Development of Western Resources is an interdisciplinary series focusing on the use and misuse of resources in the American West. Written for a broad readership of humanists, social scientists, and resource specialists, the books in this series emphasize both historical and contemporary perspectives as they explore the interplay between resource exploitation and economic, social, and political experiences.

John G. Clark, University of Kansas, Founding Editor
Hal K. Rothman, University of Nevada, Las Vegas, Series Editor

RIVER OF PROMISE, RIVER OF PERIL

The Politics of Managing the Missouri River

John E. Thorson

 University Press of Kansas

To my grandfather, John Sterling Crane,
and my daughter, Kyrstin Bergen Thorson.

Our river flows from the headwaters to the sea.

Published by the University Press of Kansas (Lawrence, Kansas 66049), which was organized by the Kansas Board of Regents and is operated and funded by Emporia State University, Fort Hays State University, Kansas State University, Pittsburg State University, the University of Kansas, and Wichita State University

Library of Congress Cataloging-in-Publication Data

Thorson, John E.
    River of promise, river of peril : the politics of managing the
Missouri River / John E. Thorson.
        p.   cm. —(Development of western resources)
    Includes bibliographical references and index.
    ISBN 0-7006-0648-3 (alk. paper)
        1. Water-supply—Political aspects—Missouri River Watershed.
    2. Missouri River Watershed—Water rights.   3. Federal-state
    controversies—United States.   I. Title.   II. Series.
    HD1695.M45T49   1994
    333.91'009788—dc20   94-36065

British Library Cataloguing in Publication Data is available.

Printed in the United States of America

10 9 8 7 6 5 4 3 2 1

"Of Time and Rivers Flowing"
(The Praetorius Hymn,
"Lo, A Rose is Blooming")

Of time and rivers flowing, the seasons make the song.
And we who live beside her, still try to sing along
Of rivers, fish, and men.
The season still a'coming, when she'll run clear again.

So many homeless sailors, so many winds that blow.
I asked the half-blind scholar, which way the currents flow.
So cast your net below,
And the gods of the moving waters, will tell us all they know.

The circles of the planets, the circle of the moon.
The circles of the atom, all play a marching tune.
And we who would join in,
Will keep the waters flowing, now let us all begin.

—Pete Seeger

CONTENTS

TABLES AND ILLUSTRATIONS

Photographs

FOREWORD

When Thomas Jefferson wrote in the Declaration of Independence that "all men are created equal" and "that they are endowed by their creator with certain inalienable rights," he obviously was not talking about water—or was he? Certainly, in delineating some of the fundamental rights, Jefferson tried to pick the most important ones: "life, liberty and the pursuit of happiness." But it is difficult to escape the fact that water is part of all that. Without water, there is no life, liberty is a hollow promise, and happiness is a forgotten dream. Water—like food, energy for shelter, land, and air—is basic to human existence.

Even though most Americans forget the next line in the Declaration of Independence, it is extremely important in American government philosophy: "and to secure these rights, governments are instituted among men." Unfortunately, when it comes to water, securing the rights of everyone gets to be a very difficult undertaking. That is, in part, why water governance is such a mess. But in addition, there are too many jurisdictions with too many partial, conflicting authorities. Sundry public agencies at all levels impose fragmented policies over fragmented concerns within the same water basin. State contends with state. A multitude of federal agencies issue conflicting policies and rules. State, tribal governments, city, and county all struggle to serve their various constituencies. Flood control, energy, irrigation, recreation, navigation, fish and wildlife, industrial, rural, and municipal users all vie for water resources.

If only all the stakeholders could sit down together and listen to each other. If only they could work together for common good, *with the authority to act!* That is the plea of this brilliant, scholarly, comprehensive work about the Missouri River by John Thorson. To the writer's credit, he has not righteously blamed others. He knows how complex the whole matter is. And yet, he has identified the one practical, possible solution: basin governance, which holds the best promise for representative democracy to secure rights in the marvelous yet often miserable Missouri River basin.

To be sure, the whole middle section of America inherits great benefits from the waters of the Missouri. The ecology of rugged scenic wonder combined with fertile food factories for the world's burgeoning population bring great blessings. These blessings all resulted from ancient glacial movement and melting. This wondrous region knows, however, the horror of Missouri water on rampages of destruction of homes as well as human and natural developments.

Governing the threat and the promise of the Missouri is a complex challenge. And sorting out environmentally sound ways to advance long-range human benefits is extremely difficult, even with the best of governance structures. Everyone who has worked in the arena has suffered failure, frustration, and anger. Hope lies in a basin structure that hears all stakeholders, finds consensus, and has the authority to act.

American democracy is based on the belief that all that is good for human beings is compatible with what is good for other human beings. And we believe that this compatibility is discoverable and achievable through a government of the people, by the people, and for the people.

Even for the Missouri River region, basinwide representative governance can succeed. John Thorson's knowledge of history is comprehensive and yet sensitive. His awareness of all of the facets of controversy is unquestionable. That is why this work advances with such strength the argument for basin governance. We must somehow soon adopt it.

George A. Sinner
Vice-President, American Crystal Sugar
Governor of North Dakota, 1985–1993

ACKNOWLEDGMENTS

The writing of this book has been a collaborative process involving many colleagues and extending many years. An earlier version of the manuscript was prepared as a dissertation for the School of Public Administration, University of Southern California. I appreciate the insight and assistance of Jeff Chapman, Kim Nelson, Chester Newland, and Alex Cloner, all of whom served on my guidance committee. The Northern Lights Institute, Montana Department of Natural Resources (DNRC), Ford Foundation, and Northwest Area Foundation supported my interest in the Missouri River. My special thanks to Don Snow and Richard Opper, former executive directors of the Northern Lights Institute; Susan Hope Higgins, Mark O'Keefe and Gerald Mueller, who were associated with Northern Lights' Missouri River Management Project; Kate McIvor, who as a paralegal in my law office assisted in early research; Melissa Rigg, who completed an extensive and invaluable edit of the manuscript; Leslee Unser, who prepared many of the graphics; Craig Sharpe, who provided photographs; and Cynthia Miller and others of the staff at the University Press of Kansas. My thanks also to Larry Fasbender, former director of DNRC, Gary Fritz, administrator of DNRC's Water Resources Division, and Richard Moy, chief of DNRC's Water Management Bureau, for the opportunities to learn more about the Missouri.

The influence of certain individuals, though embodied in this book, is transcendent. I am particularly indebted to Sarah Bates, Susan Cottingham, Sally Fairfax, John Ferrell, Dan Kemmis, Adolph Koven, Deborah Schmidt, Dan Sprague, Dan Tarlock, Lorene Mai Thorson, Gary Weatherford, and Charles Wilkinson. They, and friends like them, are the true bounty of living in the West.

INTRODUCTION

In 1833, a young Swiss artist by the name of Karl Bodmer painted portraits of the Missouri River. Accompanying Prince Maximilian Alexander Philipp, a German aristocrat, on an ambitious two-year expedition from St. Louis to the upper reaches of the Missouri, Bodmer was among the first painters to capture the native, raw qualities of the Missouri River and its inhabitants. Bodmer's canvases, many of which are now in St. Louis's Joslin Museum, depict a vast, incomprehensible frontier; proud, vital, colorful Indian tribes; abundant and varied wildlife; and the ever-present mighty Missouri.

Even in the 1830s, the frontier was vanishing. Although not then readily apparent, the region was being domesticated. Buffalo and small animals valuable for fur were already under stress. Many native communities had been beset by smallpox, the scourge of white society. Trading patterns between whites and Indians were well-established, and with the arrival of the first steamboats on the river, the wild Missouri was becoming tamed by American commerce. The Missouri promised to be America's original highway west.

A later artist captured a very different portrait of the Missouri River. In 1936, the cover of the inaugural issue of *Life* magazine presented an austere black and white photograph by Margaret Bourke-White of the just-completed, Art Deco-style Fort Peck Dam in northeastern Montana. Fort Peck was the first of six similar massive structures to be built on the Missouri River under the auspices of the federal government. No longer was interest in the Missouri River limited to early explorers and navigators, mountain men, or the quiet, sensitive impressionists who attempted to convey, in a detached way, the delicate relationships of native people in a wild, immense land. The Missouri had become the domain of engineers, lawyers, and politicians who sought actively to manipulate the land and its tribal peoples for jobs, regional development, and economic gain. Their efforts produced a fundamentally altered basin landscape.

These individuals were motivated by the Progressive Conservation Movement, and their bold vision was of unprecedented, comprehensive river basin development. Their concepts were embodied in the Pick-Sloan Plan (part of the federal Flood Control Act of 1944), named after their mentors, Col. Lewis Pick of the U.S. Army Corps of Engineers and

William Glenn Sloan of the Bureau of Reclamation. Wielding engineering studies, committee reports, laws, project proposals, and earth-moving equipment, they applied themselves to the entire Missouri River watershed, which encompasses portions of ten states.

The Pick-Sloan program has left an impressive and lasting body of work on the Missouri: six main stem and twenty-two tributary dams; the storage of 74 million acre-feet of water (enough for the annual needs of 74 million urban families), the dredging of hundreds of miles of navigation channel, and forty-one hydroelectric plants, with a maximum capacity of 2.8 million kilowatts, installed in the main stem and tributary dams. The work has cost over $1.2 billion.

Comprehensive river basin development—especially the Pick-Sloan Plan and the resulting Missouri River dams—was an optimistic, activist, and robust ideal. The policy promised jobs, regional development, and, in conjunction with similar projects elsewhere in the country, national recovery. Comprehensive river basin development had the creditable but regrettably unachieved goal of developing and managing a river basin as an integrated system.

The Pick-Sloan Plan for Missouri River development has not worn well with time. In February 1988, the U.S. Supreme Court decided the case of ETSI *Pipeline Project v. Missouri*,[1] a suit that had first been brought in federal district court six years earlier.[2] The essence of the case was whether the State of South Dakota could sell Missouri River water stored behind Oahe Reservoir to the Energy Transportation Systems, Inc. (ETSI) consortium to transport coal by slurry in a pipeline from eastern Wyoming to the Gulf States. The specific matter before the Supreme Court, however, was the fine legal point of which federal agency, the Bureau of Reclamation or the U.S. Army Corps of Engineers, had the authority to allow South Dakota to divert water from the federal reservoir (the bureau, rather than the corps, had approved the permit for the diversion). The Supreme Court's decision, which upheld the authority of the Corps of Engineers, did very little to address the underlying struggle among the governments of the Missouri River basin: how to allocate the benefits of the Missouri River and its tributaries under the Pick-Sloan Plan.

Within a week of the Court's decision, a confident editorial appeared in a lower basin newspaper to the effect that "range wars over water use and water rights are part of American history, and not always were they settled fairly. But a solution for the Missouri River fuss, today's version of a range war, emerged from the courts as it should have—even-handed and sensible."[3]

Another lower basin newspaper, the *Omaha World Herald*, was more circumspect in its commentary. With a headline reading "One River Fight Won, but Others Lie Ahead," the editor observed that it was "good to have a victory in the pipeline case" and that "the successful outcome of the slurry pipeline suit should encourage Nebraskans and people in other downstream states to take the actions that may occasionally be necessary to prevent upstream interests from taking unfair advantage."[4]

The *Omaha World Herald*'s caution was well-founded. By fall 1989, the basin states were again in open conflict. Continuing drought in the basin had resulted in record low-water levels in the main stem reservoirs in Montana, North Dakota, and South Dakota. As the water receded several miles from marinas and vacation homes, upper basin citizens and government officials demanded changes by the Corps of Engineers (the operator of the dams) to reduce outflows from the reservoirs. Lower basin states, lower Mississippi River basin states, and the navigation industry resisted these proposals to restrict flows. The intervention of North Dakota's powerful U.S. senator, Quentin Burdick, chairman of the Senate Environment and Public Works Committee (which has jurisdiction over the public works programs of the corps), resulted in the corps' commitment to review the master manual, the operating plan for the main stem dams and reservoirs. Yet it was unclear how much the corps could change without consensus among all the states and economic interests, an environmental impact statement, or congressional action.

During spring 1990, tensions were exacerbated by continuing drought in the basin. The states of South Dakota, North Dakota, and Montana sued in federal court to prevent the corps "from discharging a greater volume of water from the Oahe Reservoir than that flowing into the reservoir, with the intent that the existing pool levels be maintained, until the first day of June, 1990."[5] The states brought the suit to protect the spawning of northern pike, walleye, smelt, spot-tailed shiner, and other game fish in the shallow waters of Oahe and other reservoirs. Although a federal district judge in North Dakota granted the states' request, his preliminary injunction was vacated by the Eighth Circuit Court of Appeals.[6]

Litigation was also brought in a Montana federal district court by South Dakota, North Dakota, and Montana against the Army Corps of Engineers. This suit, *South Dakota v. Bornhoft*,[7] alleged that the corps had improperly assigned downstream uses of Missouri River reservoir water higher priority than recreation and fish and wildlife uses in upstream states. The litigation was dismissed in February 1993.

This book is about federalism in the management of rivers, about giving needed attention to both the vertical and horizontal aspects of our federalist system (including the involvement of tribal governments), and about building lasting regional water management institutions in the Missouri River basin. The failure to build viable river management institutions is the principal shortcoming of the Pick-Sloan Plan, for the absence of working intergovernmental institutions fuels the ongoing strife among the ten states, twenty-five tribes, and numerous federal agencies directly concerned in the basin. Effective basinwide intergovernmental water management institutions are necessary before past disagreements can be set aside and new policies developed for the use and protection of the Missouri River and its tributaries.

The legacy of tension and conflict in the Missouri River basin reveals several important weaknesses in the American federal system. First, the federal government has increasingly dominated the Missouri River over the last fifty years. This trend should not surprise those who have studied the imbalance of federal-state relations in many other public sectors (the vertical aspect of federalism), but the fact remains that the federal government nationalized the Missouri River, and this nationalization has resulted in deficient policies and widespread resentment.

Second, the Constitution, the basis for the American governmental system, gives insufficient attention to the horizontal aspect of federalism—that is, the relationships among the governments of a region that share a transboundary natural resource such as water. The Constitution provides few opportunities for resolving natural resource conflicts between states or within regions, and it provides even fewer formal avenues for intergovernment cooperation in the management of shared natural resources—particularly rivers. Usually, the constitutional choice is between a dominant federal or state role. The Constitution provides little explicit guidance for structuring intergovernmental solutions to regional natural resource problems.

The American federal system has developed three traditional methods of resolving natural resource conflicts between states or within regions. The most frequent method of conflict resolution, as demonstrated by the ETSI case, has been litigation. These disputes involve states and the federal government and have therefore been heard and decided by the U.S. Supreme Court under its constitutional grant of original jurisdiction. When they involve the regional allocation of water, the legal proceedings are known as "equitable apportionments." The interstate disputes between Kansas and Colorado,[8] New Jersey and New York,[9] Nebraska and Wyoming,[10] New Mexico and Colorado,[11] and other states have yielded legal principles (actually, a body of federal common law) that the Supreme Court applies, sometimes reluctantly.

Equitable apportionments and related legal actions may remain pending before the Supreme Court and its appointed special masters for years, and the financial cost is always significant. What often goes unnoticed in these proceedings is the hidden cost to mutual trust and long-term relationships among the states. Indian tribes, who often have potentially large senior claims on these waters, are rarely parties to these proceedings because their governmental immunity prevents them from being sued involuntarily. Although the final decrees in these cases may apportion a quantity of water among the governments, the decrees do not indicate how the river system can be managed in an economically productive and environmentally responsible manner.

Congressional legislation offers another avenue to resolve intergovernmental natural resource conflicts. In interstate disputes over water, this method, known as a congressional apportionment, has rarely been used: once to apportion water among the states of the Colorado River basin[12] and implicitly in disputes over water quality in the Great Lakes.[13] Although legislation could provide comprehensive solutions, congressmen believe these disputes are best left to local negotiation. Even when a dispute is not susceptible to local resolution, a congressional solution may be elusive, for a senator or representative from even one reluctant state can effectively scuttle the process.

The interstate compact is the third method for resolving interjurisdictional resource conflicts. Although used in colonial times for boundary adjustments and authorized by the U.S. Constitution,[14] the first water quantification compact, which involved the Colorado River, was negotiated in 1921. Since the approval of the initial compact by Congress in 1929,[15] over twenty other water compacts have been negotiated throughout the country; six of these have involved waters within the Missouri River basin.

Litigation, congressional apportionment, and compacting have had some success, but their limits have been even more pronounced. These traditional approaches, especially litigation and congressional solutions, often only "paper over" the dispute temporarily; the underlying causes of the conflict persist and later manifest themselves in other situations. Lawsuits and federal legislation may dictate a binding decision, but they do little to improve the actual working relationships among the states on such issues as water. Many interstate compacts, particularly those that only quantify the water of an interstate stream, do not provide for ongoing shared water management. They fail to provide the opportunities for cooperation between states that would reduce deep-seated tensions over water and other issues. All three methods generally result in specific "point-in-time" answers to a dynamic, complex intergovernmental relationship. The solution often falters as the dynamics of the relationship change, and the rigidity of the solution can impede creative solutions to new problems.

The history of Missouri River development illustrates one special weakness in American federalism. Our federal system has long been understood as a matrix of national, state, and local governments. There is, however, a fourth dimension to American federalism: the Indian tribes.

In a long line of cases dating as far back as the last century, the U.S. Supreme Court has recognized the concept of Indian sovereignty.[16] This constitutional development is neither well-understood nor popularly accepted (consider, for example, the lack of tribal representation on the U.S. Advisory Commission on Intergovernmental Relations).

Although Congress and the Supreme Court have recognized the existence of Indian reserved water rights[17] and have provided tribes with funds and authority to manage their water resources,[18] tribes have had few opportunities to participate with states and federal agencies in the management of river systems. Water allocation compacts typically have been negotiated without the participation of Indian tribes and without reference to their water rights. No tribes, for example, were party to the Colorado River Compact, and negotiations conducted in 1986 among the representatives of the ten Missouri River basin states, which might have yielded a compact or some other form of agreement, proceeded without the participation of the Indian tribes or federal agencies.[19]

The history of Missouri River development illustrates how little guidance our Constitution offers states, tribes, and federal agencies to develop cooperative, economically sound, and environmentally responsible policies for our shared waterways. The Constitution does vest certain enumerated powers in the national government, including the potentially unlimited power to regulate interstate commerce and to regulate navigable waterways. The remaining powers are retained by the states or by the people, and very little is indicated about how states, tribes, and the federal government can structure their relationships to achieve proactive, progressive policies for the management of major rivers and other shared resources. The Constitution's compact clause is the only formally specified constitutional means by which these intergovernmental relationships might be structured, and this clause has not been used to involve tribal governments. Nonetheless, new patterns for cooperative intergovernmental management of shared natural resources have developed elsewhere in the United States. The successes and shortcomings of some of these experiments—the Great Lakes Charter, the Northwest Power Planning Council, several intergovernmental agreements involving tribes, and an effort to create a broadly based Missouri River Assembly—are explored in this book.

The engineers, lawyers, and politicians of the Pick-Sloan Plan left us with much less than they promised. Although their thinking was broad, their product represented a narrow and transient set of values. Ultimately, their approach was too arrogant and insensitive, and their plan fundamentally altered the river. The politicians and engineers of Missouri River development knew how to build dams, but they knew very little about ecology, cultural diversity, or federalism. They failed to secure the promises and expectations raised by their plan, and the resulting inequities to Indian tribes and many states are readily apparent.

Although the Missouri River has been basically changed, it is not too late to redeem the promise of the Missouri River Pick-Sloan Plan. Sound river basin development and management can still enhance people's lives. Effective water management institutions can be developed in the Missouri River basin and dams and reservoirs, now emblems of destruction and dashed expectations, can again reflect optimism, cooperation, and fairness.

CHAPTER ONE

The Original Highway West

One can begin a journey on the Missouri River at either the river's head-waters in southwestern Montana or its mouth near St. Louis. If you start at Three Forks, Montana, you see the Gallatin, Madison, and Jefferson rivers run down from the high Rockies, converge, and begin America's longest river. Here, in a sparsely settled cold valley, the river performs its fundamental work: draining water from adjoining lands and moving rock and soil. You are overcome with a strong urge to see where the river goes.

If you start at the mouth of the river, first visit the nearby Gateway Expansion Arch, stand abreast of a life-sized, westward-facing Thomas Jefferson, and share his dreams of exploration. Then take the elevator to the top of the arch, preferably at dusk. Finally, journey a few miles north to the actual mouth of the Missouri and see the river as the first Europeans did—as a highway of discovery, migration, and commerce. Here you feel a strong urge to follow the river to its source.

Between the headwaters and the mouth of the river, the Missouri flows 2,540 miles through a basin encompassing a 530,000-square-mile area, roughly one-fifth of the continental United States. All of Nebraska is located within the basin, along with portions of nine other states (Montana, Wyoming, North Dakota, South Dakota, Minnesota, Iowa, Colorado, Kansas, and Missouri) and the reservations of twenty-five Indian tribes. The river itself flows through seven states;[1] its tributaries drain another three.[2] Small portions of southeastern Alberta and south-western Saskatchewan also form part of the basin (see Map 1.1).

The Missouri River basin is quite diverse, with land-use patterns ranging from nearly abandoned counties to major cities. The longest straight-line distance across the basin is 1,500 miles, about half the distance across the United States. The basin's elevation extends from 14,000-foot peaks at its northwestern boundary to about 400 feet where the river joins the Mississippi. The predominant features are the plains that extend nearly 800 miles from the Canadian boundary to the southern reaches of the basin and from the Rocky Mountains to the Mississippi River. In his classic study of this region, Walter Prescott Webb identified three distinguishing characteristics of the plains: "a comparatively level surface of great extent;" "a treeless land;" and "a region where

Three Forks, Montana, showing confluence of Gallatin and Madison Rivers. (Photo by Craig Sharpe)

rainfall is insufficient for the ordinary intensive agriculture common to lands of a humid climate."[3]

The mountain ranges of the basin, including the Rocky Mountains in western Montana, the Big Horn Mountains in Wyoming, the Sand Hills of northwestern Nebraska, the Black Hills of southwestern South Dakota, and the Ozarks of southern Missouri, while dramatic, are only interruptions of this "plain-ness." So are the 27 million forested acres of the basin (8 percent) that make up portions of the Rockies, the Black Hills, and the Ozarks and line waterways.

GEOLOGIC PROFILE OF THE BASIN

The Missouri River, as we know it today, is a rather recent natural formation dating from 25,000 years ago.[4] But the origins of the Missouri River basin can be traced back 600 million years, when repeatedly advancing and retreating seas left deposits of clay stones and shales, sandstones, limestones, and dolemites out of which the basin was to be formed. About 70 million years ago, the seas withdrew for the last time. During the subsequent Cenozoic era, plant and animal life flourished; the re-

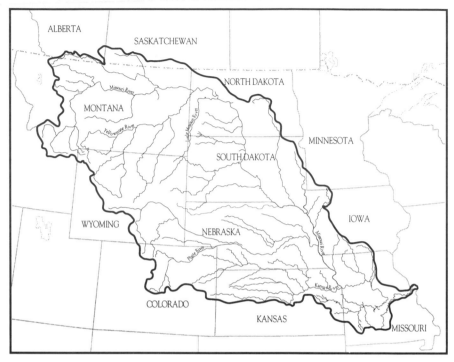

Map 1.1. Missouri River Basin. (*Source*: Northern Lights Institute)

mains of this extensive ecological system now form the beds of soft lignite coal in eastern Montana and western North and South Dakota, as well as the subbituminous coal beneath the plains of Montana and Wyoming.

During the next distinct geological period, the Pleistocene epoch, which dates from 2 to 3 million years ago, there were four distinct periods of glaciation in the upper basin. As these glaciers retreated, the water bodies now known as the Missouri, Little Missouri, and Yellowstone followed in their course and ran separately into Hudson Bay. The last of these glaciers, known as the Wisconsin, provided an east-by-southeast barrier for the main stream of the Missouri. Once the glacier began its retreat about 25,000 years ago, the altered course of the Missouri remained, and the Yellowstone and the Little Missouri became its tributaries. With the warming of the region, the Great Plains became progressively drier and took on the appearance and life forms that were there when humans first ventured into the region.

Although the Missouri River basin should be considered a distinct watershed, the area's topography varies greatly. The President's Water

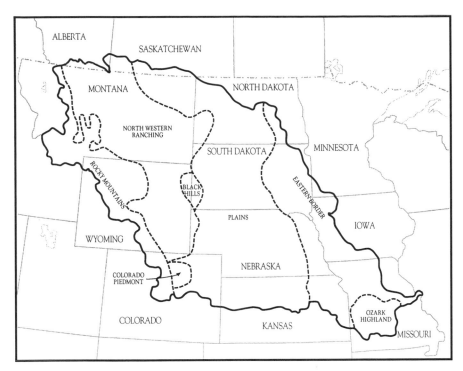

Map 1.2. Subregions of the Missouri River Basin. (*Source*: President's Water Resources Policy Commission, *Ten Rivers in America's Future* [Washington, D.C.: Government Printing Office, 1950])

Resources Policy Commission, in *Ten Rivers in America's Future* (1950), identified six rather distinct regions within the basin: the Rocky Mountains, the Colorado Piedmont area, the Northwestern Ranching section, the Plains, the Eastern Border, and the Ozark Highland region (see Map 1.2).

The Rocky Mountain region of the Missouri River basin encompasses the mountainous portions of western Montana, Wyoming, and Colorado. The area can generally be described as high elevation, rocky peaks, forest, high mountain "parks," as well as large grassland areas. Much of this region is federally owned as national parks (including portions of Yellowstone), national forests, and Bureau of Land Management grazing lands. The region is also transversed by numerous mountain streams.

The region has seen extensive hard rock mining in its history; in the last few years, there has been a moderate resurgence of mining for precious metals. The forests have supported a modest timber industry, but the industry is waning with declining market prices, changes in technology, and the gradual shift of the industry to the southeast. The grassland meadows have continued to support cattle and sheep, and the numerous high mountain streams provide water for ranch and farm operations. The region's natural beauty makes recreation of growing importance for the economy.

The Colorado Piedmont section, at the eastern base of the Colorado Rockies, is an area of contrast between the traditional agricultural economy of the greater Fort Collins area and the modern industry of the Denver metropolis. In 1950, the President's Water Resources Policy Commission predicted that "the great problem for the future of the Piedmont Area is the insufficient water supply."[5] And indeed, one of the major policy issues in the Denver metropolitan area is the availability of water. Water flowing eastward from the Rocky Mountains is captured in an array of small reservoirs. Many of Denver's suburbs have sought to acquire agricultural water rights for eventual transfer to municipal and industrial purposes.

Surprisingly, much of the Colorado Piedmont area sees its water future tied more closely to the headwaters of the Colorado than to the Missouri. The Colorado Big Thompson project diverts water from the Colorado River to the eastern slope. Denver acquires part of its water from the Frazer River tributary of the Colorado River through the Moffat Tunnel. The controversial Two Forks Dam proposal, finally killed in the late 1980s by the U.S. Environmental Protection Agency, would have augmented Denver's water supplies by diverting even more water from Colorado's west slope.

The third distinct region within the Missouri River basin is the Northwestern Ranching region, which includes the plains of eastern Wyoming and central and southeastern Montana. Here, water, soil conditions, and climate have combined to produce an agricultural economy based on mixed dryland grain farming and cattle ranching. Only a minority of these farms are irrigated, and their principle agricultural products are hay for livestock and small grains, especially wheat. Fruits and vegetables are not profitable because of climatic conditions and transportation costs. Under the right economic conditions, much of this land could be cultivated with irrigation. Indeed, much of the land to have been irrigated under the Pick-Sloan Plan for Missouri River development (see Chapter 3) would have been in this region. During the 1970s, the area gained prominence because of its energy resources. Oil resources were significantly developed near Casper and Cody, Wyoming, and Shelby, Montana, and the coal fields of northern Wyoming and southeastern Montana were also mined.

The Black Hills of southwestern South Dakota may also be considered an extension of this region. Here the mountains attain heights over 7,000 feet. Livestock graze in the high meadows, and much of the timber is in federal ownership. Recreation, especially near Mount Rushmore, and hard rock mining, including the Homestake Gold Mine, are important to the local economy.

The largest region is the Great Plains area, which includes portions of Montana, North Dakota, South Dakota, Nebraska, Colorado, and Kansas. Agriculture is the predominant, though always precarious, economic activity. Average precipitation is only sixteen inches, and the frequent high winds evaporate moisture from the soils. The production of hard grains results from extensive dryland farming. Much of the area is also used for grazing, although droughts and overgrazing have depleted the grass. The local geology together with poor farming and grazing practices have caused serious, widespread erosion problems. In the Badlands, for example, erosion has exposed the deep clay soils.

Two unique areas merit special mention. The Sand Hills of north-central Nebraska consists of low, sandy hills and numerous depressions containing marshes or small lakes. Hay is grown, and fields are used for grazing. The Flint Hills of east-central Kansas "is an area of rolling terrain with shallow rocky soils."[6] Although the thin and rocky soils prevent cultivation here, upland areas do support abundant blue-stemmed grasses and the area has become known as a fine cattle-grazing region.

The Eastern Border region can be distinguished from the remainder of the basin by the additional precipitation it receives. This climatic difference also translates into a different style of agriculture, for a greater and more consistent yield can be obtained from smaller farms. Major crops are corn, oats, wheat, grasses, and legumes, and much of the crop production is used for livestock feed. Here an overabundance of water, not a shortage, has been a problem. Floods have been a part of the region's history, and land erosion is constant. The population density of this area—especially in the Omaha and Kansas City areas—is greater than anywhere else in the basin, and the economy is much more dependent upon manufacturing and the service sector.

The Ozark Highlands, in the extreme southeastern corner of the basin, is also unique. In this humid, tree-covered hill country, rainfall can reach forty-four to forty-eight inches annually. The soils are thin, agriculture is impossible, and the area's timber resources have been depleted. The rivers, streams, and lakes, however, continue to support recreational use by people from St. Louis, Memphis, and other metropolitan areas.

The lower Missouri floodplain extends from Sioux City, Iowa, to the confluence of the Missouri with the Mississippi upstream of St. Louis. This wide floodplain contains rich bottomland soils. In the past, agricultural use of these lands has been hampered by insufficient drainage and frequent flooding. Although dams on the Missouri have alleviated the floods, municipal and industrial uses compete with agriculture for these lands.

The regions of the Missouri River basin are distinct, but their differences should not mask their commonalities. Most of the basin shares the common heritage of being Louisiana Purchase lands. The exploration and development of the region depended on the Missouri River as a corridor to the interior. The basin's economy remains heavily dependent on traditional natural resource development—agriculture, livestock, timber, and mining—and federal spending. Basin residents share the difficult problems of rural-urban migration, the transition to a technology-based economy, and reduced federal spending—including the closing or curtailment of numerous defense installations in the region.

WATER RESOURCES OF THE BASIN

From Three Forks, Montana, the Missouri River flows north and east through muddy, changeable channels into the immense placid reservoirs of northeastern Montana, North Dakota, and South Dakota. Thereafter, the river winds south and east through a slow-moving navigation channel until it joins with the Mississippi near St. Louis. Almost 2,540 miles long, the Missouri is the longest river in the United States,[7] and the combined Missouri-Mississippi system is the longest waterway in the world.

The main tributaries of the Missouri are the Milk, Yellowstone, Little Missouri, Cheyenne, James, Platte, Kansas, Grand, Osage, and Gasconade rivers. Their flow combines with that of the Missouri to produce a natural average volume of 65 million ac-ft/yr at the river's mouth.[8] Approximately 500,000 ac-ft/yr is imported into the basin, mostly from the Colorado River basin in western Colorado into eastern Colorado and Wyoming.[9] A total of approximately 30,000 ac-ft/yr is exported from the basin at two locations.[10]

Before the development of the six main stem dams, wide variations in seasonal flow were common on the Missouri River. Floods ravaged the basin on an almost regular basis. In 1844, the Missouri's flow may have reached 900,000 cfs (equivalent to a volume of 1.78 million ac-ft *per day*). Indeed, the major floods of the 1940s provided the catalyst for the dam construction program. Except for a single year, floods occurred from 1942 to 1947, inundating more than 6 million acres in the basin. The 1943 floods were particularly severe, resulting in the loss of 13 lives, $46 million in direct damage, and $8 million in indirect damage.[11] Rapidly melting snow, sometimes in combination with ice jams and rain, usually caused the floods. Floods in the tributaries also caused extensive damage. In 1935, for instance, excessive rain in the Republican River resulted in over 105 deaths.[12]

Heavy sediment loads also characterized the Missouri River and many of its tributaries before the dam construction period. The river system carried a yearly average of 200 million tons of sediment, most of which was discharged between April and July. Much of the sediment (coarse material such as sand) and fine material (mostly clay) originated in the Yellowstone River and its tributaries. The movement of these sediments gave the Missouri its common name, the "Big Muddy."

Six main stem dams are now the major features on the Missouri River, the products of the federal 1944 Flood Control Act which embodied the Pick-Sloan Plan for Missouri River development.[13] The reservoirs behind three of these dams form the third, fourth, and fifth largest artificially formed bodies of water in the United States. In northeastern Montana, Fort Peck Dam, started in 1933 and completed in 1937, was the first major flood control structure on the river. Fort Peck Lake has a gross storage of 18.9 million ac-ft. Two years after Congress enacted the Flood Control Act, construction began on Garrison Dam in North Dakota and Fort Randall Dam in South Dakota. Garrison, completed in 1955, has 24.1 million ac-ft of gross storage, and Fort Randall, completed in 1953, has 5.6 million ac-ft of gross storage.

Oahe Dam, near Pierre, South Dakota, was started in 1948, completed in 1958, and has a gross storage of 23.3 million ac-ft. Gavins Point, near Yankton, South Dakota, was constructed between 1952 and 1955 and has an additional storage capacity of 492,000 ac-ft. Big Bend Dam, upstream of Chamberlain, South Dakota, was the last major construction project on the Missouri. Construction began in 1959 and was completed in 1963; its Lake Sharpe has a storage capacity of 1,873,000 ac-ft.[14] To date, twenty-eight major reservoirs, each with more than 200,000 ac-ft of storage, have been completed in the basin. The evaporation alone from these reservoirs accounts for 2.6 million ac-ft of water lost each year.

In an average year, the Missouri River discharges 78,950 cfs, or 57.2 million ac-ft/yr, into the Mississippi River upstream of St. Louis.[15] Although water appears reasonably abundant in the river (especially compared with other western river basins),[16] this figure is based on U.S. Geological Survey (USGS) records over a period of thirty-five years and the period of record does not include the drought period of the 1930s. Thus, the estimates of water availability may be excessive.

Three periods of severe drought have beset the Missouri River basin during the twentieth century. The drought of the 1930s continued for a decade and resulted in the lowest runoff of record. The 1950s also brought drought, with the driest period occurring from 1954 to 1957. The

TABLE 1.1. Total Annual Streamflow Depletion by Type of Use

Year/	1944		1960		1978	
Use	MAF[a]	%	MAF	%	MAF	%
Irrigation	7.15	78.7	10.76	74.0	11.35	66.0
Main reservoirs (evaporation)	0.74	8.2	1.66	11.4	2.60	15.1
Other uses	1.19	13.1	2.12	14.6	3.25	18.9
Total	9.08	100.0	14.54	100.0	17.19	100.0

[a]Million ac-ft/yr

Source: Adapted from Missouri Basin States Association, *Missouri River Basin Hydrology Study Final Report* (Omaha, May 1983), 5.

third drought began in 1987 and continued until spring 1993. Runoff at Sioux City averaged 17.6 million ac-ft/yr for that period, a level only slightly higher than flows during the 1930s. In April 1991, main stem reservoir levels were at 42.1 million ac-ft, an all-time low.

Total consumptive use (depletions) in the basin is estimated at 17.2 million ac-ft/yr, or about a quarter of the total amount of water available.[17] The greatest consumptive use of Missouri River basin water is agriculture (66 percent in 1978) although evaporation (15.1 percent, or approximately 2.6 million ac-ft/yr) and other uses (e.g., municipal-in-

TABLE 1.2. Historic Trends—Acres under Irrigation, Surface and Groundwater (in 1,000s of acres)

Year/	1944		1960		1978	
Sub-basin	Surface	Ground	Surface	Ground	Surface	Ground
Upper Missouri	1,226		1,548		1,495	
Yellowstone	1,102		1,263		1,149	
Western Dakota	103		260		483	
Eastern Dakota			24	13	262	126
Platte-Niobrara	1,730	238	1,985	809	1,963	2,914
Middle Missouri			53	4	282	16
Kansas	17	56	192	863	432	3,216
Lower Missouri			10		73	
Subtotal	4,178	294	5,335	1,689	6,139	6,272
TOTAL	4,472		7,024		12,411	

Source: Missouri Basin States Association, *Missouri River Basin Hydrology Study Final Report* (Omaha, May 1983), 4.

dustrial and rural-domestic, 18.9 percent) also have a major effect (see Table 1.1).

Although irrigated acreage in the basin has increased almost three-fold since the passage of the Pick-Sloan Plan, most of that expansion is attributable to the use of groundwater (groundwater use has increased over 2,000 percent; see Table 1.2). Irrigated acreage has increased only slightly since 1944 in the upper Missouri, Yellowstone, Western Dakota, and Eastern Dakota subbasins. Farmers in the Platte-Niobrara and Kansas subbasins have been able to bring the greatest amount of additional agriculture into irrigation since 1944, primarily as a result of developing groundwater resources. One of the great ironies of the fifty-year history of the Pick-Sloan Plan, which was to promote irrigation development, is that irrigated agriculture now consumes a smaller percentage of the depleted surface water than it did in 1944 before the main stem dams were built.

CHAPTER TWO

We Who Live Beside the River

Although the Missouri River basin is itself an integrated hydrologic system extending from the Rocky Mountains to the Mississippi River, countless political boundaries have been carved across this watershed: jurisdictional lines of states, federal agencies, tribal governments, counties and cities, school boards, and local planning and conservation districts. To a greater or lesser extent, all these entities use water. They rely on the Missouri and its tributaries, and they compete for what is ultimately a limited resource. Through their activities, these governments and their residents disrupt the normal hydrologic system and hamper the sound management of the basin's water. This chapter profiles the ten states, twenty-five Indian reservations, and three federal agencies that are the most important governmental entities in the basin. The main emphasis here falls on the states and tribes, for the history of the federal government's involvement in water policy has received excellent treatment by other authors,[1] and federal activity in the Missouri River basin is more thoroughly presented in Chapters 3 and 4. By overlaying each of these systems of government, one can appreciate the jurisdictional complexity of Missouri River water management.

SUBBASIN COMPARISONS

The Missouri River basin states can be conveniently separately into two groups: upper basin (Colorado, Wyoming, Montana, North Dakota, South Dakota) and lower basin (Minnesota, Nebraska, Iowa, Kansas, Missouri). These groups can be distinguished by socioeconomic differences; the one hundredth meridian of longitude, which traces the climatic divide between the humid Midwest and the arid West; the relative amount of non-Indian federal land (83.6 million acres in the upper basin compared to 6 million acres in the lower basin); and the fact that navigation is impossible above Sioux City, Iowa.

Since the Missouri River basin does not follow state boundaries, the population of the basin is difficult to determine. The 1990 population in the ten basin states (including areas outside the basin) was 22.2 million, or almost 9 percent of the U.S. population. The most populated state is Missouri, with over 5 million people; the least populated is Wyoming, with 454,000. Denver, with 1.8 million residents, is the largest metropolitan area in the basin, followed by Kansas City, which boasts 1.5 million. The population in the lower basin states is almost three times greater than in the upper basin states (see Table 2.1). The U.S. population increased almost 10 percent from 1980 to 1990, but the population of these ten states increased only by 875,000, or 4 percent. Reflecting a decline in energy production in the upper basin and adverse farming conditions throughout the basin, Iowa, North Dakota, and Wyoming actually lost population, and growth in Montana, South Dakota, and Nebraska was flat.

The upper basin includes four of the least populated states in the nation. Except for Colorado, population density in this region is less than ten persons per square mile (see Table 2.2). The lower basin states are two to seven times as dense. Nonetheless, all the basin states are predominately urban. Surprisingly, Colorado is the most urbanized state; 82 percent of its residents live in cities (exceeding the national average). Even Wyoming is 65 percent urban. All the lower basin states are more than 60 percent urban. Only in Montana and the Dakotas do rural residents almost equal urban residents.

The Missouri River residents derive principally from European stock. Although there are over a million Blacks, 271,000 American Indians, and 752,000 Hispanics (who, according to the Bureau of Census definition, can be members of any race) in basin states, they total less than 10 percent of the population of those states. Almost 11 percent of Missouri's population is Black, followed by Kansas at 6 percent. Indians comprise 7 percent of South Dakota's population, 6 percent of Montana's, and 4 percent of North Dakota's. Almost 13 percent of Colorado's population is Hispanic, although many of these residents live in the southern part of the state, outside the Missouri River basin.[2]

The differences between the upper and lower basin states are further underlined by a comparison of their economies (see Table 2.3). The combined gross state product[3] of the lower basin states is more than three times as large as that of the upper basin, and Colorado alone contributes over half the upper basin total. The upper basin states are generally considered agricultural, but government, financial services, and other types of services are actually more important to their economies. The lower basin states, though also reliant on these activities, have more developed manufacturing, trade, and transportation sectors. Missouri has the largest economy in the basin, followed by Minnesota.

In 1990, median household income ranged from $23,375 (Montana) to $30,733 (Colorado) in the upper basin and from $27,228 (Iowa) to $31,465 (Minnesota) in the lower basin. Only Colorado and Minnesota had figures higher than the $29,943 median income figure reported for

TABLE 2.1. Resident Population, Missouri River Basin States—1970, 1980, 1990 (in 1,000s)

State	1970		1980		1990	
	No.	U.S. Rank	No.	U.S. Rank	No.	U.S. Rank
Upper Basin						
CO	2,210	30	2,890	28	3,294	26
MT	694	43	787	44	799	44
ND	618	45	653	46	639	47
SD	666	44	691	45	696	45
WY	332	49	470	49	454	50
Total	4,520		5,491		5,882	
Lower Basin						
IA	2,825	25	2,914	27	2,777	30
KS	2,249	28	2,364	32	2,478	32
MO	4,678	13	4,917	15	5,117	15
MN	3,806	19	4,076	21	4,375	20
NE	1,485	35	1,570	35	1,578	36
Total	15,043		15,841		16,325	
Ten State Total	19,563		21,332		22,207	
U.S. Total	203,302		226,546		248,710	

Source: U.S. Department of Commerce, Bureau of the Census, Statistical Abstract of the United States (1992), table 25.

TABLE 2.2. Population Density and Urbanization, Missouri River Basin States (1990)

State	Persons/Square Mile	% Urban
Upper Basin		
Colorado	31.8	82.4
Montana	5.5	52.5
North Dakota	9.3	53.3
South Dakota	9.2	50.0
Wyoming	4.7	65.0
Lower Basin		
Iowa	49.7	60.6
Kansas	30.3	69.1
Missouri	74.3	68.7
Minnesota	55.0	69.9
Nebraska	20.5	66.1
U.S.	70.3	75.2

Source: U.S. Department of Commerce, Bureau of the Census, Statistical Abstract of the United States (1992), tables 25 and 29.

TABLE 2.3. Gross State Product by Industry, Missouri River Basin States, 1989 (in billions of dollars)

State	Total	Agric	Cons	Man	Tran	Wh	Ret	Fin	Serv	Gov
Upper basin										
CO	66	2	3	9	7	4	7	10	14	9
MT	13	1	1	1	1	1	1	2	2	2
ND	11	1	1	1	1	1	1	2	2	1
SD	11	1	(z)	1	1	1	1	2	2	1
WY	11	(z)	1	(z)	2	(z)	1	2	1	1
Total	112	5	5	12	12	7	11	18	21	14
Lower basin										
IA	53	5	2	11	4	3	5	10	8	5
KS	49	3	2	9	6	3	5	8	7	6
MO	100	2	4	23	11	7	10	15	18	10
MN	94	4	3	20	8	7	9	17	16	9
NE	31	4	1	4	3	2	3	5	5	4
Total	327	18	12	67	32	22	32	55	54	34
Total	439	23	17	79	44	29	43	73	75	48

Agric—Farms, forestry and fisheries (including agricultural services)
Cons—Construction
Man—Manufacturing
Tran—Transportation
Wh—Wholesale trade
Ret—Retail trade
Fin—Finance, insurance, real estate
Serv—Services
Gov—Government (including federal military and civilian, state, and local)
(z)—Less than $500 million; consequently, figures are rounded off and may not total

Source: U.S. Department of Commerce, Bureau of the Census, Statistical Abstract of the United States (1992), table 685.

the United States.[4] All the lower basin states had poverty rates lower than the national rate of 13.5 percent. All the upper basin states, except Wyoming, had poverty rates that approximated or exceeded the national rate. Montana, at 16.3 percent, had the highest poverty rate.[5]

Although agriculture does not contribute largely to the gross product of the basin (it is the second smallest sector on Table 2.3), farming remains important to the culture and land use of the region. There are 557,000 farms in the basin states, 76 percent of them in the lower basin. Farm size in the lower basin averages 463 acres, identical to the national average. Reflecting arid conditions, farm size in the upper basin averages 1,940 acres. Irrigation is practiced principally in Colorado, Montana, Wyoming, Kansas, and Nebraska.[6]

There is remarkable asymmetry between the two groups of states where

Missouri River, Charles M. Russell National Wildlife Refuge, Montana. (Photo by Craig Sharpe)

water is concerned. Montana contains the headwaters of the river; the mouth is in Missouri. The upper basin states, which are generally thought of as western states, have a shared interest in developing Missouri River water for agriculture and other consumptive uses such as mining and municipal. More recently, their interests have shifted to the instream and recreational values associated with the river and its tributaries. By contrast, the lower basin states, generally midwestern states, are united by their interest in navigation and in flood control. Instream and recreational values are also of growing importance, and several of these states benefit greatly from the hydroelectric power produced on the river.

Neither Colorado nor Minnesota are main stem states, but they share an important interest in the hydroelectric power produced at the main stem dams. Still, both states have distanced themselves from Missouri River issues and have dropped their membership in the Missouri River Basin Association, comprised of the other basin states and a tribal representative.

The states have adopted different water law systems. Montana, Wyoming, and Colorado have adopted the prior appropriation doctrine of water law. This legal doctrine requires that water be used for socially useful purposes ("beneficial uses"), allows water to be used at locations not adjacent to the source of water (for example, transmountain movement of water), and allocates water according to a seniority system based on when water was first appropriated for use.[7] This system has allowed the development of cities, irrigated farming, and commercial enterprises in the arid environment of the upper basin states.

Missouri, Iowa, and Minnesota, meanwhile, are riparian law states. The riparian doctrine simply states that the owner of land bordering a river or lake may make reasonable use of the water on his or her land so long as the reasonable use of other riparian landowners is not prevented. Or, as one author has stated:

> Three basic principles constitute the essence of the riparian doctrine. First, water is incapable of being owned and can only be subject to rights of use. Second, only owners of riparian land acquire any riparian rights. Third, all riparians have equal rights in the adjacent watercourse or lake. . . . [Fourth,] each riparian is entitled to a reasonable use of the water, reasonableness to be determined by comparison with the uses of other riparians.[8]

Since water is relatively abundant, these three states have not developed the sophisticated water management programs found in the more arid parts of the basin. Many water uses go unregulated, which means the states have limited information about water availability and demand. In response to frequent flooding, however, these states have developed legal doctrines concerning the drainage of flood waters. Because of the historic importance of navigation, all three states recognize public rights to use the major waterways. Sometimes this protection has been buttressed by judicial adoption of the public trust doctrine that recognizes the public interest in important waterways and river and lake beds.

North Dakota and South Dakota, in the upper basin, and Kansas and Nebraska, in the lower basin, are hybrid prior appropriation–riparian law states. These hybrid states originally recognized riparian law but later adopted the prior appropriation system while preserving existing riparian rights. Of the two groups, the lower basin states are less unified in their positions about water and the Missouri River. Kansas and Nebraska, the swing states of the Missouri River basin with feet in both the West and Midwest, occasionally identify with the states of the upper basin.

UPPER BASIN STATES[9]

Montana

Originally a territory formed from the Louisiana Purchase, Montana became a state in 1889. Its features and people figure prominently in the

Near Fort Benton, Montana. (Photo by Craig Sharpe)

history and mythology of the West—and of the Missouri. Some of the most exciting pages from Lewis and Clark's journals recount episodes in what later became the "Big Sky State": passing the White Cliffs, the portage around the Great Falls of the Missouri, the arrival at the headwaters at Three Forks, the snowy ascent of Lolo Pass, and the fatal encounter with Blackfeet Indians on the Teton River. Some of the best western art depicts the river in these parts: Karl Bodmer's graphic portrayal of landscape and inhabitants virtually untouched by white man's presence, George Catlin's representations of early commerce on the river, Charlie Russell's portrayal of a noble land crisscrossed by the river.

Once thriving communities along the river are now struggling footnotes to the history of American settlement: Fort Benton, at one time the vital trade exchange between the river and the plains; Fort McKenzie, now only a state park; even Great Falls, which once considered Minneapolis its peer, now share the decline of the mineral and agricultural industries and the military complex.

Montanans of the 1990s are obsessed with water, concerned about whether the drought that lasted most of the 1980s is now broken. Other issues are also frequently mentioned in the newspapers: the three Superfund sites on the Clark Fork River (tributary of the Columbia River), the results of Butte's mining heyday; the phosphate pollution of picturesque Flathead Lake in the northwestern part of the state; and the wide-spread landowner resentment of a 1984 decision of the state supreme court that recognizes public access to most of the state's rivers and streams.[10]

In its early mining days, Montana adopted the prior appropriation doctrine and its requirements of beneficial use. Central registration of water rights, however, was not mandated until ratification of the state's new constitution in 1972. Shortly thereafter, the legislature enacted the Water Use Act of 1973,[11] which is the controlling doctrine on water allocation within the state. Because of outstanding federal water right claims and a haphazard collection of unrecorded use rights, decrees, and locally recorded notices of appropriation accumulated since territorial days, the 1973 legislation initiated a statewide general stream adjudication of all pre-1973 water rights. The general stream adjudication process was modified in 1979 when a specialized water court was created to manage the litigation. The adjudications are not expected to be completed until after the turn of the century.

Montana has taken a unique approach to quantifying federal and Indian reserved water rights. With the creation of a Reserved Water Rights Compact Commission in 1979 to negotiate on behalf of the state with tribes and federal agencies, Montana has provided a means for negotiating rather than litigating these claims. To date, three compacts have been negotiated. A water compact has been completed with the tribes of the Fort Peck Reservation recognizing the right of the tribes to more than 1 million ac-ft/yr of water from the Missouri River and certain of its tributaries (no more than 500,000 ac-ft/yr can be consumed). In 1992, a second compact, with the Northern Cheyenne Tribe in southeastern Montana, provided 91,330 ac-ft/yr of water. A third compact has been negotiated with the National Park Service. Except for the Blackfeet, all other tribes of the state have indicated a willingness to negotiate with the compact commission. The commission expires in 1999. Federal and tribal claims not resolved by that time will be referred to the water court for adjudication.

Since 1973, new uses of ground and surface water have required a permit from the Department of Natural Resources and Conservation (DNRC). The permit allows water to be appropriated for fish and wildlife as well as recreational purposes; water can also be reserved by governmental entities under the state's water reservation program for instream flows and future consumptive needs. Proceedings to reserve water for instream and future uses were completed in 1979 for the Yellowstone River and in 1992 for the upper Missouri main stem.

Montana has had a moderately ambitious water development program based on a combination of grants and loans. The original intent of this legislation was agricultural water development, but much of the funding has gone for municipal and rural domestic projects. The state initiated a new state water planning process in the 1980s patterned after the approach pioneered by Kansas. A state water plan advisory committee develops the plan's components and makes recommendations to the legislature and state agencies. The process is staffed by DNRC. Components of the plan have been completed on instream flows, efficiency of agricultural water use, hydropower development and siting, and water data collection, among others.

Wyoming

Wyoming's dry, barren landscape is not directly affected by the Missouri River. The Yellowstone River originates in Wyoming's portion of Yellowstone National Park, to be joined downstream by the Big Horn River and the Powder River, two tributaries also originating in the state. Another tributary of the Missouri, the North Platte River, transects the southeastern corner of Wyoming. Because there is relatively little water, Wyoming's wealth lies in its minerals rather than in its soil. Throughout the 1970s, the state increased its mineral production 20 percent annually, and it is one of the largest coal producing states in the nation.

Wyoming functions in boom-and-bust cycles. Its first boomtown was Cheyenne. The community's population grew from zero to 1,000 in four months when it became a Union Pacific railway terminal in 1867. Energy boomtowns such as Rock Springs, Gillette, and Evanston have been established since then and are now in decline.

Wyoming's politics are dominated by energy issues and antifederal sentiment. Its citizens primarily vote Republican, but they can be unpredictable. A few months after Wyoming voted overwhelmingly for Ronald Reagan, the 1981 state legislature voted to improve workers' compensation and created a new division of state government to help battered women. The last two governors have been Democrats.

Most Americans and foreigners take little interest in Wyoming's energy and ranch economy. They visit the state to see Yellowstone National Park and the Teton and Big Horn Mountains. Northern Wyoming is sprinkled with dude ranches that attract many wealthy, high-paying tourists every year.

Wyoming is a strict prior appropriation doctrine state, and its comprehensive water permitting system was the first in the West, giving state water managers very good information on water use. The permitting system is administered on a daily basis by the state engineer. The Board of Control, consisting of the state engineer and four water commissioners, grants water rights and approves changes and transfers.

Wyoming's water planning function is essentially a water development activity. Water planning and development are the principal responsibilities of the Water Development Commission. The commission consists of nine members—two from each of the state's four water divisions and one at-large member. The state engineer, a representative from the University of Wyoming, and the administrator of the Water Division of the Department of Economic Planning and Development serve as advisers to the commission, which completes four types of plans: regional reconnaissance, feasibility studies, detailed plans and designs, and construction plans.

Since the early 1980s, water development has been among the state's highest priorities, as witnessed by the creation of a $200-million water development fund. The major sources of money for this fund are a 1.5 percent levy on coal severance tax revenues, a 0.167 percent share of oil and gas severance tax revenues, and general fund appropriations. The fund is expected to provide $135 million for six water development projects. One proposal (estimated at $80 million) is to raise Buffalo Bill Dam by twenty-five feet on an equal cost-sharing basis with the federal government. In 1986, Wyoming finally passed instream flow legislation. The storage or release of water for recreation and fisheries are now designated beneficial uses, and the state can obtain water rights to unappropriated water to protect instream flows.

North Dakota

The Missouri River separates the southwest third of North Dakota from the rest of the state. The river also splits the state into two distinct geographical regions. After traveling through North Dakota, John Steinbeck commented on the differences of land on opposite sides of the river near the state's capital, Bismarck: "On the Bismarck side it is the Eastern landscape, Eastern grass, with the look and smell of Eastern America. Across the Missouri on the Mandan side, it is pure West, with brown grass and water scorings and small outcrops. The two sides of the river might as well be a thousand miles apart."[12]

North Dakota's inhabitants also seem to change as one journeys from the eastern half of the state to the west. Eastern North Dakotans tend to be relatively reserved, conservative, formal and churchgoing while the others are more casual people who identify more with the West. The ethnicity of the state still reflects the first settlers who arrived in North Dakota by train in the late nineteenth and early twentieth centuries. The southeast region is primarily inhabited by conservative Germans and Russians; the more liberal Scandinavians moved farther west.

Wheat production is the state's largest industry. Most years, North

Dakota ranks second only to Kansas in wheat production and often ranks first in durum wheat, barley, flaxseed, and sunflower seed. Farm cooperatives are prevalent in the state. Oil and coal represent the next important economic sector. There are many tourist attractions in North Dakota, including the Badlands, the International Peace Garden, and legalized gambling.

In certain policy areas, North Dakota is one of the most radical states in the Union. It has a history of populism and resistance to manipulative outside interests. It has a state-owned bank (the only one in the United States), a state mill, and a state grain elevator. Its citizens have also voted to outlaw corporate farms, except for family corporations. North Dakota's politicians have included radical congressman William Lemke, who ran for president in 1936 with an agrarian-isolationist platform. Since the early 1980s, Democrats have usually been elected governor and represented the state in Congress.

One cannot discuss the Missouri River or the Pick-Sloan Plan in North Dakota without discussing the Garrison Project. Garrison Dam was completed in 1955, forming Lake Sakakawea, and the Garrison Diversion Unit, an original component of the Pick-Sloan Plan, was designed to bring water from the lake to irrigate about 1 million acres in east-central North Dakota and to provide for municipal and industrial uses in several towns and cities. The first phase of the Garrison Project (to serve 250,000 acres of irrigated land) was authorized in 1965, but although canals and pumping facilities have been built, little land has been irrigated. The principal beneficiaries of the $250 million spent to date are the recreational users of the lake.

Many factors have hindered the project's completion. Canada was concerned that Missouri water, if transported interbasin into the northern-flowing Red River valley, would bring with it unwanted species of fish and other environmental uncertainties. Washington policymakers questioned whether the costs of the project, compared to projected benefits, would justify the expenditure of federal funds in times of national fiscal austerity and declining agricultural markets. State and national wildlife groups were concerned that irreplaceable wildlife habitat would give way to cultivated land if the project went forward. In the meantime, lower basin states and water users, benefiting from delayed upper basin development and having no other reason to enlist in North Dakota's cause, have been content to enjoy the status quo.

The Garrison Project has become a tired refrain, conjuring up in many critic's mind the same old water development imperative that has been deemphasized and discredited throughout the West. The underlying problem cannot be easily dismissed. In the name of national economic recovery, navigation and lower basin flood control, Indians and other North Dakota citizens paid a high price for the construction of Garrison and Oahe dams. Five hundred and fifty thousand acres of prime river bottomland have been inundated by the reservoirs; culture and lifestyle were fundamentally altered; riparian environment was destroyed. The nation has yet to mitigate these damages or to fully compensate these people for their loss.

In 1984, Congress created the Garrison Diversion Unit Commission to make recommendations for the project, with the assurance of the vying parties that they would support the commission's final report. The commission recommended that the project be reduced from 250,000 acres to 130,000 acres of irrigated land and that any proposed diversions into the Hudson Bay drainage be eliminated. Some opponents of the Garrison Project (including the National Audubon Society) were dissatisfied with even this scaled-down version and continued to push for total deauthorization. Upon the prodding of Congressman George Miller, then-chair of the U.S. House Subcommittee on Water and Power Resources, a compromise was forged. In April 1986, a statement of principles was signed by Governor George Sinner, the Garrison Diversion Conservancy District, the North Dakota Water Users Association, the National Audubon Society, the North Dakota Chapter of the Wildlife Society, the National Wildlife Federation, and the federation's North Dakota chapter. The statement pledged a joint effort to improve the management of water and wetlands of the state and support for the reformulation of the Garrison Project on a reduced scale. With this tenuous compromise, passage of the reformulation legislation was completed by Congress, although funding has been sporadic.

The bottom-line problem with the Garrison Project is that, as one North Dakotan observed, "the West is settled." It is difficult to justify nationally a major water development project based on the reclamation ethic of a bygone era. However, North Dakota has patiently waited its turn while major storage projects flooded its prime bottom land and other states like Arizona and California got their huge share of the reclamation funds for expensive distribution systems. North Dakota believes it is due.

Through all of this controversy, other aspects of North Dakota's water program have gone forward. The State Water Commission has completed and updated a comprehensive water plan for the state that strongly emphasizes public participation. The resulting plan is a catalog of water problems within the state.

South Dakota

Most Americans view North Dakota and South Dakota as very similar, but historically, the two states have viewed the world very differently. John Gunther wrote in the late 1940s:

> Nothing is more remarkable in the United States than the difference between the Dakotas. North Dakota is one of the most radical states of the Union, and South Dakota one of the most conservative. . . . South thinks North is inhabited mostly by bolsheviks; North thinks that South is a preserve for all people to the right of Hoover. South looks down across the river to Iowa and southward to Nebraska, it never looks North at all, if it can help it.[13]

Today, however, similarities outweigh differences. Both states have the largest percentages in the nation of people who earn their living from the land. Geographically, they both have fertile, humid river valleys in the east (Red River in North Dakota, James and Big Sioux rivers in South Dakota), and their western semiarid buttes and grasslands are moistened by the Missouri River.

Most of South Dakota's radical politics ceased at the turn of the century. In 1916, Republican Peter Norbeck was elected as governor, defeating a member of the left-wing Nonpartisan League (NPL). Norbeck dealt with the NPL by adopting NPL reforms whenever the "NPL-ers" became too strident. Several of these socialistic programs failed during the depression of the 1930s, giving South Dakotans more reason to be staunchly conservative. South Dakota derives most of its revenue from livestock (70 percent of farm income). Industrialization is progressing slowly in the state while tourism is the second largest moneymaker. South Dakota offers tourists the Badlands, the Black Hills, and Mount Rushmore, and favorable banking legislation has attracted major credit-card-processing centers to the state.

Before 1955, South Dakota distributed its water under both the riparian and prior appropriation doctrines. In 1955, this hybrid system was replaced by a strict prior appropriation system. Pre-1955 riparian rights were recognized as vested. Permits are required for surface and groundwater diversions, and domestic uses take precedence over all other rights. Irrigation rights also enjoy a degree of protection, for they are deemed to be appurtenant to the land and cannot be severed. Groundwater withdrawals are limited to the safe yield of the aquifer. South Dakota has a limited water reservation system under which a permit for future water uses related to energy development can be issued by the State Conservancy District.

A state water plan, largely oriented to water development projects, has been required since 1972. According to the state water facilities plan component, small water projects can be constructed under the discretionary authority of the Board of Water and Natural Resources. Larger projects, requiring specific state or federal legislative authorization and funding, are planned under a state water resources management component. Two types of funding have fueled the plan: categorical grants, loans, and bonding authority for smaller projects; state authorization and bonding for larger projects.

Federal water development activities began in South Dakota in the 1930s with the Belle Fourche Project. Even though the state lost more than 500,000 acres of land to the Missouri main stem reservoirs (Oahe, Big Bend, Fort Randall, and Gavins Point), little Pick-Sloan irrigation development has occurred. Much of the originally planned development (more than 750,000 acres) is in eastern South Dakota and would have received water from the original Oahe Irrigation Project.

The unfulfilled Pick-Sloan promises, plus the severe effects of the 1977 and 1987–1993 droughts on tourism and rural domestic and agricultural water supplies, have resulted in major efforts by the state to make other uses of Missouri River water. The sale of water to the ETSI pipeline in 1982 was one such effort; the continuing effort to reformulate the Oahe Irrigation Project into a scaled down proposal (CENDAK) is another. The state has explored the possibility of using hydroelectric power and revenues as the means for receiving Pick-Sloan Plan benefits. This proposal was part of Governor George Mickelson's Cost-Recovery Authority initiative, which foundered after Governor Mickelson was killed in a 1993 plane crash.

Colorado

Although the Missouri River seems far from Colorado, the Platte River, a tributary, provides water for urban and farm uses in the northeastern part of the state. The state has more than doubled in size since World War II, but its farm and ranch population has declined during the same period, and although the amount of land in cultivation has remained steady, farms number only 50 percent of the 1940 total. Nevertheless, mining, ranching, and farming were the original economic activities of the state, and the prior appropriation doctrine got its start in the mining camps of this state and in similar locations in California. The rural sector is still politically powerful in the Colorado legislature, for the Republican party continues to control both houses, despite the fact that the state has elected Democratic governors in recent years.

Still, Colorado is the Missouri River basin's most urbanized state. The Front Range, a 160-mile-long metropolitan stretch along the eastern slope of the Rockies, is home to 80 percent of the state's residents, and the economy of this area depends on an array of energy activities, federal installations, universities, resorts, and service industries. Colorado's portion of the Missouri River basin is even more urbanized than the remainder of the state. Here, too, the number of farms has declined since the 1940s. Unlike the rest of the state, however, the amount of farmland in the basin also has dramatically decreased—from 27.7 million acres to 11.7 million acres. A very small amount of this land is irrigated.

Colorado has perhaps the most formalized water law institutions of any state in the basin. There are four major features of this legal regime. First, since the 1880s, the state's system of acquiring and administering water rights has been well established: Colorado has relied upon state water courts, not a state engineer or other executive agency, to determine and administer surface water rights. Since the 1969 Water Rights Determination and Administration Act, the water courts have been organized into seven water districts, each with a judge and referee. Second, the state has used transbasin diversions to a degree unprecedented in the West. Water is transported across the Continental Divide and into the Missouri River drainage through the Grand River Ditch, the Alva B. Adams Tunnel, the Moffat Tunnel, the Aurora-Homestake Pipeline, and the Roberts Tunnel. One of the major public policy controversies during the 1980s was the unsuccessful proposal to divert water from the South Fork of the Platte River to fill a reservoir proposed at Two Forks.

Third, Colorado has used the interstate compact to a degree unparalleled by any other western state. Virtually every drop of surface water that leaves the state does so under the terms of one of the nine interstate compacts or two U.S. Supreme Court decisions. Finally, the state relies on the market for the distribution of water. Subject to court approval, water rights are bought and sold freely, and recently, a regional water market has developed in the Denver area as municipalities scramble to acquire water for future needs. Some firms are even in the business of developing portfolios of water rights for investment purposes. It is possible that the increasing cost of new water supplies, which fuels market activity, may have the desirable result of increasing water use efficiency.

Despite its water management experience, Colorado's water policies are severely lacking in many areas. The state does not have a water plan, and its recent instream flow program secures only junior water rights on most streams. The public trust doctrine, a judicial doctrine that guarantees public access and imposes a high standard of care in state water management, is not recognized. With most of the state's surface water fully appropriated, the state must either emphasize water development or water conservation to meet future needs. Indeed, the state government does not really manage water at all; the marketplace and water users largely dictate water policy and use.

LOWER BASIN STATES

Minnesota

Minnesota became a state in 1858. Its 87,000 square miles make it the fourth largest of the basin states, but only a small portion of this area is part of the Missouri River basin and the state has little in common—geographically, economically, or politically—with the other basin states.

The presence of such large companies as Dayton-Hudson, 3M, General Mills, and Control Data Corporation has made manufacturing Minnesota's major source of income since the 1960s. Agribusiness also remains an important industry. Livestock and corn production are the two biggest agricultural moneymakers. Actual farm employment and the food processing, marketing, and farm supply industries account for 30 percent of Minnesota's jobs. Iron ore extraction, once a major Minnesota industry, has decreased since the high-grade ore of the Mesabi Iron Range in northern Minnesota ran out immediately after World War II, leaving high unemployment in many mining communities. Tourism plays an important role in the Minnesota economy. More than 9 million people vacation in Minnesota yearly, and many Minnesotans own a vacation cabin on one of the state's many lakes.

Although Minnesota is located relatively high in the basin, its character and concerns resemble those of a lower basin state. Minnesota's riparian law allows a water user unrestricted use as long as there is no substantial interference with stream flow. Diversions greater than 10,000 gallons per day or 1 million gallons per year (excluding domestic uses serving fewer than twenty-five people) require a permit from the commissioner of the Department of Natural Resources.[14] All diversion structures, however, must be registered with the department in order to provide water-use data for the statewide water information system. Riparian water rights can be transferred to nonriparian lands. Under the public trust doctrine, the state holds the beds of navigable waters below the low-water mark in trust for public use. When waters are not navigable, the owners of adjoining property own the lake and stream beds to the center of the watercourse.

Responsibility for formulating and administrating Minnesota's water policy is shared by the Water Resources Committee of the Environmental Quality Board (EQB) (which is staffed by the State Planning Agency), the Soil and Water Conservation Board, the Southern Minnesota Rivers Basin Council, and the Water Resources Board. In early 1987, the Minnesota Environmental Quality Board prepared a two-year state strategy for water management.[15] The strategy included four basic goals and many specific recommendations to guide state water policy: safe-guarding public health (groundwater protection, toxics); enhancing environmental quality (nonpoint source pollution, drainage, comprehensive lake management); fostering wise economic development (water quality, flood control); and improving governmental capacity (agency coordination and reorganization, local planning, information systems, financing).

The EQB recommended the creation of a single independent state board to remedy the fragmentary approach the state had taken to water and soil resources management. The unified board would be created by merging the Soil and Water Conservation Board, the Southern Minnesota Rivers Basin Council, and the Water Resources Board. The EQB also recommended giving greater emphasis to local water planning through modification of the 1985 Comprehensive Local Water Management Act.[16] Financial assistance was suggested to help local governments undertake comprehensive planning, including a combination of grants for up to 50 percent of plan development and implementation costs and low interest loans for implementation. The EQB suggested greater coordination between state and local planning efforts.

Iowa

Blessed with 25 percent of the nation's best topsoil, which Robert Frost once said looks "good enough to eat without putting it through vegetables," Iowa is the most important agricultural state in the basin. The state's farm income is usually second only to California, and its livestock income is the highest in the country. Corn, soybeans, alfalfa, and other grains are the principal crops. Ninety-five percent of Iowa's land is farmed, and two-thirds of its residents are employed in farming or related activities. Because of its dependence on agriculture, Iowa was particularly hard hit during the 1980s by low prices for agricultural commodities.

Admitted to the Union in 1848, Iowa is the smallest state in the basin. The Missouri and Mississippi rivers form its western and eastern borders, and approximately 38 percent of Iowa lies in the Missouri River basin. Although the number of farms in that area has declined by almost 30,000 since 1950, the amount of farmland (almost 13 million acres) has remained constant, indicating a trend toward larger farm operations.

Iowa enacted its basic water rights law in 1957, asserted state ownership and control of all water resources, and established a permit system for both ground and surface water administered by the Department of Natural Resources. Originally, the law required permits for uses of water in excess of 5,000 gallons per day, but that threshold was increased to 25,000 gallons per day in 1983. Water permits are issued for ten years but may be renewed by applying to the department before the permit expires. There is a 200-gallon-per-minute restriction on consumptive withdrawals directly from a watercourse that has a drainage area of less than fifty square miles. Water permits cannot be sold separately from the land.

In 1985, new legislation established a priority water allocation system. In order of priority, preference in the use of water is given to self-supplied domestic use, the domestic portion of regional rural water and municipal systems, livestock, power, industry, nontraditional irrigation, irrigation of traditional Iowa crops, and out-of-state export. Out-of-basin uses are allowed, but such a diversion must not unreasonably interfere with the uses of other riparian users. Minimum instream flows have been established for all Iowa streams at the regular gaging points nearest the mouth of the stream, and artificial reduction of the protected flow is not permitted.

In 1982, legislation mandated the completion of a state water plan that was submitted to and approved by the legislature in 1985.[17] The water plan specifically noted Iowa's weak position in negotiating or litigating an allocation of interstate waters:

> This lack of knowledge and management on the part of Iowa was recently illustrated by Iowa's challenging South Dakota's proposed sale of Missouri River water to Energy Transportation System, Inc. (ETSI). Because Iowa did not actively manage (i.e., permit) Missouri River withdrawals the state had a more difficult task to determine the level of use or prove the level of benefit the state derived from such use. Iowa would be in a better position to negotiate the terms of an interstate compact with other basin states if the present and projected levels of Missouri River use could be more accurately stated.[18]

The plan also reviewed existing water uses and projected water use to the year 2005. The projections indicated that the largest growth was expected to occur in the western counties in the Missouri River drainage and that irrigation would account for nearly the entire increase in consumptive use.

Nebraska

Nebraska is bordered on the east by the Missouri River, and its northern and southern halves are separated by the Platte River. The two rivers supply surface water, and the state overlays extensive aquifers. Nebraska, even its semiarid western region, is an agricultural mecca, and indeed, agribusiness is a major source of revenue. Three-quarters of Nebraska's agricultural dollars come from livestock sales. Industry, which is primarily related to agriculture, has supplied more jobs than actual farming since the 1960s. Trade and services are also important economic activities.

Admitted to the Union in 1867, Nebraska ranks sixteenth in size. Like many of its neighbors, Nebraska's politics began as progressive and slowly became more conservative. Nebraska's conservatism has been attributed to the fact that the state was settled by "boomers," people who were unrealistically optimistic about the promise of the American frontier. When faced with the usual agricultural troubles, the optimists and builders fled to greener pastures, leaving behind the stubborn (mostly German) conservatives who purchased property and kept it.

Nebraska applies both the riparian law doctrine and the prior appropriation doctrine to allocate the state's surface water.[19] The riparian system was established in 1855 when the state adopted English common law, but the legislature adopted a prior appropriation statute in 1895. The Nebraska Supreme Court has reconciled these two systems by recognizing riparian rights established before 1895 but disallowing the establishment of riparian rights after that date. For post-1895 surface water appropriations, a permit is required from the Department of Water Resources. These water uses are administered under a priority system giving preference in times of storage to (in the following order) domestic, agricultural, and manufacturing uses.

Groundwater is considered a separate hydrologic regime and is available for reasonable use by the owner of the overlying land. Groundwater can be transferred to other locations if other groundwater users are not unreasonably harmed and the use is in the public interest. In cases of groundwater shortage, the correlative rights doctrine is applied to reduce each pumper's use proportionally.

In 1984, the state legislature created the state Water Management Board and the Water Management Fund.[20] The board reviews and expedites construction of major state water development projects, and the fund can provide up to 75 percent cost-sharing for these projects. The 1984 legislation also authorized instream flow appropriations by the state and required the Department of Natural Resources to prepare (but not implement) groundwater management plans.

Nebraska also has a water planning process, although it is pursued as an interagency activity. Legislation was passed in 1979, and the plan has been developing in a dynamic fashion under the auspices of the Natural Resources Commission. There are five major components to the plan (some of which are not funded), but the two main elements are policy issue studies and area-specific planning studies. More than fifteen policy issue publications have been completed in such areas as water use efficiency, instream flows, transferability of surface water rights, and interstate water uses and conflicts.

In recent years, the Nebraska legislature has undertaken several interstate water policy initiatives. In 1984, legislation was passed authorizing the governor to negotiate a barge navigation compact with Iowa, Kansas, and Missouri.[21] In 1985, the legislature authorized the formation of Missouri Basin Natural Resources Council with Colorado, Montana, North Dakota, South Dakota, and Wyoming.[22] Designed to discuss a broad range of natural resource issues, the council is to consist of the following individuals from each state: two legislators, a representative of the state department of natural resources, a representative of the state's geological survey, and a representative of the governor. The council will not come into existence until comparable legislation is adopted by other states.

Kansas

Kansas's economy has made a gradual transition from agriculture to other sectors. Kansas is usually America's top wheat producer, but livestock provides most of the agricultural dollars. Manufacturing is the major sector in the state's economy, and in Wichita, the state's largest city, aerospace is the most prominent industry. Food processing, electronics, and automobile assembly plants form the industrial base of Kansas City, Kansas. Two other major economic activities in the state are defense and oil and gas production.

Now a hybrid riparian–prior appropriation state, Kansas has one of the most progressive water management programs in the basin. Most elements of a comprehensive water management policy are in place: centralized permitting, a linked water development and water marketing program, and an ambitious water planning program with a conservation emphasis.

The state's centralized permitting authority dates from the 1945 Water Appropriation Act[23] which declared that all water in the state is dedicated to the use of the people. The statute requires a permit from the Division of Water Resources, State Board of Agriculture, for all water use except domestic surface and groundwater withdrawals. The legislation confirmed more than 2,000 pre-1945 riparian water rights, and since 1945, 37,000 permits have been granted by the division. Water rights are granted in perpetuity unless the right is not used for three years. Water rights can be transferred separately from the land, but if more than 1,000 ac-ft of water is to be transferred a distance of ten miles or more, permission must be obtained from two agencies and the legislature may set aside the approval.

The Kansas Supreme Court has not recognized the public trust doctrine, indicating its decision that the legislature should decide whether the doctrine applies in the state. The Division of Water Resources does have authority to establish instream flows by withholding necessary amounts of water from appropriation. A 1958 state constitutional amendment authorized state financial participation in water development programs. Rather than emphasizing state projects, however, the state collaborated with the federal government in the construction of federal projects. Under the Federal Water Supply Act and pursuant to authority granted under the 1974 State Water Plan Storage Act, the state has purchased more than 740,000 ac-ft of water, stored in federal reservoirs, which the state markets to municipal and industrial users. If not needed for municipal or industrial purposes, stored water can be sold on a short-term basis to agricultural users.

The Kansas State Water Plan has received wide acclaim. Water planning was mandated by the state legislature in 1955. From 1958 to 1962, the state developed a series of preliminary appraisals of Kansas's water problems. In 1967, a series of seven supplemental reports examined the state's long-term water requirements. The water planning legislation was then modified in 1981 to place more emphasis on conservation and management.[24] The Kansas Water Plan is a comprehensive but flexible document, organized in self-contained sections, and it is continually being revised. One component of the water plan emphasizes interstate cooperation and coordination, and adherence to that component is reflected in Kansas's leadership on basin issues. The plan is coordinated by the Kansas Water Office, approved by the Kansas Water Authority, and submitted annually to the legislature.

In addition to its water planning responsibilities, the Kansas Water Office, which was created in 1981, coordinates state water policies and oversees the state water marketing program. The Kansas Water Authority, part of the Kansas Water Office, also approves sales of water from the state's water marketing program.

Missouri

The Missouri River draws a west-to-east line across the face of Missouri from the state's second most populous city, Kansas City, Missouri, past its capital at Jefferson City, to St. Louis, its most populous metropolitan area. The state of Missouri could not be better situated for navigational purposes. The Mississippi forms its eastern border, and the Mississippi and the Missouri offer the state 1,937 miles of navigable waterways and unparalleled access to much of the Midwest and to the Gulf of Mexico.

The most populous state in the basin, Missouri has been described as a microcosm of the United States. It borders states of the Deep South, the industrial Midwest, and the Great Plains, and it shares some of the physical characteristics and cultures of all those neighbors. Farmland, which covers one-third of the state, lies north of the Missouri River. The eastern part of this farmland region is known as Little Dixie, for it was settled by migrants who had come up the Mississippi from the Deep South. The western part of this area was settled mostly by farm families from Ohio, Iowa, and Kansas. The hilly terrain south of the Missouri is more economically depressed, though it does garner tourist dollars from the Ozark Mountains and the resort areas around the Lake of the Ozarks. The two major metropolitan areas, St. Louis and Kansas City, Missouri, account for most of the state's population.

As the gateway to the West, Missouri grew quickly and was admitted as a slave state in 1821 as part of the Missouri Compromise, which banned slavery in the remainder of the Louisiana Purchase. In addition to the Blacks and the Indian tribes that lived in or were relocated to the Missouri territory, the culture of the state has been greatly influenced by the German immigrants who began settling in area in the 1830s. Manufacturing, led by aerospace and automobiles, forms the most important sector of Missouri's economy. Agriculture (especially livestock and large agribusinesses such as Monsanto and Ralston Purina) and tourism are the two next important sectors. The state is unique in having Federal Reserve banks both in St. Louis and Kansas City.

Missouri is a subhumid state, and it receives more precipitation than the remainder of the basin. Average runoff is four inches in the northwestern part of the state and fourteen inches in the southeastern portion. State policymakers tend to be more concerned with water quality, flood damage reduction, and groundwater than with water quantity issues.

The state follows the comparative reasonable use variety of the riparian doctrine in allocating ground and surface water, though the state courts have not decided whether riparian water rights can be transferred to nonriparians. Groundwater can be sold off-site as long as neighboring water users are not unreasonably deprived of water. Since flooding is a recurring problem, the state applies the "common enemy rule," which allows landowners to protect themselves from flood waters any way they can. Although the public trust doctrine has not been explicitly recognized in the state, the right of the public to navigate those watercourses with sufficient flows for recreational boating is based on guarantees found in the Northwest Ordinance of 1787[25] and in Missouri's Organic Act of 1820.[26]

Missouri has no statutory procedure for water allocation. The state does not issue permits, so state agencies therefore have no access to the data that would normally result from such permits, and the political climate has not always been favorable for the enactment of water rights legislation.[27] In 1983, the legislature did pass the Major Water Users Registration Act, which requires users of over 100,000 gallons per day to report use on a yearly basis.[28] This information is compiled in an annual report by the state geologist. The legislature also attempted to enact a limited water allocation system during the 1986 session with a bill developed by the House Interim Committee on Water Rights.[29] Had it been successful, the bill would have declared water to be a public trust asset of the state held for the benefit of citizens and would have required the Department of Natural Resources to develop a comprehensive state water plan to identify existing uses and future needs. The department would have been given authority to establish a water allocation system based on priorities and to be implemented in times of shortages, as well as to designate critical water use areas. In 1990, the voters rejected an initiative that would have created a natural streams system with an initial designation of fifty stream segments. A natural streams commission would have been formed and local management plans would have been required.

As described by Missouri's chief water planner, "the story of Missouri's approach to a State Water Plan does not inspire confidence in the bureaucratic process."[30] Water planning in the state has undergone several rounds. Legislation in 1961 authorized data collection and long-range planning; another effort was a statewide analysis of water problems published in 1977 as "Selected Water Problem Areas in Missouri." A third attempt was the development of plans addressing critical problems such as the replacement of a lock on the Mississippi, flooding, and erosion. The state also participated in the U.S. Geological Survey's National Water Assessment, which provided the state with useful information.

Another round of planning focused on the development of regional watershed assessment plans. This two-year process, completed in 1985, included the identification of problems in twenty-three designated watersheds, a projection of conditions in the year 2000, the preparation of working papers (with projections and alternative solutions) by appropriate agencies, and the integration of these papers into subbasin reports. The goal was to identify problems needing legislative solutions, those needing regulatory solutions, and those needing further study.

In 1989, the Missouri legislature adopted legislation requiring the preparation of a state water resources inventory, a ground and surface water monitoring plan, and another state water plan. The primary reason for the new legislation was Missouri's involvement in basin litigation and negotiations. Missouri does not have good information on present water uses or future projections of need—particularly for Missouri River water.

INDIAN TRIBES AND THEIR GOVERNMENTS

Ethnology

When the last glaciers retreated from the North American continent almost 10,000 years ago, the ancestors of today's American Indians gradually divided into western and eastern cultures.[31] The western culture had to adapt to a difficult environment with limited plants and animals. Eventually, these Desert Archaic people developed agriculture in what is now the American Southwest. The eastern culture enjoyed a milder climate, richer soils, and more abundant plant and animal life, and therefore the Eastern Archaic people could live more densely. They utilized copper to make tools and weapons, and they often used controlled burning of forests to stimulate the growth of edible berries, nuts, and roots.

The golden age of the Eastern Archaic culture lasted from 1200 B.C. to 1250 A.D. During this period, three successive groups of people—the Adena, the Hopewell, and the Mississippian—lived in the lower reaches of the Missouri and Mississippi valleys, where they built elaborate burial mounds that survive in such places as Chillicothe, Ohio, and Cahokia, Illinois. The Hopewell culture, which lasted from 200 B.C. to 500 A.D., extended up the Missouri River to the confluence of the Platte. The obsidian in some of the burial goods of the Hopewellian people indicates that their travels took them to South Dakota's Black Hills or even to the Yellowstone area.

At the end of the golden age, the eastern people split into smaller groups and their culture declined. The cause—whether climatic change, raids by outsiders, or disease—remains unclear. When Europeans came to the region in the 1500s, they found hundreds of tribes, and many of them still shared cultural attributes, including language. The Siouian language, spoken in various forms by the Osage, Ponca, Quapaw, Crow, and Dakota tribes, covered most of the Missouri River valley. The Algonkian language was shared by the Cheyenne and Blackfeet tribes in the upper basin and the Kickapoo tribe in what is now western Kansas.

The Missouri basin tribes belong to four such linguistic groups. The Algonkian tribes (Sac and Fox, Kickapoo, Potawatomi, Chippewa, Cheyenne, Arapahoe, and Blackfeet) were originally native to the Great Lakes

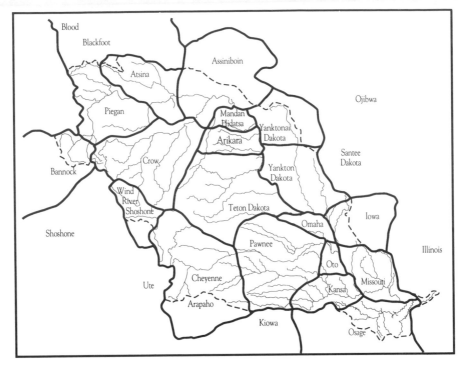

Map 2.1. Original geographic reach of Missouri River Basin tribes. (*Source:* Northern Lights Institute)

region, the upper Mississippi valley, and Canada. The Siouian tribes (Winnebago, Dakota, Iowa, Omaha, Crow, and Mandan) first lived and farmed in the Ohio River valley before pressure from the Algonkian and Iroquoian tribes pushed them westward. Once in the Missouri region, the Mandans farmed along the upper Missouri, but the economic pursuits of other Sioux expanded to include fishing and the annual hunting of buffalo on the Great Plains. Meanwhile, Caddoan tribes (Arikari) came into the basin from the south; and Shoshonean tribes (Shoshone) moved eastward into the basin from the Great Basin. Before European contact and the acquisition of horses, however, these tribes did not live permanently on the open plains. Map 2.1 indicates the general location of these tribes about 1500 A.D.—just before European contact.

European Exploration

Driven by the fur trade, French exploration extended westward from the St. Lawrence Valley into the upper Mississippi region. Joliet and Marquette were the first Europeans to pass the mouth of the Missouri; in 1673 they traveled from Green Bay to the confluence of the Arkansas River with the Mississippi. Nine years later, La Salle followed the Mississippi to the Gulf of Mexico and claimed the entire Mississippi River valley for France. When the fur trade expanded into the Missouri River region and onto the Great Plains, the French enlisted Indians into their enterprise. By this time, more than thirty tribes had migrated into the Great Plains region.

Historian Arrell Morgan Gibson notes that the French were the most successful of the Europeans in their relations with the Native Americans because the French fur trade "required Indian workers to hunt . . . , to process the pelts, and to pack them in bales for shipment to France. Hence, Indian cooperation and peace in the wilderness were essential, and French administrators placed primary reliance on diplomacy to maintain these conditions."[32] France's tenure in the trans-Mississippi region, however, did not last even a century. In 1762, as a result of its war with England, France conveyed New Orleans and the Louisiana Territory to Spain. The land was reconveyed to France in 1800 and, shortly thereafter, in 1803, Napoleon sold the territory to the United States for funds to fuel his European wars.

American Acquisition and Expansion

The history of the tribes in the Missouri River basin is largely explained by events that occurred east of the Mississippi. In 1763, the British assumed exclusive jurisdiction over the tribes in their colonial territories. The British Crown issued a royal proclamation prohibiting settlement west of the drainage divide of the Appalachian Mountains and setting aside the area west to the Mississippi for the Indians. This constraint on western settlement became one of the colonies' grievances in their war of independence. Many Indian tribes allied themselves with the British because they feared westward expansion if the colonies were successful. When the war ended in America's favor, their fears were realized as the new states claimed territory west to the Mississippi.

Starting after the Revolutionary War and continuing after the War of 1812, tribes from the north and south of the Ohio River began moving into the trans-Mississippi area. In 1819, the United States secured cessions of the Kickapoo tribe to much of a 2-million-acre tract between the Illinois and Mississippi rivers that had been pledged by Congress as bounties for soldiers who had served in the War of 1812. Land cessions by the Sac and Fox, Sioux, Potawatomi, and Winnebagos soon followed. In 1825, President Monroe established a permanent reserve west of the Missouri and Arkansas rivers, the infamous Indian Territory, where the federal government could settle tribes from the eastern United States. In 1830, President Andrew Jackson secured passage of the Indian Removal Act, which expressed a national policy for the removal of Indians from the eastern United States and gave the president power to accomplish it. By 1835, most of these tribes had been relocated west of the Mississippi into Indian Territory (see Map 2.2). This policy of relocation, in turn, straitened the Plains tribes who already lived in parts of the region.

The significant Anglo-American expansion across the Mississippi that began in 1848 introduced new pressures on tribal lands and new conflicts with the Indians. Federal Indian policy was altered to secure the settlement of the tribes on even smaller military reservations. To implement this policy, series of concessions were negotiated at Fort Laramie with many of the Great Plains tribes. Historian Arrell Gibson describes the 1851 Treaty of Fort Laramie:

> The signatory tribes pledged that their warriors would not attack the immigrant trains, freight caravans, and mail stages crossing their domains, and they agreed to permit construction of military posts at designated locations therein. The Mandans and Gros Ventres accepted reservations east of the Yellowstone, the Crows west of the Powder River, the Blackfeet in northwestern Montana, and the associated Cheyennes and Arapahoes between the North Platte and Arkansas rivers along the eastern slope of the Rocky Mountains. In return for these concessions, the signatory tribes were to receive a combined annuity of $50,000 for fifty years, subsequently reduced to fifteen years by the United States Senate.[33]

Under pressure from the U.S. commissioner of Indian affairs, the Sac and Fox, Kickapoos, Omahas, and other tribes that had been relocated to Indian Territory reluctantly agreed to treaties in 1853 that ceded northern portions of the territory to the United States.

Although tribes located in the southern portion of Indian Territory aligned themselves with the Confederacy during the Civil War, tribes in the Missouri River basin remained more aloof from the hostilities. Nevertheless, postwar reconstruction policies affected all the tribes as the United States began to dismantle Indian Territory to make way for railroads and settlers. The policy of concentrating the tribes on reservations continued, and after 1870, the United States refused to negotiate any new treaties, relying instead on unilateral statutes and presidential actions to make decisions affecting the tribes.

Military campaigns were mounted against the tribes in the Northern Plains to secure passage for white settlers and to force the Indians onto the reservations. The Sioux and Northern Cheyennes were placed on

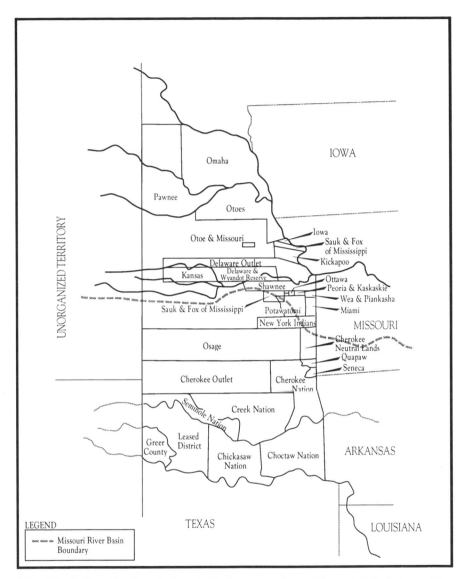

Map 2.2. Indian Territory before 1854. (*Source*: adapted from A. M. Gibson, *The American Indian*, 1980)

reservations in the Dakota, Montana, and Wyoming territories. Buffalo herds were eliminated so that the Indians would not be tempted to leave the reservations to hunt. Even on their reservations, the tribes were not protected from the constant pressure of American expansion. Gold miners soon encroached upon the Black Hills territory of the Sioux, and many Indians left the reservation—reportedly to retaliate. Colonel George Armstrong Custer's mission to return these Indians to the reservation led to the climactic battle at the Little Big Horn River on June 25, 1876. Although momentarily victorious, the Sioux and the other Plains Indians yielded to the Anglo Americans by the end of 1876.

Even with the tribes finally established on the reservations, the Anglo-American demand for tribal land was unsatiated. Advocates of more available land pressed for the partitioning of the reservations so that parcels could be owned (and conveyed) by individual Indians, a policy that some believed would speed the assimilation of these people into the white culture. In 1887, Congress passed the General Allotment Act (also known as the Dawes Act),[34] which authorized the president to subdivide reservations into 160-acre allotments for each family head and smaller parcels for single persons. The federal government was to be the trustee of the allotments for twenty-five years, but this restriction was weakened by subsequent legislation. Citizenship was conferred upon the allottees when an allotment was selected, perhaps the only positive feature of the Dawes Act, but citizenship was postponed by later enactments. Gibson evaluates the impact of the General Allotment Act:

> It liquidated all of the reservations and nations of the 67 tribes of the Indian Territory, the lands of the northern Kickapoos and Potawatomis in Kansas, the Sioux in Nebraska and North and South Dakota, northern Cheyennes and Arapahoes in Wyoming, the Gros Ventres and Blackfeet in Montana. . . . Thus the Native American estate within the present limits of the United States in 1500 consisted of nearly 3 billion acres; it had been successfully reduced by conquest, seizure, treaty, and statute, until by 1887, the year final divestment of tribal lands began through application of the General Allotment Act, the surviving tribes retained only about 150 million acres; when the General Allotment Act was repealed in 1934 this had declined to about 48 million acres, much of it desert.[35]

Only with the passage of the Indian Reorganization Act (IRA)[36] in 1934 was the national policy of reservation allotment and Indian assimilation reversed. The IRA restored the rights of the Indians to adhere to their culture and religion and to establish their own tribal governments.

Today, eighteen different tribes are located on the twenty-five reserva-

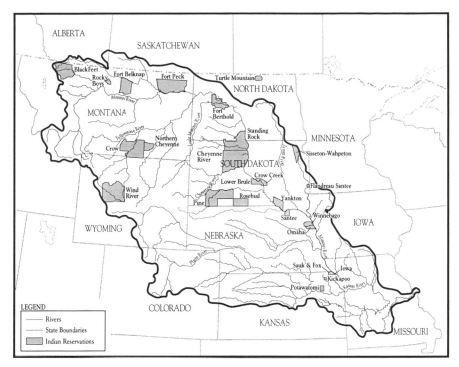

Map 2.3. Indian reservations of the Missouri River Basin. (*Source*: Northern Lights Institute)

tions in the Missouri River basin.[37] Although information is difficult to obtain and verify, tribal lands in the basin total at least 18.4 million acres (see Map 2.3 for the present location of Indian reservations). This area, roughly the size of South Carolina, is larger than the Missouri River basin portions of Iowa and Minnesota and not much smaller than the basin portions of Colorado and Missouri. The tribes have at least 127,000 enrolled members.[38]

South Dakota has the greatest number of Indian reservations in the basin with nine; Montana follows with six. Only the states of Colorado, Iowa, Minnesota, and Missouri do not have Indian reservations within the basin (see Appendix 3 for information concerning the tribes located on the basin's reservations, the date the reservations were established, the present acreage, and the present population).

Tribal Sovereignty

The stature of tribal governments in the American federal system is complex and special. Despite the many attempts that were made to terminate the reservation system and assimilate Indians into the majority society, tribal solidarity has emerged since the late 1960s, and tribal governments are asserting their authority over their members and over reservation matters. They are thus exercising attributes of sovereignty, albeit a form of sovereignty that has been forged by the difficult history of interaction between the tribes and European and American settlers.[39] As one commentator notes:

> Tribal sovereignty is neither a romantic notion conjured up by modern liberals, nor an indulgent policy creation of some halcyon political season. Tribal sovereignty is a legally recognized reality: it is acknowledged in the Constitution, federal legislation and case law. Granted, it is a modified sovereignty that is unique in its conceptual basis, but it is a true sovereignty nonetheless.[40]

The British government and the colonies recognized Indian tribes as sovereign governments, and the British Crown was responsible for relationships with the tribes. This recognition of government-to-government relations continued after the American Revolution and is reflected in provisions of the Constitution that recognize treaties made prior to 1789, provide Congress with power to regulate commerce between non-Indians and the tribes, and give the president authority to make treaties with the tribes, subject to Senate ratification.[41]

A trilogy of U.S. Supreme Court cases authored by Chief Justice John Marshall[42] provided formal recognition of this implied assumption of tribal sovereignty. Marshall recognized tribes as "domestic sovereign nations." He reasoned that, upon "discovery" by the colonial powers, "the tribes retained their internal sovereignty, but they lost the right to negotiate with other foreign powers, and the right to transfer ownership of their lands to anyone except the United States. . . . The federal government's privilege of dealing with Indian tribes was balanced by an equally explicit obligation to protect the tribes from the states and their citizens."[43] This obligation of the federal government to protect the tribes, now known as the trust doctrine, requires the executive branch to act as a fiduciary in its relations with the tribes. It represents another unique characteristic of the American intergovernmental system.

During the century after the Marshall trilogy, the status of tribes became ambiguous. One line of Supreme Court decisions adhered to the Marshall principles and continued to emphasize "the independent nature of the tribes, and . . . their territorially defined right to self-government."[44] Another line of cases recognized the decline of many of the reservations, the growing presence of non-Indians on Indian land, the growing dependency of the tribes on the federal government, and other "changed circumstances." Although the 1887 General Allotment Act authorized the president to cede 160-acre parcels of reservations to Indian families, much of the land passed out of the hands of the allottees, and Indian-held land was reduced to 48 million acres.[45] These many developments resulted in a significant erosion of tribal sovereignty and jurisdiction.

The 1934 Indian Reorganization Act was an effort "to encourage economic development, self-determination, cultural plurality, and the revival of tribalism."[46] Under the IRA, tribes could adopt tribal constitutions, which were subject to approval by the secretary of the interior, and these provided the tribes with a formal means of self-government (although many tribal decisions still remained subject to the approval of the secretary of the interior). Felix Cohen, a noted Department of Interior attorney, and others traveled the United States consulting with tribes on alternative constitutional forms. Eventually 181 tribes reorganized their governments under the act.

Even though the IRA had improved the tribes' abilities to govern, the threats to the tribes had not ended. In the 1950s, further efforts were made to terminate tribal status, assimilate tribal members into the majority society, and distribute tribal lands to individual tribal members.[47] Statutes were passed to terminate 109 tribes and bands, affecting almost 11,500 Indians and 1.4 million acres of tribal land.[48] Federal efforts at assimilation ended during the Nixon administration. Since 1959, the U.S. Supreme Court has buttressed the governmental authority of the tribes—although not fully restoring Marshall's concept of "dependent sovereign nations." In *Williams v. Lee*,[49] Justice Black "reaffirmed Marshall's principles, while noting the modifications to the doctrine: states could have jurisdiction in Indian country 'in cases where essential tribal relations were not involved and where the rights of Indians would not be jeopardized.'"[50] The Court, however, announced a new approach to tribal sovereignty in *McClanahan v. Arizona State Tax Commission*:[51]

The trend has been away from the idea of inherent Indian sovereignty as a bar to state jurisdiction and toward reliance on federal preemption. . . . The modern cases thus tend to avoid reliance on platonic notions of Indian sovereignty and to look instead to the applicable treaties and statutes which define the limits of state power. . . .

The Indian sovereignty doctrine is relevant, then, not because it provides a definitive resolution of the issues in this suit, but because it provides a backdrop against which the applicable treaties and federal statutes must be read. It must always be remembered that the various Indian tribes were once independent and sovereign nations, and that their claim to sovereignty long predates that of our own Government.[52]

An eminent Indian legal scholar summarizes the contemporary meaning of tribal sovereignty: "(1) Indian tribes possess inherent governmental power over all internal affairs; (2) the states are precluded from interfering with the tribes in their self-government; and (3) Congress has plenary power to limit tribal sovereignty."[53]

Tribal Water Rights

Legal interpretations of tribal sovereignty aside, there is a practical argument for recognizing the role of tribes in water resource decision making in the Missouri River basin. That argument concerns the magnitude of the basin tribes' claims to Missouri River water under the Indian reserved water rights doctrine.

In the 1908 case of *United States v. Winters*,[54] the Supreme Court recognized that the reservation system had been established in an effort to transform tribes into agrarian societies. The Court held that Congress reserved, by implication, sufficient water to serve the needs of the reservation with a priority extending back to the date the reservation was established (in some cases, the water rights are claimed as aboriginal with a priority date of "time immemorial"). Each of the Missouri River basin reservations can therefore be expected to assert reserved water rights claims under the *Winters'* holding. The magnitude of these claims is yet to be determined, and in a departure from the normal operation of the western prior appropriation system, the water need not immediately be put to beneficial use for the right to continue.

Ultimately, most of the Indian reserved water rights will be quantified by court decree in proceedings known as general stream adjudications, by water settlement agreements with states (approved by the federal trustee), or by congressional action. The methods for quantifying these reserved rights require careful examination of the congressional or presidential purposes for establishing each reservation. The quantification can include water for irrigation (using a methodology based on "practicably irrigable acreage" or PIA), domestic uses, stockwatering, industrial uses, and fish and wildlife uses.

In the Missouri River basin, Indian reserved water rights have been quantified only for the Sioux and Assiniboine tribes of the Fort Peck Reservation and the Northern Cheyenne tribe, both in Montana, and the Arapahoe and Shoshone tribes of the Wind River Reservation in Wyoming. Fort Peck and the State of Montana entered into a compact (discussed in more detail in Chapter 7) that quantifies the tribal water right at 1,050,472 ac-ft/yr or the amount of water necessary to supply a consumptive use of 525,236 ac-ft/yr.[55] Montana has also negotiated a compact with the Northern Cheyenne tribe.[56] Wyoming took a different approach and quantified the Indian reserved water rights of the Wind River Reservation to the Big Horn River, a tributary of the Yellowstone, in a general stream adjudication brought in state court.[57] The decree, affirmed by the U.S. Supreme Court,[58] provides the tribes with approximately 500,717 ac-ft/yr of water.

Estimates of the reserved water rights claims of the other Missouri River basin tribes are difficult to generate. In a 1984 survey of state water agencies (*not* the tribes), potential claims were estimated as follows:

- Montana, 6,632,902 ac-ft/yr (including Fort Peck);
- Nebraska, 26,481 ac-ft/yr;
- North Dakota, 190,045 ac-ft/yr;
- South Dakota, 1,269,306 ac-ft/yr; and
- Wyoming, 477,292 ac-ft/yr.[59]

This survey did not include Kansas, which also has reservations. Thus, almost 8.6 million ac-ft/yr could be claimed by the tribes against the average volume of 57.2 million ac-ft/yr at the mouth of the river (existing consumptive uses in the basin are approximately 17 million ac-ft/yr).[60]

The capacity of the tribes to assert, develop, and manage their water rights varies significantly throughout the basin. Differences exist between tribes, and between members of the same tribes, concerning the desirability of quantifying and developing the tribal water. It can nevertheless be expected that these tribes will generally manifest increasing sophistication in their efforts to quantify their reserved rights, formulate water management codes, undertake water development, and in some cases, lease water for off-reservation purposes.

FEDERAL AGENCIES

There are no fewer than eight federal departments and twenty-one bureaus and agencies with responsibilities for the water-related resources of the Missouri River basin.

Department of Agriculture
  Soil Conservation Service
  Farmers Home Administration
  Forest Service
  Economic Research Service

Department of the Army
  Corps of Engineers
Department of the Interior
  Bureau of Reclamation
  Fish and Wildlife Service
  Geological Survey
  National Park Service
  Bureau of Indian Affairs
  Bureau of Mines
  Office of Surface Mine Reclamation and Enforcement
  Bureau of Land Management
Environmental Protection Agency
Department of Commerce
  National Oceanic and Atmospheric Administration
  Economic Development Administration
Department of Energy
  Federal Energy Commission
  Western Area Power Administration
Department of Health and Human Services
  Public Health Service
  Centers for Disease Control
Department of Housing and Urban Development
Department of Transportation
  Coast Guard

Three of these agencies have extraordinary importance for the management of the Missouri River: the Army Corps of Engineers, the Bureau of Reclamation, and the Western Area Power Administration, with responsibilities for marketing and distributing the hydroelectric power produced at the federally owned dams. The impact of these agencies is further described in later chapters, but brief profiles are presented here.[61]

Army Corps of Engineers

The Army Corps of Engineers' presence on the Missouri River dates from efforts to maintain and improve navigation during the 1800s. After severe basin flooding in the early 1940s, the corps was asked by Congress to develop a flood control plan, and the Pick Plan, which recommended the construction of a series of main stem dams and levees, was developed in response to this request. The plan became part of the Pick-Sloan Plan, which was in turn incorporated into the Flood Control Act of 1944.[62]

Pursuant to the Pick-Sloan Plan, the corps constructed six main stem dams on the Missouri, built levees on the lower portion, straightened the river, and dredged a nine-foot navigation channel from Sioux City, Iowa, to the mouth of the river. The agency also operates the dams, including their hydropower-generation features. The Missouri River Division of the corps, with offices in Omaha, supervises the agency's Missouri River activities in all ten states.

Bureau of Reclamation

The Bureau of Reclamation was created to develop irrigation and to support the settlement of the western public lands. Historically, the bureau has performed its duties by building main stem dams, canals, water distribution systems, and hydroelectric power generation and distribution facilities to power pumps and provide electricity to rural areas. At the time of the severe Missouri River floods of 1943 and 1944, a bureau engineer, William Glenn Sloan, was at work preparing a comprehensive plan for the development of the upper region of the Missouri. The plan, consisting of a series of main stem dams, tributary dams, and smaller irrigation structures, was integrated into the Pick-Sloan Plan.

Since 1944, the bureau has constructed and continues to operate several of the dams in the Missouri River basin, including Canyon Ferry, Yellowtail, and other irrigation projects in the upper basin states. The agency's activities in the Missouri River basin are directed from the Missouri River Basin Regional Office in Billings. With recent bureau reorganization, many of these functions have been transferred to Denver. The bureau is not active in Minnesota, Iowa, or Missouri, for they are not reclamation states.

Western Area Power Administration

Hydropower is produced at eight major dams on the Missouri and its tributaries (forty-one production units) originally considered part of the Pick-Sloan Plan. With the exception of Canyon Ferry Dam, the hydroelectric plants at the Missouri River main stem dams are under the control of the Corps of Engineers. The hydroelectric plants at Canyon Ferry Dam and on the Missouri River tributaries are controlled by the Bureau of Reclamation. The provisions of the Flood Control Act of 1944 (as amended) stipulate that all hydropower (after subtracting the power necessary to run the dams) be turned over to the Western Area Power Administration (WAPA), a division of the U.S. Department of Energy, for wholesale marketing and distribution.

The WAPA was created in 1977 as part of the Department of Energy Organization Act,[63] and it markets and transmits federally produced

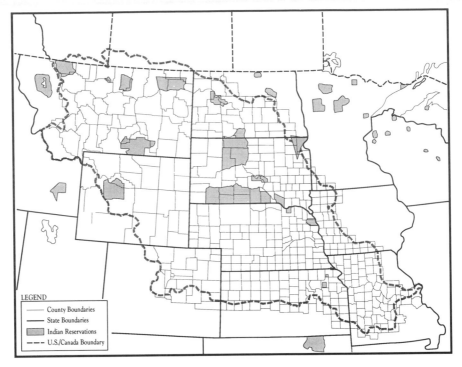

Map 2.4. Governmental complexity in the Missouri River Basin. (*Source*: Northern Lights Institute)

power in fifteen central and western states. The power marketed by WAPA is generated at fifty-two hydroelectric power plants and at a coal-fired power plant near Page, Arizona. The current operating capacity of the system is 10,486 megawatts. This power is purchased by 612 wholesale customers: cooperatives, municipalities, public utility districts, investor-owned utilities, federal and state agencies, irrigation districts, and project use customers. Western also operates more than 16,450 miles of transmission lines, 268 substations, and related facilities. For fiscal year 1992, Western had assets of $5.3 billion and power revenues of $596 million before operating expenses.[64]

Pick-Sloan project power is marketed through two area offices of WAPA. Power from the main stem dams, plus a portion of Yellowtail Dam's production, is marketed through the Billings office (Eastern Division). The power finds buyers in western Iowa, western Minnesota, Montana east of the Continental Divide, North Dakota, South Dakota, and the eastern two-thirds of Nebraska. The Eastern Division oversees the operation and maintenance of approximately 7,500 miles of transmission lines and ninety-eight substations and serves approximately 293 customers.[65]

Power from Pick-Sloan projects in Wyoming, plus the remainder of Yellowtail's production, is marketed through the Loveland, Colorado, office (Western Division). This production has been integrated with the Fryingpan-Arkansas Project, and the power from this combined system is sold in Wyoming, Colorado, Kansas, and western Nebraska. The Western Division, encompassing two dozen power plants, eighty-six substations, and 3,225 miles of transmission lines, serves forty-three customers.[66]

The political complexity of the Missouri River basin parallels both the diversity and interdependence that characterize the physical features of the region. The ten states, twenty-five Indian reservations, and twenty-one or more federal agencies provide multiplicity enough. The addition of several hundred counties, thousands of towns and cities, and innumerable special districts, each with its own problems and responsibilities, makes even the conception of this intergovernmental system nearly impossible (see Map 2.4). This governmental complexity retards regional efforts to manage water and other natural resources in the basin and is probably the most significant organizational challenge to effective management of the Missouri River system.

CHAPTER THREE

The Conservation Era and Missouri River Development

Today, the Missouri River is one of the most significantly altered river systems in America, yet only fifty years ago the Missouri was essentially an uncontrolled river. Indeed, all but one of the major main stem dams have been constructed since 1950. Missouri River development traces directly back to the passage of the Flood Control Act by Congress in 1944,[1] but the roots of comprehensive river basin development go back much further. The taming of the Missouri could have been predicted even in the 1800s with the advent of two sets of public policies: one concerning federal authority over the nation's waterways, the other concerning settlement of the nation's western lands.[2] The former policy is the story of the U.S. Army Corps of Engineers; the latter policy is the story of an often rival agency, the U.S. Bureau of Reclamation.

FEDERAL NAVIGATION POLICY

The U.S. Army Corps of Engineers became the tool for federal navigation policy. The corps traces its roots to the appointment of a chief engineer of the Continental Army during the Revolutionary War, and it was established as a permanent branch of the army in 1802.

Between 1789 and 1823, the federal government encouraged local river and harbor improvements by authorizing the states to levy tonnage taxes to support such projects. Following a U.S. Supreme Court decision in 1824 upholding the power of Congress to regulate navigable waterways, the corps began removing "sawyers, planters, and snags" from the nation's rivers and harbors. These improvements constituted the first governmental program for natural resource development and firmly established the corps' role in developing commercial navigation on the nation's waterways.

Soon, federal intervention became more direct. Congress instructed the U.S. Army Engineers to survey the Mississippi River and its tributaries, and the federal treasury dispensed grants and loans to states and state-charted corporations for waterway and canal improvements. From the end of the Civil War to 1900, Congress settled into a pattern of making regular grants for river and harbor improvements, culminating in an era of "pork-barrel" appropriations. Flooding on the Mississippi River led Congress in 1879 to create the Mississippi River Commission to address flood control and navigation issues. The corps dominated the commission, insisting on flood control projects, such as levees and channel dredging, that would also improve navigation. The commission was dissolved in 1902, and its responsibilities were assumed by the corps.

FEDERAL LAND POLICY

During the nineteenth century, the United States was acquiring the western lands. The Louisiana Territory, which contained virtually all of the Missouri River basin, was purchased from France in 1803. In 1846, after bitter negotiations with Great Britain that ended in the Oregon Compromise, the Pacific Northwest was annexed to the United States. The 1848 treaty with Mexico resulted in the purchase of the Pacific Southwest for $16 million, and additional portions of New Mexico and Arizona were purchased in 1853 (the Gadsden Purchase). These lands, plus territory purchased or annexed from Texas, completed the borders of what eventually became the contiguous forty-eight states.

Even as the United States was acquiring these extensive holdings, Congress was disposing of much of this land for a number of public purposes. The General Ordinance of 1785 provided that after survey, these public lands would be sold to settlers at no less than $1 per acre (a sum that proved prohibitive to many settlers). Grants were made to states for education and to railroads to encourage construction, and the Homestead Act of 1862[3] and the Desert Lands Act of 1877[4] allowed settlers to acquire land at little or no cost. The Desert Lands Act provided settlers with 640 acres of land if they would irrigate 20 acres within three years. Eventually, over 1 billion acres of the original public domain were transferred from the federal government to other owners.

John Wesley Powell, explorer of the Colorado River and a man who knew more about the West than any of his contemporaries, recognized the arid conditions of the region and the need for irrigation to enable settlement. His *Report on the Lands of the Arid Region of the United States*, published and submitted to Congress in 1878, argued that dry western conditions required a policy different from that which governed settlement east of the Mississippi. He urged that the public lands be surveyed, classified according to their best use (mineral, coal, irrigated agriculture, timber, pasture), and disposed of accordingly. Powell assumed that irrigation projects would be necessary to the settlement of these western lands. As director of the U.S. Geological Survey, Powell was able to convince Congress in 1888 to withdraw western lands from settlement pending the completion of an irrigation survey of the region. Settlement pressures, however, caused Congress to reopen the public domain in 1890 before the survey was complete. The nation still had not solved the problem of bringing water to most of these lands, and the federal government eventually assumed major responsibility for providing irrigation to these lands with the passage in 1902 of the Reclamation Act.[5]

GENESIS OF COMPREHENSIVE RIVER BASIN DEVELOPMENT

The nation's navigation and land policies converged at the turn of the century under the tenets of the Progressive Conservation Movement. As historian Samuel P. Hays notes in his classic book on the period, "The modern American conservation movement grew out of the firsthand experience of federal administrators and political leaders with problems of Western economic growth, and more precisely, with Western water development."[6]

The western states began looking to the federal government for assistance in developing irrigated agriculture, and the Carey Act of 1894 granted a million acres of federal land to each state. The land was to be sold to provide financing for irrigation, but few projects were built. California attorney George H. Maxwell, working though the western-based National Irrigation Congress, and Congressman Francis G. Newlands of Nevada proposed a more direct federal role in irrigation development. Newlands suggested that a reclamation fund be established to finance western irrigation projects selected by the secretary of the interior with the proceeds of western public land sales being deposited into the fund. The reclamation program would assist family farms of no more than 160 acres. With the support of the new president, Theodore Roosevelt, the Reclamation Act, also known as the Newlands Act, was passed in 1902. Frederick H. Newell, who had headed the 1888 western survey, became the first administrator of the Reclamation Service, first a branch of the Geological Survey and after 1907 a bureau reporting directly to the secretary of the interior. In the Missouri River basin, only Minnesota, Iowa, and Missouri are not reclamation states.

The investment in western water development soon drew attention to the connection between water and other natural resources. Farmers and federal officials realized that the protection of forests and range land had important benefits for the sustained river flows necessary for irrigation. As early as 1882, water was being used to generate electricity on the Fox River in Wisconsin, and larger hydroelectric power installations were installed near Portland, Oregon, in 1889 and San Bernadino, California, in 1892. Legal historian Ludwik A. Teclaff observes that "the development of hydroelectric power and its long-distance transmission probably contributed more than anything to the spread of the idea that water could and should serve several purposes."[7] Gradually, this more comprehensive understanding of the interrelationship of natural resources matured into the tenets of the Progressive Conservation Movement.

Championed by Roosevelt and Gifford Pinchot, the chief forester, the Progressive Conservation Movement developed three main themes. First, the federal policy of land disposal would be curtailed. Indeed, Roosevelt embarked on an aggressive policy of reserving lands for national forests, national parks, monuments, and game refuges. Second, the sound management of the nation's resources could yield sufficient revenues—in the form of mineral royalties, grazing fees, and timber sales—to make the resource development programs self-sustaining. Third, the Progressive Conservation Movement emphasized efficiency and scientific management. As Hays describes the period:

> Conservation leaders sprang from such fields as hydrology, forestry, agrostology, geology, and anthropology. . . . Loyalty to these professional ideals, not close association with the grass-roots public, set the tone . . . of the movement. . . . Conservationists envisaged, even though they did not realize their aims, a political system guided by the ideal of efficiency and dominated by the technicians who could best determine how to achieve it.[8]

This emerging national policy sought multiple-use stewardship of the nation's water resources where "the same water could support navigation, irrigation, hydroelectric power and also prevent wasteful flooding by the operation of regulated reservoirs."[9] Large main stem dams and basinwide planning were to be the linchpins of this multipurpose policy. This comprehensive river basin development policy would not, however, be realized during the tenure of Roosevelt or Pinchot.

The major resource challenge of the Progressive era, as stated by Roosevelt, was to prevent a private, "centralized monopoly of hydroelectric power development free of all public control."[10] In 1896, Congress had enabled hydroelectric plants to obtain rights-of-way over federal land, and companies began acquiring valuable power sites as rapidly as possible. The Roosevelt administration departed from this policy; in 1902, for example, the president vetoed a bill that would have allowed private interests to build a power station at Muscle Shoals on the Tennessee River in Alabama.

In 1906, the Roosevelt administration secured an amendment to the

Reclamation Act allowing the sale of surplus hydroelectric power from reclamation projects, and Roosevelt argued further for some kind of federal power commission. During the presidency of William Howard Taft, the Federal Power Act of 1920[11] was finally passed. "By granting the national government authority to issue licenses for construction and operation of power plants," this legislation "established the government's priority over power sites along navigable waterways."[12] The Federal Power Commission created by the act remained ineffectual during the 1920s and three major oligarchies, the Morgan–Bonbright–National City group, the Chase National–Forbes group, and the Insull group, gained control of almost 60 percent of electric production in the country, as well as control of most of the desirable hydroelectric sites.

This oligopoly, and the vulnerability of the dormant Muscle Shoals project to private takeover,[13] gave birth to the Tennessee Valley Authority (TVA) proposal, the first legislation that reflected the concept of multiple-purpose river development. TVA bills passed Congress in 1928 and 1930, only to be vetoed by Presidents Calvin Coolidge and Herbert Hoover. When a sympathetic Franklin Roosevelt took office in 1933, the TVA bill was signed into law.[14] With three commissioners and a corporate structure independent of Congress and the Corps of Engineers,

> the act proclaimed a policy for the unified development of a watershed for the national welfare, for the restoration of exhausted lands, for the development of the Tennessee in its entirety, for the reforestation of cut-over lands, for the alleviation of unemployment, for promotion of the interests of national defense, and for the revitalization of an entire region economically.[15]

The comprehensive approach to river basin development embodied in the TVA became the model for similar proposals for other river basins, the Missouri among them. Roosevelt indicated that "if we are successful here [with TVA], we can march on, step by step, in a like development of other great natural territorial units within our borders."[16] Congress authorized the appointment of a Natural Resources Committee to prepare a national plan for river basin development. Threatened by the possible transfer of water development construction to somewhat autonomous regional authorities, the Corps of Engineers resisted these planning efforts, "and the lines were drawn for a protracted battle over the use of river basin authorities as a means of national water use planning and development."[17]

Large multipurpose water development projects actually began as public works projects during the depression to alleviate unemployment. Bonneville and Grand Coulee dams on the Columbia were started in

1933 and 1935, respectively. Similar projects were authorized for central and southern California. Fort Peck Dam, a project of the Corps of Engineers, was authorized by Congress in 1935,[18] and work was under way almost before the ink dried on the legislation. In addition to jobs creation, the primary purpose of the earth-filled dam was to improve navigation in the lower Missouri basin. Provision was also made for future hydroelectric development.

PROPOSALS FOR A MISSOURI VALLEY AUTHORITY

The proposal for a Missouri Valley Authority also traces its roots to the Progressive era and the first suggestions of multiple use and comprehensive river basin management. At President Roosevelt's urging, the first bill for a Missouri Valley Authority was introduced in 1936.[19] In 1937, the president proposed dividing the nation into seven regions—based on watershed boundaries—to manage multipurpose basin developments.[20] These basin plans would be coordinated by the newly created National Resources Planning Board.

In 1940, the Omaha regional office of the National Resources Planning Board issued a Missouri valley regional development plan and suggested that a Missouri Valley Planning Commission be created.[21] In 1941, the National Resources Planning Board convened a conference in Omaha that led to the creation of a Missouri Valley Regional Planning Commission. The commission consisted of one representative from each basin state, except Colorado and Wyoming, and one representative each from the federal Departments of War, Agriculture, and Interior.[22]

The Missouri River floods of 1943 caught the attention of the nation and provided the impetus for federal flood control legislation and congressional consideration of a range of basin development proposals, including the Pick Plan, the Sloan Plan, a Missouri River Commission, and a possible Missouri Valley Authority. In that year, floods in eight major drainages in the Midwest resulted in seventy-one deaths, the inundation of more than 7 million acres of land, and damages in excess of $153 million (equivalent to more than $650 million today). Losses in the Missouri River basin were more than $46 million in direct damages.

During 1943–1944, the *St. Louis Post-Dispatch* ran a series of articles and editorials supporting the creation of a Missouri Valley Authority. In August 1944, Senator James Murray of Montana declared himself an MVA supporter and introduced a bill, S. 2089,[23] to create the authority. The bill proposed an agency similar to the TVA with a three-member commission, appointed by the president, to assume the management of dams and

Missouri River flooding, 1944. (Courtesy Bureau of Reclamation)

other projects in all portions of the basin except the small area in Minnesota.[24] Other characteristics of the proposal included the following:

> The authority was to have its headquarters in the region and was to "utilize to the fullest extent possible the advice, assistance, and cooperation of the people of the region, and their public and private organizations—local, State, and Federal." Its board was to have full power over the corporation's policy, in terms of the act's provisions, and could consult with and request the assistance of any agency of the United States. The board was charged with the preparation, over two years, of a suitable program for the whole basin. This program, if not enacted within four months after its presentation to Congress, would nonetheless be deemed as in effect. An advisory committee was also provided, to be made up of citizens of the various states who would act as curb and check upon the directors. Other provisions allowed the states five per cent of the taxes, and the M.V.A. was empowered to acquire any lands and projects necessary to its operations.[25]

Murray's proposal was supported by the National Farmers' Union, with 141,000 basin farm families among its members, and several newspapers; it was opposed by private power interests and many irrigators. Murray was accused of allowing his "hatred of the Anaconda Copper Mining Company and the Montana Power Company to blind him."[26] Committee action was not completed on the bill when Congress took an election recess in fall 1944, and when Congress returned, the Corps of Engineers and the Bureau of Reclamation had reached their Pick-Sloan compromise (discussed in the next section). Promised full hearings on the MVA proposal when Congress returned in 1945, Murray withdrew his opposition and made possible the passage of the Flood Control Act, which incorporated the Pick-Sloan Plan, in the last days of 1944.

In February 1945, Murray introduced another MVA proposal,[27] but Harry Truman had succeeded Roosevelt and administrative support for the MVA softened. Hearings on the Senate bill were held in April and September, but after two committees had significantly modified the proposal and issued adverse reports, the bill died without final action in the Seventy-ninth Congress.

Opposition to the MVA concept was based on many grounds. Some people believed the TVA model was inapplicable to the Missouri because the TVA was predominately a power project in a smaller basin with more precipitation.[28] Agriculture was divided on the proposal, and upper basin commercial and business interests opposed the legislation because of its perceived threat to western water rights.[29] Even the Corps of Engineers and the Bureau of Reclamation united in opposition to the proposition, for "no matter how much they hate each other, they hated the MVA more."[30] Although Murray introduced MVA bills in later sessions of Congress, none passed. This form of comprehensive river basin development would never come to the Missouri.

DEVELOPMENT OF THE PICK-SLOAN PLAN

The floods of 1943 did result in congressional action when Congress passed the Flood Control Act on December 21, 1944. Although the Flood Control Act was born primarily because of concerns about flooding and the need for development in the Missouri River basin, it was nonetheless legislation of national scope, with authorizations for projects in other parts of the country. The Pick-Sloan Plan, however, embodied in the Flood Control Act, was indeed developed specifically for the Missouri River basin.

Although major floods had occurred on the Missouri River in 1844, 1881, 1903, 1915, 1926, and 1934, the severe flooding in 1943 focused unprecedented public and congressional attention on the Missouri River basin.[31] A special meeting of the Flood Control Committee of the House of Representatives was held on May 13, 1943, to hear a presentation from Colonel Lewis A. Pick (then division engineer in the Corps of Engineers' Omaha office) concerning river flooding. Congress subsequently passed a resolution requesting the corps to determine flood control needs on the Missouri.

The Corps of Engineers assigned Colonel Pick the task of responding to the congressional resolution. Pick completed his report on August 10, 1943, and his plan was approved by the Board of Engineers for Rivers and Harbors later that month. After review by other federal agencies, the plan was formally submitted to Congress on March 2, 1944. With strong committee support, the Pick Plan became part of the flood control bill passed by the House.

The plan was primarily a flood control and navigation improvement plan with some provision for hydroelectric production. It called for a series of levees on the main stem of the river below Sioux City, dams on the river above Sioux City, and dams on tributaries. In addition to projects already authorized (totaling $171 million), the estimated total cost was $490 million—$410 million for multipurpose dams and $80 million for levee construction (the details of the proposal are set forth in Table 3.1).

The Corps of Engineers' proposal was hotly opposed by the Bureau of Reclamation and its lobby, the National Reclamation Association (NRA), because of a feared impact of lower basin navigation on potential water uses in the upper basin. Moreover, the Bureau of Reclamation was completing its own plan for comprehensive Missouri River basin development. Authorized by Congress in 1939, this plan was being prepared by William Glenn Sloan, an assistant engineer with the agency's Billings, Montana, office. The bureau's plan, or the Sloan Plan, emphasized irrigation, reclamation, and some power production and was submitted to Congress on May 5, 1944. The plan proposed ninety dams and reservoirs, seventeen power plants, the irrigation of 4,760,400 acres of dry land, and the supplemental irrigation of 538,000 acres. The overall cost was estimated at $1.257 billion (the elements of the bureau's plan are set forth in Table 3.2). The Sloan Plan became part of the Senate's flood control bill.

The National Reclamation Association, with affiliates in all of the Missouri basin states, supported the Sloan Plan, as did the railroads—arch competitors of barge navigation interests. The Department of the Interior and most western governors and congressmen worked closely with the NRA to encourage upstream reclamation projects and to oppose the Pick Plan. The governors of North Dakota, Wyoming, and Montana presented united testimony favoring protection of upstream beneficial use rights against downstream navigation uses.

While the flood control bill was mired in the Senate and the MVA was

TABLE 3.1. Elements of the Pick Plan (1944)

Project	Location	Storage (in 1,000s ac-ft)	Cost (in $thousands)
Dams and Reservoirs:			
Garrison Reservoir	North Dakota	17,000	130,000
Oak Creek	South Dakota	6,000	60,000
Oahe	South Dakota	6,000	50,000
Fort Randall	South Dakota	6,000	75,000
Gavins Point	South Dakota	200	15,000
Lower Canyon	Montana	2,250	35,000
Boysen	Wyoming	3,500	20,000
Medicine Creek	Nebraska		2,400
Hale	Colorado		7,200
Red Willow	Nebraska		2,100
Enders	Nebraska		6,700
Beecher Island	Colorado		6,600
Total			$410,000
Missouri River Levees:			
Sioux City, Iowa, to Platte River			14,500
Platte River to Rulo, Nebr.			8,000
Rulo, Nebr., to Kansas City, Mo.			15,000
Kansas City, Mo., to Jefferson City, Mo.			22,500
Jefferson City, Mo., to mouth			14,000
Sioux City, Iowa			600
Omaha, Nebr.			3,800
Council Bluffs, Iowa			1,600
Total			$80,000
Completion of Projects Already Authorized:			
Kanopolis Reservoir	Kansas		9,000
Harlan County Reservoir	Nebraska and Kansas		20,000
Osceola Reservoir	Missouri		28,500
Tuttle Creek Reservoir	Kansas		28,000
Chillicothe Reservoir	Missouri		28,500
Arlington Reservoir	Missouri		7,300
South Grand Reservoir	Missouri		10,400
Pomme de Terre Reservoir	Missouri		6,200
Richland Reservoir	Missouri		6,900
Cherry Creek Reservoir	Colorado		8,200
The Kansas Citys	Missouri and Kansas		18,000
Total			$171,000
TOTAL			$661,000

Source: H.R. Rep. No. 475, 78th Cong., 2d sess. (1944).

TABLE 3.2. Elements of the Sloan Plan (1944)

Reservoirs:	Number	Storage (ac-ft)	
Colorado	3	785,000	
Kansas	8	1,659,900	
Montana	24	10,321,950	
Nebraska	10	3,055,500	
North Dakota	8	1,267,000	
South Dakota	10	25,559,000	
Wyoming	27	3,064,200	
TOTAL	90	45,712,550	
Power Plants:	Location	KW Installed (in 1,000s)	KWH Firm/Yr (in 1,000s)
Montana	Mission	50.0	263,000
	Yellowtail	75.0	332,000
	Lyons	23.5	121,000
	Canyon Ferry	35.0	149,800
	Portage	20.0	146,900
Total		203.5	1,012,700
Nebraska	Harlan County	2.0	6,700
South Dakota	Oahe	150.0	1,620,600
	Big Bend	75.0	inc above
	Fort Randall	100.0	inc above
Total		325.0	1,620,600
Wyoming	Kortes	30.0	162,000
	Boysen	10.0	56,900
	Kane	30.0	139,300
	Hunter Mountain	12.0	71,000
	Thief Creek	60.0	350,000
	Sunlight	20.0	109,500
	Bald Ridge	30.0	166,500
	Tongue River	25.0	20,000
Total		217.0	1,075,200
TOTAL		747.5	3,715,200
Irrigation or Drainage:	New Acres	Supplemental Acres	Total Acres
Colorado	101,280	1,719	102,999
Kansas	193,335	155	193,490
Montana	967,130	337,500[a]	1,313,930
Nebraska	989,445	19,930	1,009,375
North Dakota	1,266,440		1,266,440
South Dakota	961,210	11,300	972,510
Wyoming	281,560	167,400	448,960
TOTAL	4,760,400	538,004	5,307,704

[a]Includes 91,700 acres of drainage measures.

Source: S. Doc. No. 191, 78th Cong., 2d sess. (1944).

ensnared in committee, President Roosevelt received a strong resolution from the Missouri River States Committee and basin states' governors calling for the Corps of Engineers and the Bureau of Reclamation to combine their separate proposals into a regional water plan. The president transmitted the message to Congress along with his own endorsement of the MVA. On October 16 and 17, 1944, Colonel Pick and William Sloan met in Omaha and worked out the compromise that bears their names. Simply, they agreed to build the projects proposed by both agencies. The agreement, sometimes referred to as "a shameless shotgun wedding," was set forth in Senate Document 247,[32] a short six-page paper, and was incorporated in the Flood Control Act that passed Congress on December 22, 1944.

The coordinating agreement set forth in Senate Document 247 adopts the plans of both agencies and seeks to eliminate duplicate projects. The final paragraph of the document indicates that the unified plan "will secure the maximum benefits for flood control, irrigation, navigation, power, domestic and sanitary purposes, wildlife, and recreation." Given the careful wording in other parts of the report, the order of proposed uses in this paragraph probably (though not explicitly) reflects the priority that the negotiators placed on the multiple uses that would result. Table 3.3 summarizes the major provisions of the consolidated plan for the six subbasins used by the negotiators, and Map 3.1 shows the major projects eventually constructed under the plan.

O'MAHONEY-MILLIKIN AMENDMENT

An important feature of the 1944 Flood Control Act was the O'Mahoney-Millikin Amendment, a consequence of the struggle between those interests wishing to improve downstream navigation and those hoping for upstream agricultural development. The resolution of this tension was a precondition for upper basin support of the Pick-Sloan Plan.

By the twentieth century, the value of the Missouri River for navigation purposes had been well established, and Congress and the Corps of Engineers developed plans to improve the navigation channel. Congress enacted legislation in 1927 to dredge a permanent 6-foot channel between Sioux City and Kansas City;[33] and a year later, Congress authorized the preparation of a comprehensive study of the possibilities for improving navigation both upstream and downstream of Sioux City (the "308" report).[34] In 1935, Congress adopted portions of the 308 report and authorized a 6-foot-deep, 200-foot-wide permanent navigation channel from Sioux City to the mouth of the river and construction of the Fort Peck Reservoir, which would be operated primarily for navigation.[35] By

TABLE 3.3. Major Features of the Pick-Sloan Plan

Upper Missouri River Basin[a]	
Reservoirs	19
Reservoir capacity	3,359,950 ac-ft
(for flood control, silt	
control, hydro, irrigation)	
New irrigated land	460,900 acres
Supplemental irrigation	208,700 acres
Yellowstone River Basin[b]	
Reservoirs	27
Reservoir capacity	4,285,200 ac-ft
(for flood control, silt	
control, hydro, irrigation)	
New irrigated land	509,560 acres
Supplemental irrigation	204,500 acres
Missouri River (Fort Peck to Sioux City)[c]	
Reservoirs	5
Reservoir capacity	26,850,000 ac-ft
(for flood control, silt	
control, hydro, irrigation)	
New irrigated land	2,292,900 acres
Supplemental irrigation	
Niobrara, Platte, and Kansas Rivers[c]	
Reservoirs	22
Reservoir capacity	5,615,400 ac-ft[d]
(for flood control, silt	
control, hydro, irrigation)	
New irrigated land	1,284,000 acres
Supplemental irrigation	21,804 acres
Minor Western Tributaries[a]	
Reservoirs	15
Reservoir capacity	1,237,000 ac-ft
(for flood control, silt	
control, hydro, irrigation)	
New irrigated land	212,980 acres
Supplemental irrigation	11,300 acres
Lower Missouri Basin[e]	
Reservoirs	7
Reservoir capacity	Not stated
New irrigated land	Not stated
Supplemental irrigation	Not stated
Other features: Levees and appurtenant works	

[a]Not addressed by Pick Plan; Sloan Plan used.
[b]Sloan Plan used as it would also accomplish objectives of Pick Plan.
[c]Both plans used with changes.
[d]Not including Red Willow and Enders projects.
[e]Both plans identical.

Source: Pick Plan, H.D. 475, 78th Cong. 2d sess. (1944); Sloan Plan, S.D. 191, 78th Cong. 2d sess. (1944).

1944, the Corps of Engineers had completed the 6-foot channel, and 90 percent of the channel had been dredged to 9 feet.

While the Flood Control Act was pending in 1944, Congress was also considering H.R. 3961, the proposed Rivers and Harbors legislation.[36] An omnibus bill for navigation projects around the country, the bill called for the dredging of a 9-foot-deep, 300-foot-wide channel below Sioux City.[37] Upper basin congressmen and senators were concerned that the lower basin might have already established a water right for the 6-foot channel; they were even more concerned about the amount of water that might be claimed to fill a proposed 9-foot by 300-foot channel. The proposed rivers and harbors legislation also seemed to run contrary to the 4 million acres of federally financed irrigation projects planned for the upper basin. The Bureau of Reclamation indicated that the 6-foot channel would leave enough water (4,168,000 ac-ft/yr) to irrigate 2,778,000 acres of land; a 9-foot channel, by requiring more than the mean annual flow of the river, "would permit no additional irrigation development at all in the upper basin."[38]

As a condition of passage, the O'Mahoney-Millikin Amendment, drafted by Senator O'Mahoney of Wyoming and Senator Millikin of Colorado, was included in the final Flood Control Act. The amendment protects upper basin consumptive uses by limiting the use of water for navigation purposes to "such use as does not conflict with any beneficial consumptive use, present or future, in States lying wholly or partly west of the ninety-eighth meridian, of such waters for domestic, municipal, stock water, irrigation, or industrial purposes."[39]

OTHER PROVISIONS OF THE FLOOD CONTROL ACT

In Section 9 of the Flood Control Act, the Missouri River projects enumerated in the Pick (H.D. 475) and Sloan (S.D. 191) plans, as coordinated by Senate Document 247, were "approved" and their initial stages authorized. The Corps of Engineers and the Department of Interior were instructed to proceed "as speedily as may be consistent with budgetary requirements." The original authorization was in the amount of $200 million for both the corps and the bureau; that amount was eventually authorized for each agency. The secretary of the interior was instructed to follow the requirements of the federal reclamation laws in constructing most of the reclamation and power development projects.

Despite its focus on flood control in the Missouri basin, the legislation makes virtually no mention of the devastating floods that inspired congressional action. Many of the statute's provisions are of general ap-

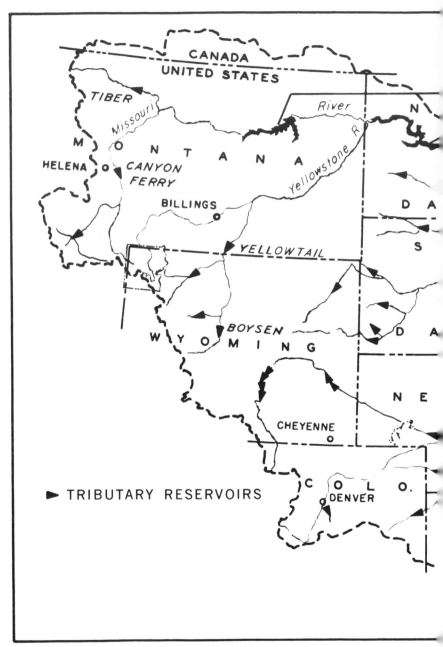

Map 3.1. Missouri River reservoirs (*Source:* U.S. Army Corps of Engineers)

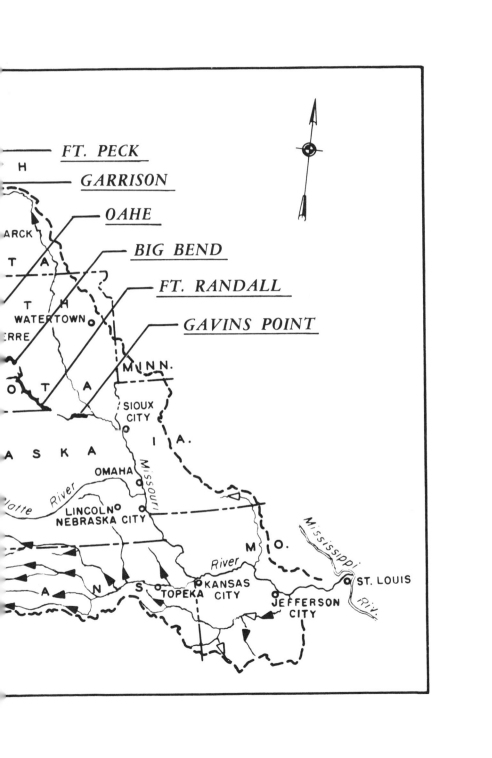

FT. PECK

GARRISON

OAHE

BIG BEND

FT. RANDALL

GAVINS POINT

plicability as flood control projects were authorized throughout the country. The statute also establishes several other important policies for river basin development and management (see Appendix 4 for more information about the act).

Comprehensive, coordinated development. Congress appears to have adopted the major premise of the Progressive Conservation Movement, for the act indicates that these "works of improvement" will be constructed for navigation and flood control and that these projects will be constructed with an emphasis on "comprehensive and coordinated development."[40] The act also reveals the tension between the need for federal action and the resistance of states and private entities to federal governmental intrusion. In the first section of the act, Congress invokes its plenary power over "the rivers of the Nation . . . , for navigation or flood control." Subsequently, however, Congress defers to the authority of states "in determining the development of the watersheds within their borders and . . . their interests and rights in water utilization and control . . . to preserve and protect to the *fullest possible extent* established and *potential uses.*"[41]

The corps is ordered to consult and coordinate with any "affected State or States"[42] and, if the project concerns waters arising west of the ninety-seventh meridian, with the secretary of the interior. Projects proposed by the corps must also be coordinated with "other plans [presumably of the states or the Department of the Interior] involving the waters which would be used or controlled by such proposed works."[43] A similar procedure is required of the secretary of the interior in undertaking investigations and developing reports for "works for irrigation and purposes incident thereto."[44] If any affected state or the chief of engineers objects to a project proposed by the secretary of the interior, that project is not deemed authorized until Congress acts. Although these coordination requirements are clear, the act fails to establish a process or institutional structure through which such communication and coordination will occur.

Division of agency authority. Congress adopted a general goal of "comprehensive and coordinated development," but it was more explicit in drawing jurisdictional lines for the relevant federal agencies. The army engineers are given authority over "flood control and allied purposes," defined "to include channel and major drainage improvements."[45] The Department of Agriculture is given authority to investigate watersheds and to develop measures for "run-off and water flow retardation and soil-erosion prevention on watersheds."[46]

Sale of electric power. Section five of the act establishes important policies for the marketing of electric power produced at dams under the control of the Corps of Engineers. Excess power is to be transferred to the secretary of the interior (since 1977, to the secretary of the Department of Energy).[47] The secretary markets the power so as "to encourage the most widespread use thereof at the lowest possible rates to consumers consistent with sound business principles."[48] The rates are to be approved by the secretary with "regard to recovery . . . of the cost of producing and transmitting" the electricity, including the amortization of the capital investment allocated to power. Three principles emerge from this statement of policy: (1) the costs of electrical production will be recovered; (2) the use of the power will be widespread;[49] and (3) the rates are to be low for the ultimate consumer.

The secretary of the interior is authorized to purchase or construct the necessary transmission lines and related facilities so that power can be distributed on a wholesale basis (and on "fair and reasonable terms and conditions") to public entities, cooperatives, and privately owned companies. Another important provision is the preference in the sale of electric power to public entities and cooperatives—a provision that has been a major feature in American energy policy.

Sale of surplus water.   The secretary of the army is authorized to market "surplus water" from any reservoir under the control of the Corps of Engineers to states, municipalities, private concerns, or individuals. No definition is given for the "surplus water" term, but the U.S. Supreme Court in its 1988 ETSI *Pipeline Project v. Missouri* decision indicated that it means "all water that can be made available from the reservoir without adversely affecting other lawful uses of the water."[50] Barring any specific allocation to irrigation under the statute, the Court also determined that the corps has exclusive authority to contract for the industrial use of surplus water.[51] Receipts from the sale of water are deposited as miscellaneous receipts in the U.S. Treasury.

Regulation of stored water.   The act creates an ambiguity, still unresolved, when it authorizes the secretary of the army to issue regulations for the storage of water in federal reservoirs for flood control or navigation. The question has arisen whether this authority extends only to the portion of the reservoir pool needed for these two purposes or whether the corps also has authority over all the water in the reservoir.

The Supreme Court's decision in ETSI, based as it is on the Court's intolerance of divided administrative authority over these reservoirs as well as on other sections of the law, appears to give the corps exclusive authority over all the water in corps-operated reservoirs as long as no formal allocation has been made to irrigation and no other lawful uses are disturbed.

Use of water for irrigation.   Section eight provides for the use of water for irrigation purposes. Although the secretary of the interior may recommend such a use from a specific reservoir, the secretary of the army determines whether water will be used for irrigation. Interior must also receive specific authorization by Congress before it may construct or operate irrigation works. Federal reclamation law applies to these irrigation projects. The Interior Department's proposed irrigation projects must also be "predicated" upon repayment by irrigators (considering their financial ability) "of an appropriate portion of the cost of structures and facilities used for irrigation and other purposes."[52] This language suggests that irrigators would not necessarily have to repay the entire cost of the irrigation features of a project.

LIMITATIONS OF THE BASIC PRINCIPLES

The Flood Control Act, incorporating the Pick-Sloan Plan, is the organic act of the Missouri River basin, but its principles, though important, are frequently forgotten or neglected. They are also difficult to apply to situations that were not contemplated by the original authors.

The act provides the Corps of Engineers with significant authority over the basin, and the Supreme Court's ETSI decision (coupled with the recent retrenchment of the Bureau of Reclamation) reinforces that authority. Yet the mandate contained in the act should not be neglected: the corps' activities are to be well-coordinated with the plans of states and other federal agencies.

A second principle of the statute concerns the distribution of hydroelectric power from the basin's federal dams. The power was to be distributed "to encourage the most widespread use thereof at the lowest possible rates consistent with sound business principles." As delineated in the next chapter, the Pick-Sloan hydropower may be cheap, but the use of the power is concentrated in just a few selected states. This shortcoming needs to be addressed.

The limitation on downstream navigation is a third major principle of the act. Navigation improvements must at once yield substantial benefits to navigation and not interfere with other appropriate uses of the water. The use of water for navigation is also constrained by the O'Mahoney-Millikin Amendment, which establishes a transbasin preference, rather than a strict allocation, in the use of water. Beneficial consumptive uses in the upper basin, present or future, are to be preferred over downstream navigation. Thus upper basin use of water for irrigation or municipal-domestic purposes takes precedence over lower basin navigation.

What is less clear is whether upper basin nonconsumptive uses, such as recreation and fisheries, outrank lower basin uses. Does hydroelectric power generation at the main stem dams, which all lie in states all or partly west of the ninety-eighth meridian, also have a preference over navigation? These hydropower rights also would be senior to lower basin consumptive uses established since the dams were built in the 1950s. The preferential status of water exported for out-of-basin purposes is also unclear. The Flood Control Act contemplated the comprehensive development of the basin; possible uses out-of-basin were not contemplated and probably run against the original congressional purposes for the legislation.

The Pick-Sloan Plan was the blueprint for building the large main stem and tributary dams, constructing levees and a nine-foot navigation channel, installing hydroelectric turbines and transmission lines, and undertaking irrigation projects. The plan is a reminder of what was promised to the people of the Missouri River basin in 1944, how much of what was promised has not been honored, and how some of the promises have been fulfilled only at great cost to the residents and ecology of the basin.

CHAPTER FOUR

Implementation of the Pick-Sloan Plan

In the fifty years since passage of the Flood Control Act, many of the projects of the Pick-Sloan Plan have been constructed. Many projects, however, still exist only in the language of the original congressional documents. Uncertainties about provisions of the Flood Control Act and the disparity of actual Pick-Sloan Plan benefits have resulted in conflict among the states, federal agencies, and basin residents.

COSTS AND BENEFITS TO THE STATES

Several features of the Pick-Sloan Plan have been very successful. Flood control, the premier goal of the legislation, has been largely achieved. The Corps of Engineers estimates that since integrated operation of some of the main stem reservoirs began in 1954, $2.7 billion in flood damage has been prevented because of the flood control features.[1] This figure does not include an estimated $7.7 billion in flooding damage that was avoided during the severe 1993 Mississippi and Missouri River floods thanks to the available storage capacity in the upper basin reservoirs. Of course, most of the flood control features benefit the lower basin states.

Hydroelectric power production was considered a secondary purpose in the original legislation, being barely mentioned either in the army's plan or in the composite plan. Only the Sloan plan contains any detailed discussion of the proposed power features. In its original submission, the bureau projected the installation of 758,000 kilowatts of capacity and the annual production of 3.8 megawatt-hours. At full development, the power was to have a value of $17.4 million per year. The Pick-Sloan projects now have a maximum operating capacity of 2.8 million kilowatts and a net generation of 9.3 million kilowatt-hours in 1988 (down to 7.3 million kilowatt hours in 1992 because of drought conditions). In 1986, gross revenues were $190 million.[2] The distribution of this power is quite skewed. Montana, Wyoming, North Dakota, and South Dakota produce virtually all this power, but two-thirds of it is consumed by Minnesota, Colorado, Iowa, and Nebraska.

Another underestimated benefit of the Pick-Sloan Plan is the recreational use of the main stem and tributary reservoirs. Recreation is men-

Million Visitor Hours

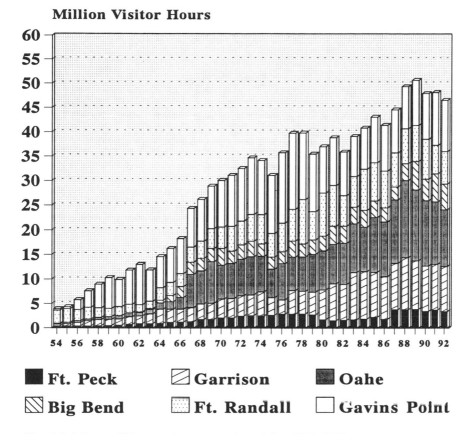

Fig. 4.1. Missouri River main stem project visits, 1954–1992.

Note: 1954 through 1988 data in calendar years; 1989 to present in fiscal years; Ft. Peck data prior to 1989 estimated.

Source: U.S. Army Corps of Engineers, Missouri River Division, *1992–1993 Annual Operating Plan* (Omaha, December 1993)

tioned as an incidental use in the original congressional documents, but in 1992, public recreational use at the main stem reservoirs alone amounted to 49.5 million visitor hours.[3] In some areas of upper basin states, recreation has become perhaps the primary benefit local residents have obtained from the Pick-Sloan Plan (see Figure 4.1 for an indication of the substantial growth in the recreational use of these reservoirs, especially since the late 1960s).

As for the original purposes of the Pick-Sloan Plan, the results have been much less dramatic. For example, improved navigation was one of the major features of the plan. Estimates in the 1940s indicated that after

Million Tons

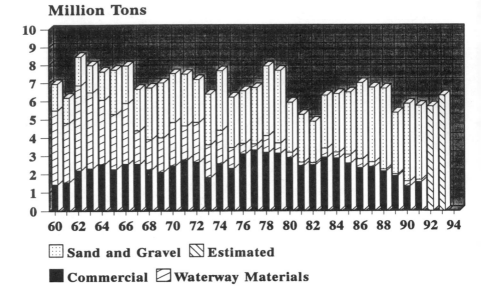

☐ Sand and Gravel ☒ Estimated

■ Commercial ▨ Waterway Materials

Fig. 4.2. Missouri River total tonnage, 1960–1994.

Source: U.S. Army Corps of Engineers, Missouri River Division, *1992–1993 Annual Operating Plan* (Omaha, December 1993)

a nine-foot channel was dredged in the lower river and other navigation improvements were made, annual commercial tonnage would be nearly 5 million tons.[4] Yet in recent years, commercial tonnage in and out of the river has been declining (see Figure 4.2). In 1990, for instance, commercial tonnage was only 1.3 million tons.[5] Farm products provide the largest amount of commercial cargo, followed by chemical products and stone products, and more of the combined commercial cargo moves upstream than downstream.

It is, however, in the area of irrigation development, the centerpiece of the Bureau of Reclamation's plan, that the results of Pick-Sloan have been most disappointing. Approximately 5.3 million acres were to be developed. As of 1987, only 501,600 acres (full and supplemental irrigation), less than 10 percent of the irrigation features, had been developed (see Table 4.1). Having obtained 16 percent of its promised 1 million acres, Nebraska is the winner in terms of total acreage developed under the plan. Although the total irrigated acreage promised to them was small, Wyoming (which has developed 56 percent of the planned acreage) and Kansas (which has developed 17 percent of the planned

TABLE 4.1. Existing Pick-Sloan Irrigation Projects and Amount of Irrigation Aid Associated with Each

Project	State	Year	Full (1000 ac)	Supplemental (1000 ac)	Aid ($1000)
Kirwin	KS	1957	11.4		9,747
Webster	KS	1960	8.5		8,363
Cedar Bluff	KS	1963	6.8		7,172
Almena	KS	1967	5.8		5,636
Glen Elder Dam & Reservoir	KS	1970			4,653
Total			32.5		$35,571
Savage	MT	1950	2.2		665
Crow Creek	MT	1955	5.0		2,703
Helena Valley	MT	1959	16.0		16,110
East Bench	MT	1965	21.8	28.0	16,895
Lower Marias	MT	1979	3.2		16,513
Total			48.2	28.0	$52,886
Cambridge	NE	1952	56.5	9.6	50,638
Sargent	NE	1957	13.4		3,661
Ainsworth	NE	1965	34.5		15,699
Frenchman-Farwell	NE	1966	50.1		21,741
Total			154.5	9.6	$91,739
Heart Butte	ND	1952	6.7		1,588
Dickinson	ND	1954	0.4		253
Fort Clark	ND	1954	1.9		1,140
Total			9.0		$2,981
Rapid Valley	SD	1948		8.9	2,110
Angostura	SD	1953	12.2		13,483
Shadehill	SD	1976	3.0		2,247
Total			15.2	8.9	$17,840
Riverton	WY	1925[a]	64.3		45,366
Owl Creek	WY	1957		11.3	7,978
Hanover-Bluff	WY	1957	7.4		6,714
Keyhole	WY	1976		5.2	3,185
Total			71.7	16.5	$63,243
Bostwick	KS,NE	1953	62.9		41,664
Glendo	NE,WY	1958		44.6	860
Total			62.9	44.6	$42,524
TOTAL			394.0	107.6	$306,784

[a]Reauthorized under the Pick-Sloan Plan in 1970 (Pub. L. 91-409).

Source: Western Area Power Administration, Proposed Power Rate Adjustment (Golden, Colo., 1987), 7.

acreage) have done better than the remaining states in obtaining the irrigated acreage promised under Pick-Sloan. Colorado, for example, was promised that 103,000 acres would be irrigated, but none of that acreage has been developed under Pick-Sloan. North Dakota (less than 1 percent developed), South Dakota (2 percent developed), and Montana (6 percent developed) were each entitled to around 1 million acres of irrigated farmland, and each of these states lost more than 500,000 acres of land to main stem reservoirs.

The evaluation of any public policy measure is difficult, particularly when the program, like the Pick-Sloan Plan, is multidimensional and many decades old. It is difficult to measure retroactively the ancillary benefits of the program, for example, the multiplier effect of federal dam construction expenditures through local and state economies. But because the original purposes of Pick-Sloan were rather clearly spelled out and because record keeping has been reasonably thorough, it is possible to develop some conclusions. Although the evaluation in Table 4.2 may be somewhat rough, it is evident that Nebraska has received numerous benefits from the plan and that Montana, North Dakota, and South Dakota have received very few.

The fact that very few of the irrigation features of the plan have been completed is bad enough. Congress, however, added insult to injury in 1964 when it essentially deauthorized the irrigation features of the Pick-Sloan Plan.[6] Now, before any of the irrigation projects contemplated in the original plan can be constructed, they must be specifically reauthorized by Congress.

Thus, the results of the Pick-Sloan Plan have been very different than the original expectations. Although it is informative to make this assessment, the conclusion is not necessarily an argument to complete the original features of the plan. The public interest and the interests of the basin states are no longer served by blindly completing a fifty-year-old plan. Whether the skewed and incomplete implementation of Pick-Sloan is explained by changed circumstances, unanticipated events, or congressional politics is a question that deserves additional research.

SPECIAL DAMAGE TO THE TRIBES

For the Indian tribes on the Missouri main stem, it is ironic that a project conceived to prevent flood control actually ended up flooding Indian lands and displacing Indian families. That, in essence, has been Pick-Sloan's impact on the tribes. Author Vine Deloria has labeled Pick-Sloan the single most destructive act ever perpetrated on any tribe by the United States.[7] Another historian concludes that the "Pick-Sloan Plan

TABLE 4.2. Distribution of Benefits and Costs of Pick-Sloan Plan

State	Acres lost to Reservoirs	Irrigation Promised (ac)	Irrigation Developed (ac)	P-S Hydro Generation Capacity (%)	P-S Hydro Received (%)	Navigation Benefits	Flood Control Benefits
Big Winner							
Nebraska	15,162	1,009,375	164,100		18.72	Yes	Yes
Winners							
Kansas		193,490	32,500			Yes	Yes
Minnesota					23.53	No	No
Iowa					13.53	Yes	Yes
Missouri						Yes	Yes
Losers							
Colorado		102,999			1.47	No	No
Wyoming		158,100	88,200			No	No
Big Losers							
North Dakota	584,060	1,266,400	9,000	19.49	12.33	No	No
Montana	590,000	1,313,930	76,200	15.06	10.94	No	No
South Dakota	520,390	972,510	24,100	65.45	19.45	No	No
Multistate projects			107,500				
TOTAL	1,709,612	5,016,804	501,600	100.00[a]	100.00[a]		

[a]Figures may not total because of rounding.

Sources: Magedanz, "Historical Perspectives on the Pick Sloan-Plan," *Public Affairs* 97 (April 1988); Western Area Power Administration, *Proposed Power Rate Adjustment* (Golden, Colo., 1987); Western Area Power Administration, *1992 Annual Report* (Golden, Colo., 1992); U.S. Army Corps of Engineers, Missouri River Division, *1992–1993 Annual Operating Plan* (Omaha, December 1993); *Missouri River Report 2* (November 1993).

Fort Peck Dam, Montana. (Photo by Craig Sharpe)

caused more damage to Indian land and resources than any other public works project in America."[8] When one considers the competition for that award, the magnitude of the impact becomes clearer.

When the Fort Peck Dam was constructed, 350 Sioux and Assiniboine families were displaced. Elsewhere in Montana, the Crow tribe lost 7,000 acres to the construction of Yellowtail Dam, and almost two decades passed before the tribe received anything approaching adequate compensation for their loss. The tribes of the Wind River Reservation in Wyoming lost 25,000 acres of timber and grazing land to the construction of Boysen Reservoir, and in 1952, the government provided an initial award of $18 per acre as compensation.

In North Dakota and South Dakota, the impact of dam construction has been even more severe. The Three Affiliated Tribes of the Fort Berthold Reservation lost 156,000 acres to the construction of Garrison Dam and the inundation of Lake Sakakawea. Eighty percent of those Indians (325 families) were relocated from villages near the river to the surrounding windy plateaus, disrupting the entire socioeconomic fabric of the reservation. The tribe received $12.6 million (roughly $81 per acre) between 1947 and 1949 for the land and the relocation costs of schools, community facilities, tribal cemeteries, monuments, and shrines. In 1986, the Garrison Diversion Unit Joint Tribal Advisory Committee, appointed by the secretary of the interior, recommended additional compensation of $360 million to $762 million.[9] (By contrast, the Arizona Department of Transportation recently paid the Salt River Pima-Maricopa Indian Community $247 million for 583 acres of right-of-way for the construction of the Papago Freeway on the eastern edge of Phoenix.)[10] The Standing Rock Sioux tribe in South Dakota lost 220,000 acres of land and 600 Indian families were relocated to allow the construction of Oahe Reservoir. In all, the construction of Pick-Sloan's five main stem dams (not including Fort Peck) has resulted in the taking of 550 square miles of Indian land (an area half the size of Rhode Island) and the relocation of more than 900 Indian families. In 1991, Congress acted on the advisory committee's recommendations and established a $149-million recovery fund.

Pick-Sloan's benefits to the tribes have been nominal. Irrigation has been brought to 40,000 acres on the Wind River Reservation and 10,000 acres on the Fort Belknap Reservation (19,000 acres have also been irrigated on the Fort Peck Reservation). The tribes have certainly received no navigation benefits and few flood control benefits. Pick-Sloan virtually ignored Indian reserved water rights, and the tribes did not have the same access to the cheap hydropower produced by the dams. Furthermore, the tribes have often been excluded from the development of water policies for the river. The Missouri River Basin Commission provided a limited opportunity for the participation of a few tribal members in an observer capacity; in 1990, a tribal seat was added to the Missouri River Basin Association.

ENVIRONMENTAL DAMAGE

Surveys by the federal Missouri River Commission during the 1890s provide baseline information about predevelopment ecological conditions on the Missouri River. Even at this early date, the Missouri River had been altered by the efforts of the Corps of Engineers, started in 1838, to remove large trees and other impediments to navigation.

The damming and channelization of the river have divided the Missouri into three approximately equal sections. As biologists familiar with the river have indicated, "one-third is channelized, one-third impounded and the remaining one-third consists of remnant 'free-flowing' reaches. In actuality, one percent of the entire river's length, the 25 miles upstream of Canyon Ferry Reservoir in Montana has truly uncontrolled water releases."[11]

The primary result of this development has been the loss of riparian habitat necessary for many fish and wildlife species. The navigation chan-

TABLE 4.3. Natural Habitat Losses Caused by Construction of Missouri River Main Stem Dams

Dam/Reservoir	Grassland Timber (acres)	Bluffland (acres)	Tributary Mouths (number)	Main Channel (miles)	Erosion Zone (acres)
Canyon Ferry	10,918	19,136	6	42	5,146
Ft. Peck	55,686	173,109	20	161	20,205
Garrison Dam/ Sakakawea	127,379	205,565	10	207	46,221
Oahe	215,000	85,131	47	265	65,869[a]
Big Bend/Sharpe	30,016	9,415	9	92	23,917[b]
Randall/ Francis Case	20,347	42,846	26	110	34,682[c]
Gavins Point/ Lewis & Clark	11,053	10,688	4	26	9,011
TOTAL	470,399	545,890	122	903	205,051

[a]Including 23 major timbered islands
[b]Including 20 major timbered islands
[c]Including 34 major timbered islands

Source: Larry W. Hess and J. Schmulbach, "The Missouri River: The Great Plains' Thread of Life," in Boundaries Carved in Water: The Missouri River Brief Series, no. 16 (Missoula, Mont.: Northern Lights Institute, April 1991).

nel between Sioux City, Iowa, and St. Louis, Missouri, has reduced the river length by 127 miles, and between 1892 and 1982, "deciduous tree cover declined 41 percent, wetlands 40 percent, sandbar habitat 97 percent, and grasslands 12 percent" on floodplain lands.[12] Natural habitat losses caused by the construction of the seven main stem dams and reservoirs (including Canyon Ferry) is estimated at over 1.2 million acres (see Table 4.3). By the year 2003, perhaps only 112,000 acres will remain of the 664,000 acres that once comprised the active erosion zone (the area through which the river meandered) in the navigation reaches of the river.

The loss of riparian habitat has been particularly acute for fish. These losses, some biologists have concluded,

> have sealed the fate of the ephemeral and the large rheophilic fish species. Lake sturgeon have been extirpated from the basin while blue catfish and pallid sturgeon are rare through their traditional range in the Missouri River. The pallid sturgeon has just been listed as nationally endangered, an ominous prelude to extinction. The sturgeon chub and sickelfin chub may shortly join the pallid sturgeon and the Niangua darter on the federal list of rare, threatened, or endangered species in this basin. . . . The paddlefish now faces the real possibility of extinction and is presently under review for listing on the national threatened

list. Indeed, 33 of the 156 native fish of the basin are on "species of special concern" lists in at least one of the basin states.[13]

The biologists estimate similar impacts on terrestrial animals, such as beaver, mink, and muskrat, and birds. The least tern and the piping plover are two bird species that are now classified as endangered and threatened, respectively.

Although habitat loss can be attributed to the original damming and channelization of the Missouri River, other ecological effects result from the ongoing operation of the dams:

- Altered river flows cause lower-than-normal river elevations and volume discharges during spring and summer months.
- Power-peaking discharges cause daily water-level fluctuations during critical spring and summer months and cause the desiccation of fish eggs and larvae and macroinvertebrates.
- Main stem dams are complete barriers to fish migration.
- Elimination of flows—which causes flooding and a reduction of scouring flows—and control of meandering of the river channel in the unchannelized reaches of the river have accelerated the conversion of barren sandbar habitat to permanently vegetated sandbars.
- Unnatural sedimentation in the main stem reservoirs has altered natural energy cycling in the river's downstream reaches.
- Unnatural erosion causes degradation and occurs in remnant free-flowing reaches downstream from Fort Peck, Garrison, Fort Randall, and Gavins Point dams.
- Channelization has prevented the lower one-third of the Missouri from meandering, which is a necessary process for restoring energy to the ecosystem in floodplain rivers.[14]

CONFLICTS

Conflict has been a major part of the history of the Missouri River basin, and many of today's conflicts stem from the failure to complete the Pick-Sloan Plan and from issues the plan did not adequately address. Increasingly, disputes among the sovereigns of the basin—the states, tribes, and federal agencies—go unresolved or find their way into court.

Geographic Differences

One major source of controversy among these jurisdictions stems from the basin's geography. The one-hundredth meridian runs north and south through the Dakotas and the states of Nebraska and Kansas. East of that line, water is usually abundant, water management institutions are less developed, economies have grown up around navigation and the hydroelectric power supplied from the main stem dams, and water problems have been those of flooding rather than scarcity. West of that meridian, water is scarce, sophisticated water management institutions have developed to manage the shortage, and water is coveted for agricultural and other economic purposes. Large Indian reservations and federal land management agencies compete for this scarce resource.

Lower basin states have been interested in preventing flooding from the Missouri, in ensuring stable flows for navigation and hydropower generation, and in preserving wetlands and other riparian values, including recreation. Upper basin states, however, have been interested in using the Missouri River for irrigated agriculture and energy development; they would especially like to make greater use of the basin's hydropower production. These states are developing more slowly and are interested in preserving sufficient water for anticipated future growth. The Pick-Sloan Plan, a historic compromise between the upper and lower basins, has not been fully implemented, and its benefits have therefore been inequitably distributed. In recent years, the question has been whether the compromise would withstand growing pressure. It has not.

ETSI Proposal

External pressures began to overwhelm the water management structures starting in 1982, when, as a result of the U.S. Supreme Court's decision in *Sporhase v. Nebraska*,[15] water became a valuable interstate commodity. Coincident with that decision, South Dakota's Governor William Janklow, motivated both by money and a desire to protect the state's groundwater,[16] arranged with the approval of the Department of the Interior the sale of 50,000 ac-ft of water from Oahe Reservoir for as much as $1.4 billion.[17] The water, starting at an average price of $150 per ac-ft, would have been sold to the Energy Transportation Systems, Inc. (ETSI), consortium for use in a coal slurry pipeline from Wyoming to the Gulf States.

The amount of water was not large—Janklow claimed it was only one-tenth of the amount that evaporates from that reservoir each year—and somewhat surprisingly, since water marketing was controversial, the Department of the Interior supported the idea. Secretary James Watt said that "the governor pulled off a brilliant and creative suggestion. I support it 100 percent. I think that's the way the states ought to do it."[18]

His assistant secretary, Garrey Carruthers, concurred: "If you want to sell your water, that's your business."[19]

Opposition developed in many quarters. The target date for project completion originally was July 1, 1984, but the Army Corps of Engineers indicated that a permit, taking two to three years to secure, would be required to take water out of Oahe Reservoir.[20] Downstream navigation interests feared that such water sales could curtail the navigation season (the season had been shortened by three weeks in 1981 because of low water),[21] and in Governor Janklow's own state, the Sioux Indians contended they owned part of the water to be sold to ETSI.[22]

The most serious opposition came from the lower basin states of Missouri, Iowa, and Nebraska. Kansas, another lower basin state with only eighty miles of Missouri River frontage, attempted to stay neutral and out of the fray. Missouri's governor and attorney general led the charge. Attorney General John Ashcroft pointed out that the Missouri River provides drinking water for more than 60 percent of the state's residents and drives seventeen hydroelectric plants. "This is not some snail darter issue. This is a basic issue of Missouri continuing to be a productive state."[23] Governor Christopher Bond was more circumspect. Although he conceded that ETSI would not significantly lower the level of the river, he indicated that "it will open the door for taking water out of the Missouri River Basin to other states."[24]

Iowa officials were also concerned about the precedent ETSI would set. The Iowa Conservation Commission opposed the project, indicating that "we are painfully aware of many other precedents that have been set and are pessimistic about the future [of the river] if significant withdrawals or diversions are allowed."[25] The city commission of Sioux City indicated that the project would have a detrimental effect on the traditional uses of the Missouri River by Iowa residents.

Nebraska, whose own water regimes are divided between an irrigation-based appropriation system in the west and a navigation-based riparian system in the east, seemed to have mixed sentiments about the whole affair. Governor Charles Thorne was upset because for several days immediately preceding the ETSI announcement, the South Dakota governor had sat next to him at a governors' conference and had never mentioned the impending development to him. However, a prominent Nebraska legislator actually supported ETSI[26] and later invited Governor Janklow to appear before the legislature to explain South Dakota's position.

Governor Janklow rose to the challenge. He justified ETSI's benefits to South Dakota as partial compensation for the broken promises and lost acreage resulting from the Pick-Sloan Plan. He pointed to the municipal water supplies that would become available to communities in the western part of the state and added that the reason lower basin cities "don't flood anymore is because half a million acres plus of land became flooded in South Dakota. So these people are just being selfish right now."[27]

Like many important controversies, this one was destined for court. What ensued could best be called a feast of litigation:

- Missouri, Iowa, Nebraska, railroads, and environmental groups sued federal agencies to prevent the sale. They questioned the availability of water for such out-of-basin transfers. Finally, they prevailed before the U.S. Supreme Court, though on a narrow basis.[28]
- South Dakota, kept out of this litigation on a legal fine point, petitioned to be heard immediately in the U.S. Supreme Court.[29] Turned down in 1986, the state renewed its petition, which was also turned down.
- To up the ante, South Dakota and ETSI filed two separate antitrust actions against the original plaintiffs—claiming that the railroads were seeking to prevent the building of the coal slurry pipeline.[30] Janklow also half-seriously suggested that his state intervene in every minor water-permitting proceeding in the lower states—mocking the concern of the lower states about water availability. For a while, South Dakota's antitrust strategy worked as it won a $844-million verdict. This judgment was overturned by an appellate court.

Other Proposals for Large Diversions

Generally, the lower basin states were not concerned about the amount of water actually at stake in the ETSI project, but they were concerned about the precedent they thought would be established by allowing water to be diverted from the Missouri River.[31] The ETSI project was announced at a time when other potential demands for Missouri River water were receiving much attention, and in fact, during the energy crisis of the 1970s and early 1980s, ETSI was only one of several proposed major projects to divert water from the Missouri River basin. Exxon Corporation talked about diverting 1.7 million ac-ft/yr from the basin for oil shale development in Colorado and Utah,[32] and three other coal slurry pipelines, each projected to use 20,000 ac-ft/yr of Missouri water, were planned to deliver coal to eastern Texas, Minnesota, Wisconsin, and the West Coast.[33] Two proposals heightened concerns in many states: the Six-State High Plains–Ogallala Aquifer Regional Resources Study[34] and the Corps of Engineers' water marketing proposal. In retrospect, the alarm was misplaced.

The High Plains–Ogallala Aquifer Regional Resources Study was a $6-million project funded by Congress and completed in March 1982. The project was undertaken because of Congress's concern about the continued depletion of the aquifer, which underlies six states and provides most of the region's irrigation water.[35] The region comprises an area of 220,000 square miles and 180 counties in eastern Colorado, western Kansas, western and central Nebraska, eastern New Mexico, the Panhandle of Oklahoma, and west Texas. Forty million acres of irrigable farmland are in the region; about 15 million acres were irrigated in 1980 (20 percent of the nation's total irrigated agriculture). The area produces much of the feed grains, corn, sorghums, wheat, and cotton grown in the United States.

Studies for the High Plains investigation indicated that by the year 2020, 3.7 million additional acres of land would be irrigated and that serious overdraft of the aquifer would continue. Nebraska, with irrigated acreage projected to increase from the present 7 million acres to 14 million acres, would need 1.8 million ac-ft/yr to meet these expected irrigation increases; Texas would need an additional 800,000 ac-ft/yr. The study team analyzed five management alternatives, including voluntary and mandatory conservation and local supply augmentation. The two alternatives suggesting intra-or interstate transfers (with potential points of diversion from the Missouri at Fort Randall Dam[36] and at St. Joseph) drew a great deal of attention and fear from opinion leaders in the Missouri River basin.

These leaders overplayed the conclusions reached by the High Plains study. For one thing, Congress had limited the analysis of possible interbasin transfers to sources in "adjacent areas"—thus eliminating any consideration of the lower Missouri. For another, the conclusion of the High Plains study was that diversions from the Missouri River were generally unworkable. Energy costs would be high, for the terminal storage reservoirs for such diversions were from 1,745 to 3,618 feet higher than the points of diversion. At Fort Randall, the study concluded, no surplus water was available for interbasin transfer after allowing for present commitments and projected future in-basin uses. Any such transfer "would involve tradeoffs with navigation downstream and with lessened hydropower generation. The environment for fish and wildlife and the riparian habitat would be seriously affected. Stream morphology would be affected even more than it has been altered already."[37] Although a diversion lower on the river at St. Joseph might avoid some problems, the available water would still be inadequate for the needs of the High Plains. The authors of the study concluded:

The only implementable water management strategy to alleviate the stress on the Ogallala Aquifer to some degree is greater emphasis on conservation and increased efficiency of use by farmers themselves within economics. . . . It is highly doubtful that any new large-scale interstate interbasin transfers are necessary and justified in the near future or will be undertaken for many years because of the costs involved, lack of adequate studies and planning, and opposition by the states and basins of origin.[38]

The Corps of Engineers developed a marketing proposal for the sale of water from the main stem reservoirs on the Missouri in response to the developing interest in water marketing. The initiative was met with suspicion by many states, quite a few of which asserted their authority for allocating water within their boundaries. They also questioned whether their citizens would have to pay for water that could otherwise be appropriated for free.

In fall 1986, the corps floated a "Trial Water Supply Strategy—Missouri River Main Stem System"[39] and invited the states to respond to the document. The corps proposed to consider all water in storage in the Missouri River main stem system as surplus and available for marketing by the corps. The price of water would be set in relation to the expected loss of hydropower revenues due to water being taken out of the system (estimated at between $7 and $42 per ac-ft, depending on the amount of generation lost).

The states, though recognizing that federal law requires reimbursement for the benefits of the federally financed dams, responded that no charges should be imposed for "natural flows," that is, water that would be available even without the federal dams. The basin states actually united in response to the corps' proposal. With the assistance of a conflict-management firm, the states developed a consensus resolution in opposing the corps' proposal and suggested a category of uses that should be exempt from federal water service charges.[40] Eventually, the corps withdrew the water marketing proposal.

Indian Reserved Water Rights

The quantification of Indian reserved water rights has also been a divisive, misunderstood issue. A 1984 study by the Western States Water Council indicated that tribes could eventually claim 6.6 million ac-ft/yr of water in Montana, 1.2 million ac-ft/yr in South Dakota, 190,000 ac-ft in North Dakota, and 26,500 ac-ft/yr in Nebraska.[41] When the Fort Peck–Montana Compact was ratified in 1985,[42] lower basin water managers were alarmed to the point of visiting Helena, Montana, for an explanation of a 1-million ac-ft/yr settlement made with the Sioux and Assiniboine tribes. The Wyoming courts quantified the reserved water rights of the Wind River Reservation at 500,717 ac-ft/yr for some 48,000 potentially irrigable acres, an award that was later affirmed by the U.S. Supreme Court.[43] Many officials in the lower basin concluded that Montana and other upper basin states were only seeking to tie up large amounts of water in anticipation of an equitable apportionment action.

Once again, these concerns were exaggerated. Virtually none of the water awarded to the Fort Peck or Wind River tribes has been developed. Since the 1980s, only the water rights of the Northern Cheyenne Reservation have been quantified—by a settlement with Montana reached in 1992.[44] Tribes may eventually secure large water rights awards by settlement or litigation, but it will take many decades and millions of dollars before this water is actually developed in a way that reduces flows available to the lower basin.

Meaning of the O'Mahoney-Millikin Amendment

The interpretation of the O'Mahoney-Millikin Amendment is a continuing source of disagreement between upper and lower basin states. The amendment guarantees that consumptive beneficial uses of water in basin states lying wholly or partly west of the ninety-eighth meridian will have priority over lower basin navigation. Does the amendment constitute an equitable "mass" apportionment of water between the upper and lower basins? Is hydropower generation in states west of the ninety-eighth meridian a consumptive and beneficial use of water? These and other questions of interpretation have and will continue to divide the upper and lower basins.

Water Accounting Problems

Many recent conflicts among Missouri River basin states concern the availability of water in the system. When the states have discussed the allocation of water among themselves, the amount of water that is available becomes an important issue. Water managers disagree about the proper way to account for water in the system, however, and they are aware of the mistake apparently made by the negotiators of the Colorado River Compact in overestimating the amount of water in that river.[45]

Even though the U.S. Geological Survey and other government agencies have measured the flow of the Missouri and its tributaries for much of this century, there is a surprising amount of disagreement about the water supply. The state of Missouri has questioned figures that had previously been commonly accepted. By basing water availability on monthly averages rather than daily averages, Missouri charged that the Missouri Basin States Association's model overstated water availability by 2.6 million ac-ft/yr at Sioux City, 5.7 million ac-ft/yr at Kansas City, and 9.9 million ac-ft/yr at the river's mouth near Hermann, Missouri.

Data concerning water usage in the basin also vary. Some states, such as Colorado and Wyoming, have well-developed decree and permit systems that closely account for water use. Other states, such as Montana, are in the process of developing that information. One state, Missouri, is still attempting to develop a permit system as surface water use in the state has been unrecorded.

Regardless of the mountains of water-related data that have been generated by the governments of the Missouri River basin over the last fifty years, there is a perception that data are incomplete or not useful. In a 1988 poll of the people interested in Missouri River issues,[46] the data problem was identified as being of prime importance for decision makers in the basin.

Climate Variability

Extreme climate variability—especially drought—has caused conflicts among the governments of the basin. From 1987 to early 1993, the Missouri River basin suffered severe drought. In 1988, runoff above Sioux City was 12.4 million ac-ft, half of the average flow, and in spring 1991, the main stem reservoir system was at an all-time low, holding only 42.1 million ac-ft of water (compared with the 1967–1992 average of 57 million ac-ft). Hydroelectric production at Pick-Sloan dams steadily decreased from 9.3 million kilowatt hours in 1988 to 7.3 million kilowatt hours in 1992. The Western Area Power Administration was forced to purchase additional power to satisfy its customers, costing the agency $6 million in fiscal year 1988 and $43 million in fiscal year 1992.[47]

The drought increased competition for water between the upper and lower basins. The upper basin states wanted to retain water in the reservoirs so that recreation and tourism could continue. As upper basin reservoirs were drafted to sustain lower basin navigation flows, many marinas and boat docks were left high and dry and far from the water's edge. Lower basin states also wanted river levels maintained so that municipal and industrial water intakes would still receive water. Throughout the basin, fish and other animals populations were under stress because of the lack of water.

Several upper basin states sued the Corps of Engineers to reduce flows during the spring of 1990, but the case was ultimately dismissed.[48] These states were successful, however, in convincing the corps to review its master manual of reservoir operations[49] and hoped that revisions in the manual would enable the corps to hold more water in the upper basin reservoirs in times of drought. The corps has yet to issue its final report, but it is completing an environmental impact statement as part of the planning process.

The 1993 floods in the Midwest ended the drought but caused loss of life and significant damage, particularly in the lower basin. In the Missouri River basin, rainfall during July was 462 percent of normal, and the summer was the wettest in a century in Montana, North Dakota, South Dakota, Minnesota, and Iowa. The Missouri was closed to navigation for fifty-two days. The Corps of Engineers estimated that the floods caused $12 billion in damages in the upper Mississippi River basin and in portions of the Missouri River basin.[50] Still, an estimated $7.7 billion of damage was prevented by Missouri River basin flood control works, including reservoirs and levees. Whereas most of the reservoirs, at low levels because of the drought, easily held the excess water, public and private levees in the lower basin were significantly damaged.[51]

The future may bring similar occurrences of climate variability. That there has been a significant increase in global average temperatures no longer seems in doubt.[52] The "greenhouse effect," generated by carbon dioxide and other gases trapping an increasing amount of heat in our atmosphere, is thought to be a major cause. Many global climatic models agree that average surface temperatures will increase 1.2°–4.2°. The relevant question is, What will the regional effects of this change be? Several models predict that the grain belts of North America will become drier, especially in the spring and summer.[53] One study for the National Academy of Science even suggests that the Missouri River basin may experience a 50 percent reduction in flows over the next forty years. These climatic changes make predictions of future water supply and use in the Missouri River basin very uncertain.

PROSPECTS FOR WAR OR PEACE

Decision makers once believed they had crafted a historic agreement that would benefit all parties in the Missouri River basin. With the passage of the Flood Control Act of 1944, which incorporated the large, Pick-Sloan catalog of water development projects, these decision makers believed they had found an approach that would both tame the destructive forces of the river and release its potential. Through the construction of six major main stem dams, lower basin flooding would be avoided and continuous flows for navigation ensured. With the construction of delivery systems appurtenant to the upper basin dams, water would be available to irrigate farmland. Consumptive use of water west of the ninety-eighth meridian would have precedence over navigation by virtue of the O'Mahoney-Millikin Amendment, and hydroelectric power produced from the main stem dams would be available for rural electrification. The Corps of Engineers would build dams and dredge and maintain navigation channels, and the Bureau of Reclamation would build irrigation projects and operate some of the dams.

The Pick-Sloan Plan has not worn well with the passage of time. In the years following its authorization, not all of the terms of the historic agreement have been carried out. To be sure, six great dams have been constructed on the Missouri main stem, flooding has been avoided,[54] and navigation on the lower reaches of the river has greatly improved.[55] Very little, however, of the upper basin's irrigated agriculture potential has been realized. Moreover, the hydropower that was to benefit rural agricultural communities now finds its way to such out-of-basin places as Minneapolis–St. Paul.

The basin's Indian tribes, especially those that had reservations on the main stem, have benefited little if at all. At Fort Berthold, North Dakota, for instance, the tribal lands of the Mandan, Hidatsa, and Arikara were inundated by Lake Sakakawea, and a seemingly self-sufficient social and economic system was totally disrupted. Although these tribes were compensated for their lands, recent studies have indicated that the compensation was inadequate.[56]

The virtues of the Pick-Sloan Plan have also been undermined by dramatic trends since its implementation. The systemic problems of agriculture, owing to international competition, U.S. monetary policy, and changeable farm policies, have been powerful barriers to the development of agriculture in the upper basin states. Furthermore, a nation plagued by continuing federal fiscal imbalance has less tolerance for funding water development projects—especially those with potential adverse environmental impacts. Thus, proposals like North Dakota's Garrison Project, well within the original expectations of the Pick-Sloan Plan, are now faulted on both economic and environmental grounds.

In addition to these national trends, the upper basin states (which believe they provided the necessary political support for the lower basin to obtain its flood control benefits) now face lower basin neutrality, if not outright opposition, toward completion of the promised projects. When upper basin states seek to make alternative uses of the water (such as South Dakota's proposed sale of water to ETSI), those efforts are challenged by lower basin states.

The passage of time has also resulted in a greater appreciation on the part of the lower basin states of the river's wetland, recreational, and other riparian values. These states believe they, too, are victims of the excesses of the Pick-Sloan Plan: "Over 500,000 acres of aquatic and terrestrial habitat will have been lost [in the lower basin] by the year 2003 as a result of the U.S. Army Corps of Engineers' Bank Stabilization and Navigation Project authorized by the Flood Control Act of 1945."[57] Lower basin states argue for reasonably undiminished flows so that wetlands and water-dependent species are not threatened and water-based recreation is not disrupted. Three states also desire sufficient flows to dilute pollutants in the river. They argue that when water is diverted as a result of projects like ETSI, all states suffer; therefore, all states should share in the revenues received for that water.

Further conflict arises from the disparity in the water management capacity of the states and tribes. Even though the water management ability of the lower basin states is improving, they still lag in terms of information about their water resources, the coverage and sophistication of their water laws and institutions, and the importance of water on each state's political agenda. For the most part, the basin's tribes have even less water management capability. Resources are insufficient for the tribes to estimate their water needs and entitlements, money is not readily available for water development, and some of the tribes are just now starting to develop water management codes.

Thus, the Pick-Sloan Plan, rather than achieving the anticipated cooperation and economic development among basin residents, has resulted in an inequitable distribution of benefits favoring the lower basin.[58] This continuing inequity undermines efforts at cooperation and produces new tensions. Moreover, even lower basin policymakers are beginning to realize that some components of the Pick-Sloan Plan no longer serve their own interests.[59] The failed Pick-Sloan Plan has poisoned relationships among basin states and tribes, creating a burden that is now shared by the entire basin.[60]

There are, however, many reasons to predict a more peaceful future along the Missouri. Most important, future consumptive needs will be much lower than the horrifying scenarios of earlier days. With the federal fiscal crisis continuing, upper basin states are coming to accept that Pick-Sloan's promises of irrigated agriculture will not be fulfilled. Very pessimistic reports about the future of Great Plains agriculture, coupled with the need for existing farmers to reduce their energy inputs to be profitable, indicate that completion of Pick-Sloan would hardly be desirable. North Dakota's very modest settlement of its demands for completion of the Garrison Project exemplifies that acceptance. Furthermore, a recurrence of the energy crisis is not soon expected. The peaks and valleys of energy consumption since 1972 indicate the great capacity for energy conservation in times of shortages. Even if faced with a severe energy crisis, the federal government and the energy companies probably would avoid the exaggerated predictions and reckless investments that characterized their responses in the 1970s.

Large interbasin transfers also appear unlikely. Only three subregions of the West are predicted to have water deficits by the year 2000,[61] and the same trends experienced a decade ago in energy allocation are now seen in water allocation. Local water markets are developing in many of the urban areas, and increasing prices are bringing surrounding agricultural water onto the auction block. Impressive water savings are being realized in some areas as the result of pricing structures. In short, water deficient areas of the West will likely be able to meet their foreseeable demands from local or surrounding sources. Some present uses of the Missouri River will also become less important. Navigation, once a primary use of the river, is a shadow of its former self and sand and gravel, not commercial goods, are the commodities now most often transported on the river.

Thus, many feared conflicts among the basin states are not likely to occur. The two traditional uses around which Pick-Sloan policy was formulated—irrigated agriculture and navigation—are not likely to expand. Major interbasin diversions, either for energy development or growing southwestern cities, are equally unlikely. The probability that these events will not occur, however, does not automatically reduce the widespread perception that they will occur. The basin's opinion leaders must assess realistically the demands for water and the basin's water supply.

Some forces remain divisive. The first is the continuing, simmering resentment in the upper basin states caused by the deauthorization of the Pick-Sloan projects. Whereas the tendency is for Congress and the lower basin to sweep Pick-Sloan promises under a stack of other priorities, the upper basin's dissatisfaction will color relationships with lower basin states for years to come.

Moreover, the continued quantification of federal and Indian reserved water rights creates uncertainty. The basic, unresolved issue is whether these water rights will be ultimately charged against the water share of individual states or whether they will be charged against the entire basin. If the latter is the case, how will adjudications or negotiations of these rights be structured so the interests of the lower basin states are represented? What restraints, if any, will be imposed on off-reservation transfers or marketing of these reserved rights?

The aftermath of a decade of litigation may also adversely influence relations. The U.S. Supreme Court's affirmation of lower court decisions in ETSI *Pipeline Project v. Missouri*, involving the authority of the Bureau of Reclamation and the Corps of Engineers over main stem reservoirs, may be more a psychological loss than a real one. The ruling that only the corps has authority to lease water from federal reservoirs would appear to place the upper basin's future water use in the hands of the agency that has been the lower basin's longtime benefactor. Yet it must be remembered that the corps informally concurred with the bureau's contract to provide water for the ETSI project. As its proposed surplus water marketing policy suggested, the corps appears adaptable to changing circumstances and is becoming more concerned with municipal and industrial supplies and less concerned with navigation. The agency will likely be seeking new political constituencies, and the upper basin may be one of them.

A sudden catastrophe would also strain if not break the river's meager management and dispute-resolving institutions. The breach of a dam, floods or droughts even more severe than the ones recently experienced, or an accidental toxic spill on the magnitude of the 1987 Rhine River disaster could result in recriminations and ill-conceived solutions. Finally, dramatic changes in the basin's climate could undermine all the assumptions about water supply and unravel the slender threads of cooperation among the states.

Decision makers in the Missouri River basin face an important set of issues that eventually must be resolved:

- How will the Missouri be allocated and managed? Will the states simply divide up the waters, take their share, and turn their backs on their neighbors? Or will they formulate a basinwide organization that practices bioregional ethics and is premised on the fact that the river may in the future be the region's most valuable natural resource?
- How are federal agencies and Indian tribes to be involved in this management regime? Do they want, and will they have, a seat at the decision-making table? How much water do federal agencies need for reserved lands and tribes for on-reservation purposes? Can tribes sell or lease their water for off-reservation uses?
- How are upper basin states and Indian tribes to be compensated for the prime bottomland they lost when the large reservoirs were created? If money can be found, does it make sense to spend it on bringing agricultural land into production when commodity prices are so low? Can other forms of compensation be found?
- What is the meaning of the O'Mahoney-Millikin Amendment given the harsh realities of the new agricultural economy? Is lower basin navigation subordinate to upstream hydroelectric generation? Upstream recreational use? Out-of-basin diversions?

- Can water use, including navigation and hydroelectric production, be made more efficient? Can water be sold and transferred out-of-basin? Who benefits from these sales? The selling agency, state, or tribe? Should the revenues be shared?

More important, basin decision makers need a continuing forum in which these questions can be addressed and resolved and their answers implemented and evaluated. The Flood Control Act and Pick-Sloan failed to provide such a forum, and Washington and basin policymakers have failed to structure such an institution in the fifty years since passage of the act. These problems will not be resolved by one Supreme Court decision or in one round of negotiations. This agenda will take Missouri River basin decision makers well into the twenty-first century.

CHAPTER FIVE

Nationalization of the Missouri River

Passage of the Flood Control Act and Pick-Sloan Plan in 1944 was made possible in part by Senate leaders' promises that the management structure for the Missouri River basin would be considered in the next session of Congress. Such assurances were necessary to remove legislative impasse over the controversial proposal for a Missouri Valley Authority. In 1945, and for many years thereafter, Congress did indeed consider various proposals for an MVA. None of these proposals passed, and, except for what is stated or implied in the Flood Control Act and the Pick-Sloan Plan, Congress never decided what type of intergovernmental water management institution it wanted for the Missouri River. Since the early 1940s, the federal agencies and states have experimented, with no permanent success, with a range of organizational approaches for coordinating their interests and efforts and for managing conflict.

MISSOURI VALLEY REGIONAL PLANNING COMMISSION

Formed in 1941, the Missouri Valley Regional Planning Commission was composed of one representative from eight basin states (Colorado and Wyoming were excluded), appointed by their governors, and federal representatives from the Departments of Army, Agriculture, and Interior. The commission's activities included coordination of federal and state agencies, local governments, and regional organizations; information exchange; planning; and technical assistance. The commission published a report in 1942 that called for the apportionment of the waters stored by Fort Peck and other reservoirs that might be constructed. The organization was terminated in 1943 when Congress failed to continue funding for the National Resources Planning Board.[1]

MISSOURI RIVER STATES COMMITTEE

The Missouri River States Committee (MRSC), created before the Pick-Sloan Plan, was influential in the plan's passage but had less influence after the plan's enactment and the establishment of the Missouri Basin Inter-Agency

Navigation on the lower Missouri. (Courtesy Bureau of Reclamation)

Committee. The origins of the MRSC actually extend to 1941 when the governors of North Dakota, South Dakota, Wyoming, Montana, and Nebraska agreed to organize a Five States Committee. This committee was to provide a "general executive committee" that would coordinate the various basin interests "and direct them toward some methodical procedure to get results."[2] With the inclusion of Missouri, Iowa, and Kansas in 1943, the organization became the Eight States Committee, and shortly thereafter, with the addition of Colorado, it became the Missouri River States Committee.

The MRSC concentrated on the need for basinwide development, but it did not support the proposal for a river authority. Rather, it gave strong political support to the Pick-Sloan compromise.[3] After the creation of the Missouri Basin Inter-Agency Committee, there was less reason for the committee to meet, and it became inactive. Before it became dormant, however, the MRSC (with the assistance of the Council of State Governments) did draft a Missouri River Basin Compact.[4]

MISSOURI BASIN INTER-AGENCY COMMITTEE

The Flood Control Act of 1944 did not solve the problem of coordinating federal agency actions in the Missouri River basin. Several of the federal land and water agencies, however, had agreed as early as 1939 to the formation of the Federal Inter-Agency River Basin Commission (FIARBC), which was organized for river basin activities throughout the United States and consisted of the chief of engineers of the corps, the commissioner of reclamation, the land-use coordinator for the Department of Agriculture, and (after 1943) the chairman of the Federal Power Commission.

This interagency approach became the model for the Missouri Basin Inter-Agency Committee (MBIAC), which came into being on March 29, 1945.[5] The Pick-Sloan Plan approached the coordination of the corps and the bureau in only a general way, and the responsibilities of the Department of Agriculture and Federal Power Commission were infrequently mentioned. Thus, FIARBC led to MBIAC, which was to provide "a means through which the field representatives of the participating Federal agencies may effectively interchange information and coordinate their activities."[6] The MBIAC soon included representatives from the Departments of War, Agriculture, Interior, and Commerce; a member of the Federal Power Commission; and five governors chosen by the Missouri River States Committee. The interagency committee usually met on a monthly basis.

In 1953, however, Frank Trelease, a noted water law scholar, recounted two recurring demands heard throughout the basin "for coordination of federal efforts, and for participation by local people and governments in the development program."[7] He identified forty-three federal agencies that had responsibilities for basin development.[8] Although the Flood Control Act requires some interagency cooperation between the Corps of Engineers and Bureau of Reclamation,[9] Trelease found that the federal presence was overly complex and fragmentary among agencies with "fundamental dissimilarities" and "no legal process for evaluating the individual projects against the overall program."[10] Trelease concluded that

> no agency . . . exist[ed] within the federal government . . . equipped to determine the policies, make the decisions, and give the supervision which will be required as development progresses. . . . A simple organization is needed to recommend to Congress those uses entitled to preference and to coordinate water resources in accordance with whatever priorities are set up. The unilateral decision by a single agency should not control.[11]

The fact that MBIAC had no legal mandate was probably its principal shortcoming. As one observer indicated, "Stemming as they [regional commissions like MBIAC] do from the central Federal Inter-Agency River

Basin Committee . . . they, like their parent, have been impotent to resolve inter-departmental jurisdictional disputes, or to build truly comprehensive, balanced regional plans."[12] Other criticisms included poor
attendance by governors, funding difficulties, the requirement of unanimity for action, and infrequent contact among members.[13]

The MBIAC did have some small successes: an agricultural and soil
conservation program, a public relations program, and improved intra-
basin communication. Before its termination in the early 1970s, MBIAC
produced a multivolume framework study that pulled together a large
amount of basin information. In the final analysis, MBIAC was ill-
equipped to oversee the massive construction projects put in motion by
the Pick-Sloan Plan or to coordinate integrated management for the
basin.

MISSOURI RIVER BASIN COMMISSION

The Missouri River Basin Commission (MRBC),[14] in existence from 1972 to
1981, was a bold experiment to create a permanent management institution for the Missouri River.[15] The commission was created by executive
order[16] under the provisions of the Water Resources Planning Act of
1965,[17] legislation that sought a comprehensive water planning process—
rather than one that followed narrow agency lines—and a substantive
role for states in the planning process.

River basin commissions were told to prepare comprehensive, coordinated joint plans[18] for the development of water and related resources.
Specifically, they were (1) to serve as the principal agency for the coordination of planning; (2) to prepare and update a comprehensive, coordinated joint plan; (3) to recommend priorities for construction and further
planning; and (4) to undertake such other studies as might be necessary.[19] The commissions, however, had authority only to plan or make
recommendations, not to implement or enforce the plans.

Missouri River Basin Commission members represented the Departments of Agriculture, Army, Commerce, Health and Human Services,
Housing and Urban Development, Interior, Transportation, and Energy;
the Atomic Energy Commission; the Environmental Protection Agency;
the Federal Power Commission; the Federal Emergency Management
Agency; the Energy and Development Administration; the ten basin
states; the Yellowstone Compact Commission; and the Big Blue River
Compact Administration. Observers from Canada and the basin's Indian
tribes were nonvoting members.[20] The MRBC usually operated by consensus. If unanimity could not be reached on a proposal, a majority vote
was required for commission action.

The commission's last budget, in 1981, was $1.5 million, and at that time the staff consisted of over forty permanent employees and contract staff.[21] Half of the operating funds came from the federal government and the remainder from the states (individual state contributions ranged from $22,154 to $31,613 per year). In 1981, the federal government provided an additional $1.4 million for special studies. The commission's greatest accomplishment was providing a forum for communication and information sharing. The commission developed a management plan, published numerous reports, started a computerized water accounting system, and handled public relations.

Yet with two dozen interests represented, the commission was often indecisive. Because MRBC operated by consensus, its plans were generally of the nonbinding, "laundry list" variety. The Comprehensive Coordinated Joint Plan (CCJP), specifically required under Title II of the Water Resources Planning Act, remained elusive. The CCJP was to have three major components: a "directions for the future" segment to express water resource planning objectives; a "baseline of plan elements" to include all types of projects and programs from data collection to project implementation; and a "next step toward plan implementation" to present conclusions and recommendations for implementation. The commission's planning efforts, by comparison, simply amounted to a catalog of all conceivable projects within a specific subbasin.[22] The commission was further weakened by the separation of planning from implementation. Although the consensus decision-making approach eliminated controversy, "the structure provided little incentive to address existing conflicts."[23]

After taking office in 1981, President Reagan eliminated Title V regional commissions, organized for economic development under the auspices of the U.S. Department of Commerce, and river basin commissions, organized under the Water Resources Council.[24] His intent was to buttress state prerogatives by terminating federally funded, intermediary organizations whose programs were often seen as overlapping if not conflicting with those of the states. In the Missouri River basin, the result was the abolition of the Missouri River Basin Commission, which involved all ten states, and the Old West Regional Commission (Title V), which involved Wyoming, Montana, the Dakotas, and Nebraska. To be sure, the merit of some of these commissions' programs had been questioned, but their elimination destroyed the only permanent interstate organizations in the region. Then-Governor Ed Herschler of Wyoming described the result as follows:

No matter how the water controversy [ETSI] is ultimately resolved, it is lamentable that it probably could have been avoided completely if the commissions [Title V, Old West Regional Commission] still were in operation. In its haste to implement the administration's budget reductions, the Congress destroyed in the commission the one legal structure capable of handling such disputes without the necessity of court action or new legislation.[25]

Thus, vehicles for frequent interaction and cooperative activity among the states were eliminated in the basin. There were now fewer opportunities for state officials to meet, become acquainted, and work together, and an important experiment in interstate and federal-state co-operation had ended.

MISSOURI BASIN STATES ASSOCIATION

After the abolition of the MRBC, the Missouri River basin states continued their cooperative activities by creating the Missouri Basin States Association (MBSA) as a nonprofit corporation organized under the laws of Nebraska. Two representatives appointed by the governor of each of the ten states made up the board of directors. The association received a large residual payment from MRBC and developed a dues schedule for the member states. Additional funds came to the association for special projects, such as completion of the water accounting system (a model of water supply and demand in the river). Until April 1988, MBSA usually had three professional staff members and a secretary.

The association's purpose was stated as follows:

> The Missouri Basin States Association (MBSA) serves as a forum for the identification, discussion, and possible resolution of issues of concern to the basin states. Issues to be discussed will include matters of interstate comity among the basin states, as well as matters of common concern to the basin states that arise due to the actions and programs of the Federal Government, other states, Indian tribes, and private interests. If agreement can be reached on how an issue should be resolved, the Association may take a position and advocate that position to those in a position to resolve the issue.[26]

Much of MBSA's effort was devoted to completing work started by the MRBC, including the water accounting system. The association also published a series of monographs, circulated biweekly news clippings, maintained the library inherited from the commission, sponsored conferences, and conducted conflict management and consensus-building exercises. The association was hampered by the failure of some states to pay their dues, because they found it difficult to justify the association before their legislative budget committees.

In 1982, MBSA fell victim to the ETSI controversy. The organization, which (in spite of its stated purposes) had been largely technically oriented, found itself in a highly political environment. The organization was not an adequate forum for managing the serious conflicts that accompanied the ETSI litigation. The MBSA directors, many of them midlevel water managers, could not make political and legal commitments for their states, and the MBSA staff was hampered by its inability to generate useful policy information for its members.

The MBSA did provide staff assistance to the 1986 negotiations among the representatives of the ten states (see the next section), but its role was less than optimal. Indeed, the negotiations produced many concerns about MBSA's purpose and structure and also resulted in a decision by member states to encourage senior policy officials (i.e., the natural resources adviser to the governor, the director of natural resources, or the director of water resources) to participate in the association.

1986 NEGOTIATIONS AMONG THE STATES

As a result of the controversies set in motion by the ETSI proposal, Governor John Carlin of Kansas sent a letter to his nine colleagues in July 1985 suggesting negotiations. Carlin's letter said that the disputes were interfering with sound development and that "the river is big enough to support growth and development in every state."[27] The governor suggested that permanent resolution could be achieved either through "adjudication as is now being contemplated by South Dakota" or through negotiation of a "formal agreement (compact)" among the states.[28] Carlin proposed that each governor appoint a negotiator to begin drafting a formal compact. The agreement could be limited to issues that needed resolution in the near future, but Carlin cautioned that "we must immediately address the right of each state to develop reasonable portions of the river without interference from other states."[29]

Carlin was the appropriate person to make the suggestion, for he was then chair of the National Governors' Association; his director of the Kansas Water Office, Joe Harkins, was the chair of MBSA; and Kansas had attempted to remain neutral in earlier skirmishes in the basin. Moreover, Kansas had just adopted a new state water plan with an emphasis on Missouri River issues, and Kansas policymakers were interested in avoiding litigation and encouraging cooperation.

By late October 1985, Governor Carlin had responses from most of the states. Six states had agreed to participate in negotiations. South Da-

Garrison Dam and Lake Sakakawea, North Dakota. (Courtesy Bureau of Reclamation)

kota's Governor William Janklow indicated that negotiations would be possible if downstream states would acknowledge each state's right to manage the river within reasonable limits. Nebraska said it would negotiate only if South Dakota joined the process and suggested the downstream states meet to address Janklow's concerns. Minnesota opposed negotiations on the basis that compact discussions were premature. Colorado did not respond.

Carlin then undertook an additional effort to get all states to the table by convening a meeting of the downstream states to address Governor Janklow's precondition. Representatives from Iowa, Kansas, Missouri, and Nebraska met in Topeka, Kansas, on November 20, 1985, and agreed on the following language designed to bring South Dakota to the table:

> The Missouri River is a natural resource that benefits the people of all the states of the Missouri Basin. Along with the benefits derived from this resource, we recognize our responsibility to work together in a spirit of cooperation and good faith to allow management of the river within reasonable limits by each state, while at the same time

recognizing that certain safeguards are necessary to protect the integrity of the Missouri River.

We pledge our good will and cooperation to any effort which will promote an enforceable agreement among the states to share and manage this resource for the benefit of all people in the Basin.[30]

This language was probably not the unequivocal statement that Janklow had intended,[31] but it was victory enough after a long line of setbacks. Janklow, however, had not finished making the lower basin states dance. After a six-week delay (and only two weeks before the first negotiating session Carlin had proposed), Janklow responded that he needed the personal assurances of the four lower basin governors that they concurred in the statement resulting from the November meeting.[32] Governors John Carlin, Terry Branstad (Iowa), John Ashcroft (Missouri), and Bob Kerrey (Nebraska) signed a letter of further assurances,[33] but because legislative sessions were beginning in many of the states, negotiations were postponed. Before basinwide negotiations commenced, the upper basin representatives held their own prenegotiation meeting in Billings, Montana, on March 13, 1986.

The negotiators met first in St. Paul, Minnesota, in late April 1986, and six additional sessions were held through December.[34] All sessions were held in airline "hub" cities (e.g., Denver, Minneapolis–St. Paul). All were scheduled over two days, usually starting in the afternoon of one and concluding at lunch on the next. Before the first negotiations, the MBSA Executive Committee met and prepared a "Suggested Meeting Format," essentially a one-page model agenda, to guide the meeting.

The meeting began with the election of Joe Harkins of Kansas as chair and a discussion of procedural issues. The group decided to have MBSA staff the negotiations, to close the meetings to all persons except state participants and others invited by the group, and to operate by consensus. The group also agreed that federal agency representatives could be involved in the discussions later. Apparently no mention was made of involving Indian tribes, and the group chose not to have a mediator. The negotiators agreed on a three-step approach to their work: (1) identification of issues; (2) development of possible solutions; and (3) development of instruments or mechanisms for implementing the proposed solutions.

At the second meeting, in May, the negotiators began to separate into two camps with differing views on the direction negotiations should take. Some upper basin states wanted to take an "incremental," practical, and nonphilosophical approach to the negotiations—premised on sufficient water availability, a partial allocation of water, and recognition of existing laws, compacts, and decrees. Other states desired a "systems" approach, insisting that broad policies and objectives needed to be developed to consider future basin needs and the region's quality of life. This group complained (justifiably, based on the three-stage methodology agreed upon at the first meeting) that the negotiators were rushing to solutions without having thoroughly framed the issues. The entire group did concur that allocation of the water between states would be the main issue and that each state would come to the next meeting prepared to discuss (for the main stem only) state allocations in terms of amount, type, place, time, and whether from storage or natural flows.

At the third meeting, in June, water supply data became a divisive issue. Missouri presented its own analysis of MBSA's water accounting system: the system was inadequate because it was based on monthly average flows and not on actual daily flows. Missouri was also concerned that MBSA had known of the deficiencies in its model for two years and had failed to correct them. This complex issue was ultimately referred to a technical committee. At the conclusion of this meeting, the negotiators agreed on three principles they believed should be included in any agreement: (1) recognition of all existing interstate compacts, court decrees, and international treaties; (2) a requirement that states share information on new appropriations and new consumptive uses; and (3) a provision that the agreement be continuous but subject to reexamination at specified intervals.

The fourth basinwide negotiating session was held in Denver in late July. The first items of business were a report by the technical committee and continued debate about the accuracy of MBSA's water accounting system. Two lower basin states, Missouri and Iowa, took the position that a water allocation agreement would be impossible until an improved water supply model, allowing predictions of future flows, was completed. Other states indicated that to delay negotiations pending completion of such a model would protract the negotiations indefinitely and cost millions of dollars.

The discussion led to several comments about the role of the organization. One negotiator indicated that his state had given up on MBSA; another delegate noted that "MBSA was a weak sister . . . because states haven't sent in the 'A' team," and indicated that, depending on the results of the negotiations, MBSA would need a new charter. The discussion continued about whether MBSA would be responsible for implementing an agreement and what changes would have to be made to MBSA. The negotiators eventually concluded they liked the concept of a nonbinding "statement of principles" for water management in the basin (patterned after the Great Lakes Charter). A drafting committee of three states was appointed to draft a statement of principles.

The September meeting began with the negotiators reviewing the committee's draft statement of principles. The parties agreed to try to reach agreement on a draft that could be reviewed with their governors before the next meeting. Some of the discussion concerned future exchanges of water data information, and the parties agreed that the states should pledge to share information and to improve the collection of that information. The negotiators reached an impasse on the issue of out-of-basin transfers.

The sixth meeting of the negotiators was held in November. The discussion focused on the draft statement of principles. Actually, five versions of the statement were on the table, but the negotiators agreed to work from a draft developed by Kansas and worked their way through it, frequently using language from other drafts to amend the document. The negotiators agreed on the need to improve information sharing about current and planned uses of water, the need to develop a nonjudicial dispute resolution process, and the need for structural improvements to MBSA; they also settled on a series of topics for future discussion.

Eventually, agreement was reached on all issues except one: the second principle of the document, which indicated that the subscribing states "will not interfere with the efforts of any basin State to develop a reasonable amount of water for new consumptive uses."[35] Two alternatives were proposed as "implementing actions" under the principle, each specifying different amounts of water that could be developed without being deemed unreasonable. The Kansas draft proposed that Montana, North Dakota, and South Dakota could develop new water uses on the Missouri and its tributaries totaling 600,000 ac-ft/yr and that Iowa, Kansas, Missouri, and Nebraska could develop new consumptive uses totaling 300,000 ac-ft/yr. Kansas also proposed two options: (1) that these limits would not apply to new consumptive uses on the tributaries, or (2) that each of the seven states be awarded 600,000 ac-ft/yr in new consumptive uses. In any cases, these limits would be effective only until 1992. By comparison, the Montana draft proposed 250,000 ac-ft/yr in new consumptive uses on the Missouri River main stem for Montana, North Dakota, and South Dakota; Iowa, Kansas, Missouri, and Nebraska would be allowed 125,000 ac-ft/yr in new consumptive uses; and the limits would be valid until 1990 (see Appendix 5).

The final meeting of the negotiators took place in Denver on December 17, 1986. Since the sixth meeting, legal proceedings before the U.S. Supreme Court had become more active, as ETSI and the federal government had filed petitions with the U.S. Supreme Court for review of the *Missouri v. Andrews* case, and South Dakota was preparing to renew its request for an original action before the Supreme Court against three of the lower basin states. Several upper basin states were reluctant to sign the statement of principles, fearing that an agreement would compromise their chances for the Supreme Court to accept the case. Although involving Oahe Reservoir, the litigation might be expanded into an apportionment of some or all of the river. The meeting, the final effort to negotiate a basin agreement, ended inconclusively.

The 1986 Missouri River negotiations were hampered by substantive differences and varying assessments by the states about how the negotiations would further their interests. The negotiations were also impeded by numerous procedural weaknesses. None of procedural flaws was fatal, but in combination they seriously weakened the negotiations.[36]

Substantive and Strategic Differences

Initially, the upper basin states sought to explain their frustrations with the Pick-Sloan Plan and to secure an agreement on development of Missouri River water without federal or lower basin interference. The lower basin states on the other hand were more entrenched in the status quo. They had succeeded in blocking South Dakota's ETSI plans, and even if an agreement were not reached, the river would continue to flow by. The upper basin's ability to develop major amounts of water and the quantification of federal and tribal rights were years away. The benefits of inaction were accompanied by the incomplete understanding in some lower basin states of the river system and the law of interstate rivers. For the short term, some lower basin states preferred to study and not act.

The states' support of the negotiations waned in the fall of 1986 as the negotiation process fell into the hands of lawyers. Since the negotiators were getting close to a final agreement, it was natural that individual states would refer the document to legal counsel for review, and there was also the increased activity regarding the Supreme Court. As a result, the states became exceedingly cautious and positioned themselves for litigation. Policymakers in some states were heavily influenced, if not actually displaced, by attorneys general or retained counsel.

Procedural Problems

Although well-run and harmonious negotiations will never produce an agreement if substantive differences remain, poorly conducted negotiations can certainly prevent agreement. In several respects, the Missouri River negotiators made their own job more difficult by allowing procedural problems to develop.

Unrealistic deadline. The negotiators were under a difficult mandate from the beginning: to conclude an agreement between April and the end of the year. Given the limited time available for meetings, their task became almost impossible. Most meetings were essentially twenty-four-hour affairs, with some negotiators coming late and others leaving early. Water compact discussions on other rivers have continued for years, frequently with multiday sessions. The Missouri River negotiations may be the most complex water-related negotiation ever undertaken in North America, and the ten-state negotiators devoted decidedly insufficient time to the task.

Few opportunities for negotiators to "socialize." For the most part, the negotiators did not have established working or personal relationships, particularly between the upper basin representatives and their lower basin counterparts. These people, some virtual strangers, were immediately thrust into a difficult setting. Meetings were not structured to facilitate informal exchanges among the participants, and meeting locations were not conducive to socialization. Other river basin compacts have been negotiated, at least in part, in casual resort settings (e.g., both Colorado River compacts and the Rio Grande Compact were negotiated at a resort, Bishop's Lodge, outside of Santa Fe).

Inadequate staff support. Governor Carlin's initiative offered the assistance of MBSA in staffing the negotiations, and that offer was implicitly accepted by the parties. From the start, however, MBSA's staff assistance was inadequate. The MBSA could have been much more helpful in providing information about how such issues as confidentiality, public information, and meeting records have been handled in other negotiations, and although the negotiators had agreed not to keep verbatim minutes of the session, the summaries that were prepared did not adequately capture the decisions that had been made or the content of the discussions.

Tenuous role of Kansas. Kansas was the convening state of the negotiations, and its delegate, Joe Harkins, was elected as chair. The Kansas position paper was the discussion document early in the sessions, and the state clearly wished to play a neutral, statesmanlike role in the negotiations.

Unfortunately, Kansas's role became more tenuous as the negotiations proceeded, for the state realized that it had positions on many of the issues—and it sought to achieve them. At one point, Harkins had to give the gavel to the MBSA staff director so that Harkins could speak freely on the issues. At that point, if not earlier, Kansas surrendered its role as mediator and was never able to regain its role of statesman for the basin.

Failure to define problems; failure to use statements of objectives and issues. At the first session, negotiators agreed to a three-step process to identify issues and to explore and develop solutions. During the first three meetings, many issues were identified, and some representatives even spoke of their state's objectives for the basin, but the minutes indicate that the group failed to use these expressions of issues and objectives in any meaningful way. The three-step process appears to have been short-changed, and the group jumped into the discussion of solutions (e.g., limited apportionment) to problems that had not been well-articulated or discussed.

Inadequate resolution of the "systems" states' concerns. Early on, several states wanted to make a more sweeping "systems" examination of Missouri River issues, a desire that may be interpreted as a need to learn more about the basin's law and characteristics. Although these states agreed at the third meeting to limit the discussion to some form of apportionment, it is likely that their concerns were never addressed. They may have assented nominally to the agenda change, but they may never have been totally "on board" during the remainder of the negotiations.

Selection of an inappropriate document to begin negotiations. In the third negotiating session, the group agreed to use Kansas's position paper as the basis for further discussions. The intention behind this suggestion was probably only to use the paper as an *outline* for future discussions, but in fact the paper immediately became *the* negotiating document. Although the paper was a good outline of discussion topics, it was not written as an agreement, and significant amounts of negotiating time were expended in improving it.

Insufficient use of committees. Given the limited time available for negotiators to meet as a group, one might expect that the group would have relied on committees to do much of the work. Committees were indeed formed and were useful in addressing the water data issue and in redrafting the statement of principles, but in general, they were underutilized throughout the negotiations. Although group members are often suspicious of committees on which they do not serve, their suspicion can be reduced by creating enough committees to involve all group members. Such organization equalizes the stake, burden, and input of all members.

Decline of the MBSA

Once negotiations had collapsed, participants intended to resume discussion after legislative sessions in the spring of 1987. Some participants believed that one positive result of the otherwise unsuccessful effort would be the strengthening of the Missouri Basin States Association, as the negotiators did agree to upgrade the association by encouraging the direct gubernatorial appointment of state engineers, directors of departments of water resources or natural resources, and similar high-level officials.

Nevertheless, the MBSA declined. When the directors convened again in 1987, the issue was not when negotiations would recommence but whether the association should be disbanded. Nebraska took the lead for dissolution, stressing MBSA's expense and inability to manage basin conflict. Other states wanting to quit the association, such as Colorado and Minnesota, cited their peripheral concerns in the basin. Although the directors did not agree to disband, they decided to close the association's Omaha office and to lay off staff.

In April 1988, after sponsoring a conference on Missouri River main stem operations,[37] the doors of the MBSA office were closed. Gone were the biweekly "Directors' New Bulletins" that had provided such an excellent set of news clippings on basin water developments. Gone also were the association's excellent library and the water accounting system. The recipient of these few but valuable assets?—the Army Corps of Engineers.

Many factors contributed to the termination of MBSA's staff. When MBSA was formed in 1981, many technical studies begun by the Missouri River Basin Commission remained to be completed—an agenda well-suited for a technically trained staff. During the next few years, Missouri River issues changed from technical questions concerning water development to legal and political issues (e.g., conflict management, significance of federal reserved water rights) for which the staff was not well-trained. Other factors contributing to the closing of the Omaha office were an increasing difficulty in obtaining dues from state legislatures, disappointment with the little-used water accounting system, and inadequate staffing of the 1986 round of negotiations.

THE MISSOURI RIVER AND AMERICAN FEDERALISM

The history presented here recounts the gradual nationalization of the Missouri River by the federal government. More and more, the Missouri has come to be run as a federal river; for instance:

- The Army Corps of Engineers ensures the navigability of the lower portions of the river.
- In conjunction with the Bureau of Reclamation, the corps determines the flow regime through the federal reservoirs on the main stem.
- The Western Area Power Administration markets hydroelectric power produced at the basin's dams.

- The U.S. Fish and Wildlife safeguards threatened or endangered species.
- The Environmental Protection Agency monitors water quality and regulates discharges into the river.
- The Bureau of Land Management safeguards the flow through the river's wild and scenic portions.
- The Departments of Justice and Interior have a trust obligation to ensure that ample water from the river will be available for Indian tribes and the land holdings of federal agencies.
- The Corps of Engineers holds much of the information left by the Missouri Basin States Association.

The state and federal governments have undertaken many approaches to regional water management, attempted to structure intergovernmental cooperation, and experimented with conflict resolution, but there has always been a fatal flaw in each of the initiatives and each approach has arisen as an exaggerated response to its predecessor. The Missouri Basin Inter-Agency Committee was too unstructured and informal, lacking legal authorization, enumerated powers, a dedicated staff, and the participation of all the basin states. By comparison, the Missouri River Basin Commission was overly structured and threatened state power. Too many agencies were involved. The commission's work was driven by a planning imperative, and insufficient attention was given to implementation and conflict resolution. With the large amounts of federal funds available to the commission, the states contributed a minor amount of the resources, and state leaders were but minor shareholders in the commission's activities.

The Missouri Basin States Association was an inadequate replacement for the commission. Although federal agency representatives frequently attended MBSA's meetings, they were not a federal-state forum. With the closing of MBSA's office, interstate coordination and the ability to assert basin states' positions were at their lowest points. In the late 1980s, representatives from state fish and wildlife agencies established a basin organization, and these representatives felt that their ecological concerns were not always addressed by the MBSA directors. This new organization, however, did not have as much political clout as even the weakened MBSA. Finally, as of the late 1980s, the basin's tribes had no role in any of these organizations except for their observer status in the Missouri River Basin Commission.

Thus, the Pick-Sloan Plan failed to provide a permanent forum through which state and tribal concerns could influence decision making. The abolition of the Missouri River Basin Commission, the weakening of the Missouri Basin States Association, and the redirection of the

Bureau of Reclamation created a vacuum that was filled by the U.S. Army Corps of Engineers.

The failure to achieve a viable intergovernmental structure for Missouri River water management is partially explained by basic changes in the American federal system, historic trends that can be better understood by studying the work of such scholars as Daniel Elazar and federalism literature written at different points in the twentieth century.

Elazar notes that the administration of Theodore Roosevelt marked the beginning of "progressive agrarianism"[38] in American politics and it was during this period that the concept of comprehensive river basin development was born. Roosevelt offered "positive government action to meet the problems of an industrialized society, and laid the foundation for co-operation"[39] with other governments in following years. A period of "normalized entrenchment" extended from 1921 to 1932, a time of "general reluctance to increase the role of government coupled with a negative attitude toward intergovernmental collaboration."[40] During this period, inaction by the Federal Power Commission allowed major oligopolies to gain control of most of the desirable hydroelectric sites in the United States.

The inauguration of President Franklin Roosevelt marked another benchmark in this century's history of federalism. The period was one of "crisis-oriented centralism," evidenced by calls for river valley authorities in the Tennessee and Missouri River basins and for passage of the Pick-Sloan Plan. Nevertheless, Elazar describes the period as one of continued collaboration between the federal and state governments although "the great acceleration of the velocity of government made co-operative federalism all-pervasive . . . [and] the co-operative system was subtly reoriented toward Washington."[41]

Indeed, much of the relevant literature of the time supports that assessment. Papers presented at a 1940 symposium on federalism[42] give significant attention to the roles of state and local governments. Yet, in other papers concerning the use of federal grants-in-aid,[43] the use of federal regions,[44] and the deference accorded congressional enactments by the Supreme Court, it is clear that the federal government was emerging as the dominate party in the federal scheme.

The post–World War II era was one of "noncentralist restoration," with the states and localities expanding in their functions and accepting some of the functions, usually with federal grant assistance, that had been performed by the federal government during the depression and the war. In the Missouri River basin, this was the period when the major dams were built. There was a fair amount of coordination between the federal government and the states concerning the implementation of the construction program, and a water compact proposal was developed by the states.

Most of the 1960s saw "concentrated cooperation" with "increased federal activity in a number of fields . . . coupled with an intensification of the debate over 'states rights' on one hand and widespread acknowledgment of intergovernmental collaboration on the other."[45] In the Missouri River basin, the dams were completed, and basin decision makers were searching for ways to collaborate in the ongoing management of the river. The Corps of Engineers, however, was becoming firmly entrenched as the day-to-day operator of the river.

For Elazar, the period from 1969 to 1981 (and in some instances to the present) was an extremely unfortunate one for the American federal system. On the one hand, the U.S. Supreme Court "stood the Constitution on its head so as to give the Congress . . . the last word in determining the federal-state relationship."[46] On the other hand, Congress "order[ed] the states to do this and that without any pretense of winning them over through federal aid or making those orders contingent upon accepting federal grants."[47] This, he laments, was "prefectorial federalism."[48] Another commentator remarks that

> observers of all political persuasions agree that the federalism of two centuries ago is either dead or pretty close to death. Especially since the New Deal, Washington has made a habit of usurping state authority, and now conservatives and liberals alike join hands in the continuing national power grab.[49]

Elazar concludes that in the 1980s a form of "neo-dualism" of state and federal authority was restored to the federal system, partly as a result of Reagan administration initiatives to transfer some responsibility back to the states and partly through states' and localities' own efforts to become more vital governments.

Unfortunately, prefectorial federalism still characterizes water management in the Missouri River basin. The U.S. Supreme Court and lower appellate federal courts have consistently recognized the broad authority of federal agencies over the Missouri River. The Missouri River Basin Commission, which was originally established to coordinate government activity, gradually became a federally driven planning agency with an agenda that was ultimately rendered obsolete by congressional failures to fund the completion of the Pick-Sloan Plan. The Reagan administration made things even worse by eliminating this singular opportunity for regular communication among some of the basin governments.

Throughout the 1980s, the basin states were adrift, unable to regularize their communications and order their relationships. At frequent intervals they were buffeted by litigation or other conflicts. And while the states searched for an institutional form to order their affairs, the river continued to run and the corps continued to run the river.

CHAPTER SIX

Traditional Patterns of Federalism in River Management

As one longtime participant in the fray has observed, "there never has been sufficient glue" in the Missouri River basin to keep the governments together. This situation, though unfortunate, is not surprising. The American federal system provides few avenues for intergovernment cooperation and conflict resolution in a river basin. The classic understanding of American federalism is that power is divided between the national government and numerous states, most of which are defined by artificially described boundaries.[1] Conflicts between states and between states and the federal government can be resolved by the U.S. Supreme Court. The Constitution also provides for interstate compacts, if approved by Congress; but it took almost 150 years before an interstate water compact was developed under that authority. The Constitution simply was not drafted with river basins in mind. Whereas opportunities for interstate cooperation concerning rivers may have been constrained by the Constitution, federal supremacy has not, and as we have seen, the Missouri River, like many river systems, has been nationalized by the federal government.

This chapter examines the development of American federalism with reference to interstate rivers. The resulting pattern is one of constrained interstate cooperation and federal supremacy, and because the interstate compact has become the principal means of interstate agreement, its qualities are explored in detail in connection with existing or attempted compacts on several important rivers (see Map 6.1).

DEVELOPMENT OF THE CONSTITUTION'S COMPACT CLAUSE

Disputes among political entities arose early on the North American continent. Because of vagueness in their charters, the colonies engaged in frequent boundary disputes as they expanded their territories.[2] Two methods were used to resolve these disagreements: negotiation between the quarreling colonies and appeal to the English Crown.

As early as 1644, boundary negotiations were conducted between

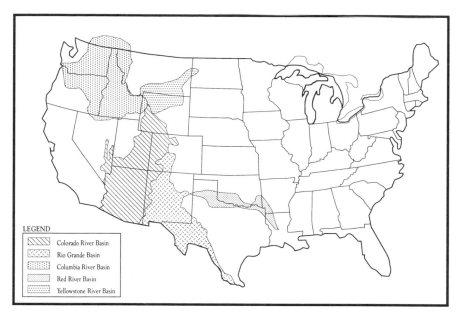

Map 6.1. Selected river basins. (Map by Leslee Unser)

New York and Connecticut. Nine such agreements were reached between colonies as the result of negotiations between joint commissions
that sometimes extended for decades.[3] Once an agreement was reached,
it was submitted to the Crown for approval. If negotiations failed or a
more direct method of resolution was sought, an appeal was made to the
English Crown, usually followed by a referral of the controversy to a
Royal Commission and, possibly later, to the Privy Council. This method
of boundary adjustment was used as late as 1773.

When the proposed Articles of Confederation were finalized by the
Second Continental Congress in November 1777, the central feature of
the document was the extensive retention by the states of their sovereignty. ARTICLE 2 of the proposal stated that "each State retains its sovereignty, freedom, and independence, and every power, jurisdiction, and
right, which is not by this confederation expressly delegated to the
united States, in Congress assembled."[4]

One of the purposes of the Articles of Confederation was "to protect
the new Union of States . . . from the destructive political combinations
of two or more States."[5] Concerned about potential aggregations of regional power, the articles limited the states' authority to enter into interstate agreements without the consent of Congress.[6] A similar provision
eventually found its way into the Constitution.

The articles did provide for an appeal to Congress "in all disputes and differences now subsisting or that hereafter may arise between two or more states concerning boundary, jurisdiction or any cause whatever."[7] ARTICLE 9 of the Articles of Confederation set forth the complicated means of settling these interstate disputes. The first step in the procedure required each of the conflicting states to appoint commissioners or judges to constitute a court to hear the dispute. If this body could not resolve the conflict, congressional delegates were selected from all thirteen states; this group was reduced to a commission of seven to nine members after rotating disqualification by the contesting states.

Two interstate disputes were addressed under these procedures of the articles. The first case arose between Pennsylvania and Connecticut over title to an area known as the Wyoming Valley. A five-man court heard forty-two days of testimony, then issued a unanimous judgment in Pennsylvania's favor. A second dispute, between New York and New Hampshire over an area known as the Hampshire Grant, was rendered moot when the area was admitted to the union as the state of Vermont.[8]

It took three years to adopt the Articles of Confederation, and they lasted only eight years. One of the document's major deficiencies was its inability to resolve interstate conflicts. Alexander Hamilton, in the *Federalist* (No. 7, "Sources of Interstate Conflict"), listed the sources of these tensions. They included disputes over territories[9] and boundaries, commercial rivalries, arguments over the allocation of the public debt of the union (resulting from the Revolutionary War), retaliations among states for wrongs committed upon private citizens, and disagreements incurred by state entanglements with rival European powers.[10] Hamilton was not merely concerned about unpleasant tensions among the states, his "argument [was] that these conflicts of interest . . . [would] rather lead to *war.*"[11]

Delegates to the Constitutional Convention came to Philadelphia in the summer of 1787 to fine-tune the Articles of Confederation. They soon turned to the more fundamental challenge of designing a government strong enough to overcome the provincialism of the articles but with self-regulating safeguards to protect the states from the excesses of government. Eventually, the debate between the federalists and the antifederalists was resolved in favor of a strong national government. The Senate however became the principal body for the representation of state governments, with senators being elected by the state legislatures.[12] The Constitution was ratified and became effective in 1789.

Under the Constitution, boundary disputes continued to be the principal source of conflict among the states. As the Supreme Court recounted in an early opinion, "It is part of the public history of the United States . . . that at the adoption of the Constitution there were existing controversies between eleven states respecting their boundaries, which arose under their respective charters, and had continued from the first settlement of the Colonies."[13]

The Constitution did, however, change the method of conflict resolution between states. The most notable feature of the Constitution was to vest the Supreme Court with original jurisdiction to hear disputes between states[14] (thus assumed the role delegated to Congress under the articles).[15] Since the ratification of the Constitution, interstate disputes over water have replaced boundary disputes as the principal subject matter of these interstate cases before the Supreme Court.

The Constitution makes explicit provision for resolving other interstate disputes. For instance, ARTICLE 4, SECTION 1, requires a state to give "full Faith and Credit . . . to the public Acts, Records, and judicial proceedings of every other State." SECTION 2 of the same article requires extradition of criminal defendants "who shall flee from Justice and be found in another State." Other forms of interstate cooperation are allowed by the Constitution.[16] Traditionally, they have included the passage of uniform laws, the adoption of reciprocal legislation, the formation of associations of government officials, and the negotiation and approval of interstate compacts.[17]

Interstate compacts, authorized by ARTICLE 1, SECTION 10, of the U.S Constitution,[18] were a method that the Founders provided to resolve interstate disputes that did not rise to national significance—thus continuing a practice that had preceded both the Articles of Confederation and the Constitution.[19] An interstate compact must be ratified by Congress, and prior congressional consent to negotiations has traditionally been sought. One perennial constitutional question concerns which interstate agreements this requirement affects. Early decisions indicate that the U.S. Supreme Court read this language quite strictly. In *Holmes v. Jennison*, the Court indicated that the clause includes "every agreement, written or verbal, formal or informal, positive or implied, by the mutual understanding of the parties."[20]

The 1893 decision of *Virginia v. Tennessee*[21] has become the standard for identifying those agreements that require congressional approval. In that opinion, the U.S. Supreme Court indicated that the Compact Clause applies to agreements "which may tend to increase and build up the political influence of the contracting states, so as to encroach upon or impair the supremacy of the United States or interfere with their rightful management of particular subjects placed under their entire control."[22] This standard, however, has failed to provide a "bright line" clarifying which interstate agreements require congressional approval and which do not.

The resolution of boundary disputes between states no longer requires congressional approval because such agreements do not distort the balance between state and federal power.[23] The Multistate Tax Compact, which assists interstate tax enforcement, also does not require federal approval. The tax compact, the Supreme Court said, neither enhances state power respective to the national government nor "is an affront to the sovereignty of nonmember States."[24] Yet, in a 1981 decision, the Court indicated that the Interstate Agreement on Detainers required federal approval because the subject matter was appropriate for congressional legislation.[25]

The Court has also been lenient concerning the manner by which Congress gives its consent to interstate agreements. Congress can provide advance unconditional or conditional approval of an agreement even before it is drafted, or it can approve the agreement after it has been drafted and approved by the states. Congressional consent can also be inferred from a single legislative act that is not specifically addressed to an interstate agreement or from a pattern of such legislation.[26]

WATER RESOURCE COMPACTS

Congress has approved approximately thirty-five water-related compacts, more than twenty of them in the West. As shown in the following list, all of the Missouri River basin states except Iowa are members of at least one water-related compact.

Colorado:	Animas–La Plata Compact
	Arkansas River Compact of 1949
	Colorado River Compact
	Costilla Creek Compact
	La Plata River Compact
	Republican River Compact
	Rio Grande Compact
	South Platte River Compact
	Upper Colorado River Basin Compact
Kansas:	Arkansas River Compact of 1949
	Arkansas River Compact of 1965
	Big Blue River Compact
	Kansas-Missouri Waterworks Compact
	Republican River Compact
Minnesota:	Great Lakes Basin Compact
Missouri:	Kansas-Missouri Waterworks Compact (1922)
Montana:	Fort Peck–Montana Compact (Indian reserved water rights)

	Northern Cheyenne–Montana Compact (Indian reserved water rights)
	Yellowstone River Compact
Nebraska:	Big Blue River Compact
	Republican River Compact
	South Platte River Compact
	Upper Niobrara River Compact
North Dakota:	Yellowstone River Compact
South Dakota:	Belle Fourche River Compact
Wyoming:	Bear River Compact
	Belle Fourche River Compact
	Colorado River Compact
	Snake River Compact
	Upper Colorado River Basin Compact
	Upper Niobrara River Compact
	Yellowstone River Compact

The primary purpose of an interstate water compact is to resolve disputes between sovereign states over a shared waterway. To this fundamental purpose can be added two more visionary goals: to achieve meaningful coordination of federal and nonfederal water policies and actions and to bring about a regional, ecological perspective in the management of water resources. Water resource compacts fall into four categories: water allocation, pollution control, flood control, and comprehensive water regulation and project development.[27] Since a water pollution compact has never been proposed for the Missouri River, and water quality regulation falls increasingly under the federal Clean Water Act,[28] these types of compacts are not discussed.[29] Flood control compacts, created in the 1930s to provide state support for federal flood control programs, also are not discussed because they are now of minor importance.[30] Federal-interstate comprehensive water management compacts are examined in the next chapter.

Water allocation compacts are the most common type of water resource compact. The first water allocation compact was negotiated among the Colorado River basin states in 1922, and it has been followed by over twenty other water quantification compacts. Some of these compacts have been simple water allocation compacts; others, more sophisticated water planning and management agreements with commissions and permanent staff. Some compacts have only state members; in others, the federal government is a signatory as well.[31]

Water allocations are often made on a specified volume or percentage basis. Half of these compacts provide that the state allocations also include water for federal uses. Earlier compacts require the chief water managers of the signatory states to develop regulations and procedures to implement the water apportionment agreement, whereas later compacts establish a permanent administrative entity to implement the compact's terms.[32]

Some water allocation compacts have attempted to solve the problems of overappropriation of an interstate stream brought about by the independent actions of two or more states. These compacts establish a mechanism by which overappropriation may be reduced, usually by applying the prior appropriation doctrine across state lines. The Rio Grande, La Plata, South Platte, and Bear rivers are examples of waters governed by such water distribution compacts. Other water allocation compacts allocate the unappropriated waters among the riparian states. The Upper Colorado River Compact and the Yellowstone River Compact are examples.[33] Recently, as in the 1985 Fort Peck-Montana Compact, water allocation compacts have been negotiated between states and Indian tribes. Although not required under the Compact Clause, congressional approval of state-tribal compacts may be necessary because of Congress's trust responsibility for the tribes.

Colorado River Compact

The Colorado River system is among the most contentious of river basins, and the Colorado River Compact is the grandparent of all other western water allocation compacts. Seven states, more than nineteen Indian reservations, and Mexico share the Colorado River basin compared to ten states, twenty-five Indian reservations, and Canada in the Missouri River basin. The history of the Colorado has been told many times and is relatively well-known;[34] it offers many lessons that may be relevant to Missouri basin policymakers.

The Colorado River system is affected by two compacts: the basinwide seven-state 1922 Colorado River Compact,[35] and the five-state 1948 Upper Colorado River Basin Compact.[36] The 1922 compact, which became effective as a six-state accord in 1928 (and was finally approved by hold-out Arizona in 1944), divided the consumptive use of the Colorado River's flow between upper and lower parts of the basin, muting upriver fears about preemptive downstream appropriations and facilitating federally subsidized water and power development for southern California.

Several forces combined to produce the compact. Farmers in the highly irrigable Imperial Valley lobbied heavily for a federal dam on the river to provide storage, flood control, and silt reduction and for a diversion canal located entirely north of the U.S.-Mexico border. Los Angeles, competing with private power interests, wanted electric power from the planned dam and reservoir at Boulder Canyon.

The Bureau of Reclamation's desire to construct a Colorado River dam to promote irrigation in the lower reaches of the basin was embodied in a formal report and legislative proposal in 1922. Pending in the U.S. Supreme Court at the time was the *Wyoming v. Colorado* lawsuit over the Laramie River,[37] which held out the prospect (in June 1922 the reality) that the high court would recognize the prior appropriation doctrine in interstate water disputes, giving the earlier (senior) appropriator preference over the later (junior) one. Fast-paced water development in southern California could thus give that area senior rights over the planned and potential uses upstream.

All of these forces and prospects made the upstream states, which expected to develop more slowly, quite nervous. Led by Colorado, these states began to appreciate the need for a guaranteed allotment or reservation of sizable shares of the river's flow for themselves. This growing mutuality of interest in an agreement and sense of urgency—southern California's need for a federal water project on the Colorado and the upper basin states' need for a protected share of the flow—made negotiations possible.

Commissioners representing the seven basin states and President Harding's representative, Herbert Hoover, began negotiating the compact in January 1922 and completed a compact document in November of the same year. Agreement could not be reached on water entitlements for each state; instead, the compact divides water between the lower basin and the upper basin. The boundary line runs through a point called Lee's Ferry, which is about ten miles downstream from Arizona's Glen Canyon Dam.

The 1922 compact, which declares that the upper and lower basins are each apportioned perpetually "the exclusive beneficial consumptive use of 7,500,000 acre-feet of water per annum," restricts the upper states from causing the flow of the river at Lee's Ferry to be depleted below an aggregate of 75,000,000 ac-ft for any period of ten consecutive years.[38] Practically speaking, this guaranteed minimum delivery requirement means the upper states bear the risk of shortage. The flow records on which this apportionment was based came from a limited period when flows were abnormally high. Instead of the 16.4 million ac-ft/yr average flow that the negotiators assumed for the river at Lee's Ferry, average flow is now estimated to range between 13.5 and 14.8 million ac-ft/yr, leaving the upper states with considerably less potential supply than the 7.5 million ac-ft/yr recognized for them in the compact.

The 1922 compact did more than create an upper and lower basin apportionment formula, for it anticipated an international water treaty by specifying how water for Mexico would be charged against the system. It also made electric power generation subordinate to agricultural and domestic uses and deferred the question of Indian water rights with a disclaimer that has been frequently used since: "Nothing in this compact shall be construed as affecting the obligations of the United States of America to Indian tribes." The 1922 compact did not create an administrative structure, such as a commission, to implement the compact, although it did mandate continued interstate and federal-state cooperation.

Since the 1922 compact did not apportion water to each state, that task remained. The Boulder Canyon Project Act of 1928,[39] passed over Arizona's objections, authorized the construction of Boulder Canyon (now Hoover) Dam, the All-American Canal for Imperial and Coachella valleys, and approved the 1922 compact as a six-state agreement. It also made possible another compact that would apportion an annual 0.3 million ac-ft/yr to Nevada, 4.4 million ac-ft/yr and half of the surplus to California, and 2.8 million ac-ft/yr plus half the surplus to Arizona. This lower basin compact was never negotiated, although the apportionment Congress suggested became a reality in 1963, when the U.S. Supreme Court in the fourth *Arizona v. California*[40] case ruled that Congress delegated the power to the secretary of the interior to apportion water to those states by contract.

Mexico was given the right to 1.5 million ac-ft/yr in the international treaty of 1944.[41] Soon after, the upper basin states, wanting more federally subsidized water projects for their region and realizing that water rights had to precede development, negotiated their own compact during three short weeks in 1948. The resulting Upper Colorado River Basin Compact, unlike its 1922 relative, did apportion water to individual states and authorize a compact commission. Uncertain about climatic variability and the amount of water actually available to them under the 1922 compact, the upper basin states wisely used a percentage formula for apportionment: 11.25 percent for New Mexico, 14 percent for Wyoming, 23 percent for Utah, and 51.75 percent for Colorado. The 1948 compact established the Upper Colorado River Commission, composed of a representative from each state and the United States, with offices in Salt Lake City. The compact prepared the way for the Colorado River Storage Project Act of 1956[42] that authorized Glen Canyon Dam and a host of other upper basin projects.

The apportionment of water to Indian tribes in the Colorado River basin, an issue sidestepped by the 1922 and 1948 compacts, is only partially complete. Five lower Colorado River tribes were awarded reserved water rights in the 1963 *Arizona v. California*[43] decision—these allocations are charged against the entitlements of the states in which the reservations are located. Other reservations have been variously litigating, negotiating, or delaying quantification of their claims. The tribes recently organized their own basinwide organization, and they have attempted to present a cohesive front in negotiations with the basin states. Other issues not addressed by the 1922 or 1948 compacts are water quality and groundwater. Salinity control is being attempted by an interstate salinity control program paid for by the federal government,[44] and groundwater is regulated by the individual states.

The Colorado River experience is particularly relevant for the decision makers of the Missouri River basin because of the conflict between the upper and lower basin (although the intense conflict between two states of a subbasin, Arizona and California, has not been repeated in the Missouri). Although the 1922 compact was negotiated in less than a year, questions left unanswered in that document have taken more than seventy additional years to address—and important questions remain unanswered. Unfortunately, the original compact created no forum in which the states could address these unanswered questions; thus, disputes have been taken to the courts and to Congress, reducing the ability of the basin states to chart their own destinies. The law of the river has been developed as a weave of compacts, court decrees, and legislation. The Colorado River Compact also illustrates the necessity of obtaining accurate hydrologic information and projections. A central weakness of the 1922 compact stems from inaccuracies about the average flow of the river.

The Colorado River basin states have been very successful in reaping benefits—such as the Central Arizona Project (CAP), the Central Utah Project (CUP), and the All-American Canal—from the river. Perhaps they have been too successful, as Arizona is now finding out. With farmers unwilling to pay for the expensive CAP water, state leaders are wondering how the repayment obligation for the project will be met. An old adage comes to mind: Don't wish too hard for something; it may come true.

For the most part, the Colorado River basin states have relied upon their separate political power rather than upon cooperative strategies (e.g., California had a large congressional delegation; Arizona had Congressmen Carl Hayden and Morris Udall). The pursuit of individual state agendas will likely fail in the Missouri River basin for the reason that Congress is less receptive to water development requests—especially when there are outstanding differences among the states and when the rights of Native Americans have not been adequately addressed.

Rio Grande Compact

The Rio Grande begins in southern Colorado, flows south for 400 miles through New Mexico, and forms the 1,250-mile Texas-Mexico border before entering the Gulf of Mexico.[45] The Rio Grande River Compact apportions the river's water above Fort Quitman, Texas, which lies approximately 80 miles southeast of El Paso. The compact, signed by Colorado, New Mexico, and Texas in 1938,[46] is the oldest of Texas's interstate water compacts. Like other compacts in the West, the Rio Grande Compact has been enmeshed in controversy and litigation.[47]

Negotiations for a Rio Grande compact actually started in 1924 in meetings convened by Secretary of Commerce Herbert Hoover. In 1929, the three Rio Grande states signed a preliminary compact that preserved the status quo,[48] and a commissioner from each state was appointed to negotiate a permanent compact for the apportionment of the Rio Grande. The negotiations went relatively smoothly until 1935 when Texas filed a lawsuit against the state of New Mexico and the Middle Rio Grande Conservation District for violating the provisions of the 1929 accord.[49] Texas claimed, not only that New Mexico had diverted excessive amounts of water above Elephant Butte Dam, located about 100 miles north of El Paso, but also that the salt content of the water delivered to Texas had increased.[50]

The amount and quality of the water in Elephant Butte Reservoir were important to Texas because New Mexico wanted to satisfy its compact obligation to Texas by delivering water to the dam, not to the state line. Elephant Butte Dam was the result of a 1906 treaty with Mexico that allowed the United States to supply Mexico with 60,000 ac-ft of water per year from the Rio Grande.[51]

The 1935 litigation fostered the timely completion of the permanent compact. Because of the suit, Franklin D. Roosevelt embargoed all additional Rio Grande water projects pending an agreement, and this action prompted the President's National Resources Committee and several federal agencies to prepare the Rio Grande Joint Investigation Study. The resulting report gave negotiators an adequate description of the problems surrounding the equitable apportionment of the Rio Grande and enabled them to complete the compact quickly.

During the negotiations, each state had clear goals. Colorado wanted to build several federal dam facilities that had been halted by the president's embargo. New Mexico wanted to deliver water to Elephant Butte Dam rather than to the Texas border so that New Mexican irrigators downstream of the dam would also benefit from the delivery. Texas wanted a guaranteed annual release from Elephant Butte Dam of 800,000 ac-ft. When the negotiations were completed, Texas received a guarantee of 790,000 ac-ft, and the other two states' demands were met in full.

The compact was signed in 1935 and Texas's suit was terminated.[52] The compact is administered by the Rio Grande Compact Commission, consisting of one representative from each signatory state and one nonvoting federal representative. Unanimous consent is needed for commission action. Thus, each member has the power to veto any proposal.

Under the compact, the water of the Rio Grande is allocated on an inflow/outflow basis. The amount of water that Colorado is required to send to New Mexico depends upon the amount measured at gaging stations in Colorado; the amount of water New Mexico delivers to Elephant Butte depends on the amount gaged at locations in northern New Mexico. The inflow/outflow amounts change, of course, from year to year. The size of accrued and annual debits that the compact allows, however, remain constant. Colorado's annual or accrued debit cannot exceed 100,000 ac-ft of water, and New Mexico's cannot exceed 200,000 ac-ft.

By the early 1950s, both Colorado and New Mexico had exceeded these limits. In 1952, Texas filed a suit against New Mexico, claiming that its neighbor had built up a debit of 331,800 ac-ft in 1951,[53] and hearings were conducted on the case by a special water master. The Supreme Court dismissed the case in 1957 because the United States was an "indispensable party,"[54] and by that time, New Mexico had accrued a debit of 549,400 ac-ft. This debit began to decrease as the drought of the 1950s ended.

By 1965, Colorado had an accrued debit of close to 940,000 ac-ft, and Texas and New Mexico filed an original action against Colorado in 1966 for violation of the compact.[55] The U.S. Solicitor General again argued that the United States was an "indispensable party" in the suit. A continuance was requested by Texas and New Mexico, however, pursuant to an agreement by Colorado to meet its delivery obligations. The continuance was granted by the Supreme Court in 1968.[56]

By the end of 1984, Colorado's accrued debit had fallen to 600,000 ac-ft. In 1985, natural events combined with an unusual provision of the compact to eliminate both Colorado's and New Mexico's debits. Elephant Butte Reservoir was almost full after several wet years when a large amount of snow fell in the winter of 1985 and the spring runoff caused Elephant Butte Reservoir to overflow. According to the compact, the resulting spill automatically eliminated both states' debits, and the 1966 lawsuit was dismissed.[57]

The Rio Grande Compact is complicated and unique. The spill provision was considered superfluous by some until spring 1985 when it drastically changed the status of all three states. Texas is understandably concerned that the elimination of Colorado's and New Mexico's deficits will be seen as an invitation to accrue new ones. We can expect court action if more deficits accrue.

This compact reinforces some of the lessons of the Colorado River Compact. First, multistate arrangements take time to develop. The Rio Grande Compact took fourteen years to negotiate, and several of its provisions are still in question. Second, compact negotiations can benefit from external pressures. The finalization of the compact was aided by the presidential moratorium on water development and by the federal Rio Grande Joint Investigation Study. Third, the success of compacts depends greatly on the reliability of hydrologic data, data that are often hard to come by.

Yellowstone River Compact

The Yellowstone River Compact, concluded on October 30, 1951, is essentially between Wyoming and Montana, although North Dakota is also a member because the Yellowstone River passes briefly through that state before joining with the Missouri River.[58] The essence of the compact is its allocation of the unappropriated waters of the Clark Fork of the Yellowstone and the Bighorn, Tongue, and Powder rivers between Montana and Wyoming. The apportionment rests on a percentage basis of the flow at the mouths of each of these four tributaries of the Yellowstone. Existing and future domestic and stock water uses were excluded, and the compact recognizes water that had been appropriated prior to January 1, 1950. The agreement does not affect any Indian reserved water rights.[59] Since 1950, there has been sufficient water in the four major streams to adequately supply pre-1950 water rights and post-1950 development without invoking the percentage allocation contained in the compact. Thus, no specific quantity of water has been determined for the member states.

Three previous attempts to compact the Yellowstone were unsuccessful.[60] The first compact discussions began pursuant to congressional authorization in 1932. In February 1935, commissioners from Montana and Wyoming signed an agreement, but the compact was never acted upon by the legislature of either state. A second authorization was obtained from Congress in August 1937, and this consent required completion of a compact by June 1939. Montana, Wyoming, and representatives of several federal agencies participated in these negotiations. In 1939, the negotiators had not completed an agreement, but they recommended that additional data be accumulated, that Congress provide an indefinite extension of its consent for negotiations, and that North Dakota be included in future negotiations. Congress extended its consent in 1940, and commissioners from the three states reached an agreement in 1942. This compact was doomed, however, when the Wyoming legislature, the first body to consider it, failed to ratify the agreement. A third compact was successfully ratified by the legislatures of all three states, but the Wyoming governor vetoed it.

In June 1949, Congress again consented to negotiations, and four rounds of formal meetings were held in Billings between November 1949 and December 1950. Sixteen commissioners participated from Montana, eighteen from Wyoming, and three from North Dakota. The agreement was signed on December 8, 1950, and by March 1951, the compact had been ratified by all three states. When the agreement reached Washington for congressional approval, however, the U.S. Department of Justice voiced concerns about three of the provisions. The department objected to the allocation of unappropriated waters on a percentage basis, fearing that this provision might deprive the federal government of surplus water flowing into the Missouri. The department's second concern was that a provision of the agreement allowing the compact commission to be sued might constitute a waiver of the sovereign immunity of the federal government.[61] The department was also concerned about the ambiguity of a section of the agreement that affirmed the sovereignty and jurisdiction of the federal government "in or over the area of waters affected by such compact."[62]

For its part, the Department of the Interior expressed doubt about requiring the unanimous consent of all signatory states before diversions from the Yellowstone River could take place, but it did not oppose ratification. The Bureau of the Budget objected to the inclusion of a representative of the U.S. Geological Survey on the commission; the bureau would have preferred an appointee of the president who would represent the interests of the United States as a whole. The Senate Committee on the Interior rejected all these concerns, and the compact was ratified by Congress on October 31, 1951. Thus, it took over sixteen years for the states to successfully conclude an agreement.

The Yellowstone River Compact is administered by a three-person commission made up of representatives from Montana and Wyoming, who are appointed by their governors, and a representative from the U.S. Geological Survey (appointed by the director), whose vote is limited to instances when the state representatives cannot agree. The commission is empowered "to formulate rules and regulations and to perform any act necessary to carry out the provisions of [the] Compact."[63] The commission has no interpretative or explicit dispute resolution authority.

Attorney Richard Dana recently analyzed the structure, successes, and failures of the Yellowstone River Compact.[64] He identifies the most important accomplishments of the Yellowstone River Compact as its reorganization of jurisdiction over interstate waters to correspond more closely to the natural river basin and its establishment of a structure that reduces intraregional fragmentation of water resources control.[65] Dana asserts that "the compact has not eliminated interstate controversy, . . . [but] it has channeled that controversy into constructive channels."[66] Dana observes that the stated original goal of the compact, "to remove all causes of present and future controversy," was unrealistic but that the compact has created an important mechanism for regional conflict resolution. He points to the commission's decision to manage interstate ditches and to work toward developing a system to administer interstate waters. Nonetheless, says Dana:

> Recent representatives to the Compact Commission have become pre-occupied with strict interpretations of the compact according to past conditions. . . . Montana and Wyoming would benefit by explicitly recognizing that . . . they formed a regional government, and as a result, they inherited responsibilities to act for regional (rather than state) goals.[67]

Dana suggests a future-oriented agenda for the commission including promotion of environmental quality, development of a basinwide water protection strategy, and basin economic development.[68]

Although the compact attempts to account for Native American rights by disclaiming any jurisdiction over them, Dana concludes that the failure to involve the tribes on the compact commission is "essentially discriminatory."[69] He adds that "due to their control over water resources, Indians play a role comparable to the states in determining water allocation and uses on a regional scale, and they deserve adequate recognition. To be a fully effective agreement, the Yellowstone Compact should include the basin's Indians as full partners."[70]

Water law professor Frank Trelease has also analyzed the Yellowstone River Compact and draws attention to the following issues:

- The need to develop an accounting system with forecasting capability that will allow the compact commission to administer the agreement, including a determination of the amount of water available to each state.
- The need to resolve the reserved rights of the Crow and Northern Cheyenne tribes and the effects of those rights on the compact allocation.
- The need to resolve the apportionment of the Little Big Horn River among Montana, Wyoming, and the Crow tribe.
- The need to determine whether Wyoming will be allowed to divert some of its compact share on the Yellowstone main stem in Montana and transport it back to Wyoming.[71]

Another issue addressed by Trelease, the constitutionality of Article 10 of the compact, which requires the consent of all the signatories before water can be diverted out of the basin,[72] has been upheld by the federal courts.[73] The Court held that the compact, because approved by Congress, is federal law. Thus, Congress has consented to an interstate restraint that would normally contradict the dormant commerce clause.

Red River Compact

The Red River begins in northwestern Texas and stretches along the Texas-Oklahoma border, through Arkansas and Louisiana, and into the Gulf of Mexico. About halfway along the Texas-Oklahoma border sits the only reservoir on the main stem of the river, Lake Texoma. The lake, the result of Denison Dam, divides two different regions. Above the lake, the land is semiarid, and people are concerned about having enough water for domestic, municipal, and agricultural uses. The lands below the dam receive up to sixty inches of rain per year, and farmers worry that floods will inundate their crops.

In 1955, Congress passed legislation allowing representatives of Texas, Oklahoma, Arkansas, and Louisiana to begin negotiations on a water-appropriation compact for the Red River.[74] The diversity of the four states' water needs made the negotiations long and arduous. After twenty-two years and sixty formal meetings, the compact was signed,[75] marking an important step in the concept of basinwide water use coordination.

A number of factors in the 1940s made officials in these states interested in coordinating the use of the Red River. Oklahoma was worried that Texas had little interest in maintaining water quality in watersheds that yielded water stored in reservoirs in Oklahoma. Texas was uneasy about an Oklahoma irrigation district's application for a large amount of Red River water. Arkansas and Louisiana were both concerned about severe drought conditions. The Mississippi River was so low during the period that New Orleans' municipal water supply was threatened by an intrusion of sea water.

In March 1950, the governor of Oklahoma responded to these concerns by inviting leading water officials from the four basin states to discuss the feasibility of a compact for the Red River. As a result of the meeting, a bill granting congressional approval of compact negotiations had been drafted by May 1950, but because of many delays in both Washington, D.C., and the Red River basin, the act was not approved until August 11, 1955. State leaders mistakenly believed that congressional approval was necessary to begin negotiations (approval is needed only of the final agreement). Thus, five years were lost—a preview of the glacial speed of the subsequent negotiations.

The Red River Compact Negotiating Committee (RRCNC) was composed of a nonvoting federal representative appointed by the president and one representative of each state appointed by the governors. Two subcommittees of the RRCNC were established—the Engineering Advisory Committee and the Legal Advisory Committee—and they were composed of experts from each state who gathered and processed the technical information needed for the negotiations. The engineering committee studied water flow and quality at a number of gaging stations; the legal committee studied the legal mechanisms available to improve water quality. By the end of 1956, the lawyers had completed a rough draft of the general features of the compact, and by 1959 the engineers had finished their initial assignments. The work of each committee, however, continued for the length of the negotiations.

One problem both the technical experts and the negotiators encountered was the dramatic difference in state water laws. Texas and Oklahoma both adhere to the appropriation doctrine prevalent in the arid western states. According to this doctrine, water rights are derived from using water for "beneficial" purposes such as agriculture, livestock, or mining. The rights are quantified, and if a stream is overappropriated, rights are based on priority in time. Arkansas and Louisiana have adopted the doctrine of riparian rights prevalent in humid regions. Since water is not quantified under this doctrine, the negotiators did not know how much water to allocate to those two states.

The personalities of the negotiators and the feuds among some of the states also made apportionment difficult. Between 1962 and 1978, there were six different chairmen and numerous changes in state representatives, turnover that disrupted continuity and caused a frequent reemergence of problems. Arkansas's representatives refused to compromise on language intended to protect future development in the basin, and Texas and Oklahoma fought between themselves over the amount of water appropriated to the Lugart-Altus Irrigation District in Oklahoma. By 1976, however, Arkansas had agreed to compromise, and Texas and Oklahoma had agreed on an apportionment between them. The Red River Compact was signed on May 12, 1978.

The compact apportions five segments or "reaches" of the river, which are broken down into subbasins to further simplify apportionment. The compact sets general rules for water apportionment within the subbasins as well as delineating some specific compromises. In general, 60 percent of the water in interstate tributaries is allocated to the upstream state and 40 percent to the downstream state. Percentages of flow are usually measured on an annual basis. Texas and Oklahoma each receive 200,000 ac-ft of the storage of Lake Texoma and 50 percent of the flow of the Red River. Texas and Louisiana are each entitled to 50 percent of the conservation capacity of Caddo Lake, located on their border. The states can use their water for any purposes they deem "beneficial." Water rights established by December 22, 1980, remain intact, and the states can use the Red River and its tributaries to convey stored water. Finally, the states have primary responsibility for the quality of the water within their boundaries. The apportionments are overseen by the Red River Compact Commission (RRCC), made up of two representatives of each state and one federal commissioner.

The compact outlines the commission's authority while still giving the commission flexibility in the exercise of that authority. The RRCC can adopt rules to enforce the compact, maintain an office, distribute proceedings and reports, enter into contracts with state or federal agencies for gathering factual information, and employ the engineering, legal, clerical, and other support necessary to carry out the provisions of the compact. The commission can also recommend water quality objectives to the states.

The commission depends on money from the four compact states. By adopting the compact, the states implicitly agreed to fund the commission, but that implicit agreement does not remove the pressure on commissioners to secure regular appropriations from the state legislatures.

The Red River Compact has been generally successful. The agreement is a step toward assuring sufficient water for the region, providing a firm foundation for basinwide water planning and management, and providing a forum for interstate cooperation.[76] Some of the major accomplishments not found in the text of the agreement are

- an inventory of water supply, water use, and present and future needs completed during the negotiations;
- modification by the Corps of Engineers of its operation of a reservoir to facilitate water apportionment under the compact;
- a survey of water quality conducted by the U.S. Public Health Service and the Corps of Engineers that resulted in better control of chloride contamination; and
- federal legislation that gives the federal district court jurisdiction over water quality disputes arising under the compact.[77]

Although the length of time necessary to negotiate a water allocation agreement seems excessive, there may not be a viable alternative—certainly not in the court system. As one observer notes, "the American legal system is simply not equipped institutionally to address the complex and multifaceted problems the negotiators had to consider in their deliberations for the Red River basin."[78]

In contrast to other negotiations, reliable technical information was available to assist the negotiators of the Red River Compact in their legal and policy deliberations. Even though personnel changed during the negotiations, the states had a continuing forum for twenty-two years to improve their relationships and build an institution for the river system.

Prairie Provinces Water Apportionment Agreement

Canada provides a useful illustration of how a set of interprovincial agreements, similar to interstate compacts, has been used in apportioning western waters of that country.[79] The Prairie Provinces Water Board operates under the Apportionment Agreement of 1969 entered into by the federal government of Canada and the provinces of Alberta, Manitoba, and Saskatchewan. The agreement covers interprovincial rivers and streams flowing eastward from Alberta, through Saskatchewan and Manitoba, and ultimately emptying into Hudson Bay. The principal rivers are the Saskatchewan, Churchill, Assiniboine, and Qu'Appelle.

The Prairie Provinces Water Apportionment Agreement is actually four interdependent sets of documents: (1) a master agreement; (2 and 3) two agreements determining the amount of water that must be allowed to flow in the eastward-flowing interprovincial rivers, one between Alberta and Saskatchewan and the other between Saskatchewan and Manitoba; and (4) an agreement establishing the Prairie Provinces Water Board.

The core of the interjurisdictional arrangement is the agreement on the apportionment of the shared flowing surface waters: Alberta must permit one-half of the natural flow of each watercourse to pass into Saskatchewan. Likewise, Saskatchewan must permit one-half of the water received from Alberta and one-half of the natural flow in Saskatchewan to flow into Manitoba. Natural flow is defined as the water that would flow if unaffected by human intervention; it excludes water unavailable under any international treaty. The actual flow is adjusted on an equitable basis at various times during the year. The Prairie Provinces Water Board, composed of two federal representatives and one from each of the provinces, administers all features of the agreement.

The Prairie Provinces Apportionment Agreement is a simple, useful, and apparently successful model for the apportionment of interjurisdictional waters. Although there has been some criticism that the apportionment does not yield the most economically efficient use of the waters (by not allocating the water to the highest bidders), this limitation may eventually be overcome by the development of a regional water market. Perhaps more serious, the agreement has not resulted in the anticipated shared construction of water development projects, nor has it been effective in implementing the water quality provisions.[80]

Unsuccessful Columbia River Compact Efforts

From 1950 to 1968, Montana, Idaho, Oregon, and Washington participated in the ill-fated negotiation of a Columbia River Basin Compact.[81] Nevada, Utah, and Wyoming were also minor participants. A compact for the Columbia River system had been proposed as early as 1911, but it was not until 1949 that several governors in the Northwest asked Governor Arthur B. Langlie of Washington to lead an effort to develop a compact. The first meeting of the Columbia Interstate Compact Commission was held on July 10, 1950, with representatives from all five states (including Wyoming). One commentator summarizes the lengthy negotiations:

> That meeting of representatives of five Pacific Northwest states marked the modest beginning of nearly two decades of active negotiations. The U.S. Congress was twice asked to pass enabling legislation authorizing the states to enter a compact. Attempts were to be made to ratify the Compact by the states in five different legislative sessions over a 10-year period. The Compact was to become the subject of heated political debate. Finally, after nearly two decades, the Columbia Interstate Compact attempt would lapse into a period of inactivity without ever having gained the necessary ratification by Oregon and Washington.[82]

Although the compact negotiations concerned water for consumptive uses in the upper basin and water for nonconsumptive uses in the lower basin, the central debate focused on public and private power. Since the 1930s, the federal government had urged a public power policy that included an active role for the federal government in the generation, transmission, and marketing of hydroelectric power; multipurpose basin development; and favorable policies for existing and future local public and cooperative utilities.[83] The extension of this public power policy had led to the proposal of a Columbia Valley Authority in the late 1940s, a measure that was defeated in 1949.

With the election of Dwight Eisenhower as president in 1952, basin authorities were out, public power was in retreat, and "the time was right . . . for the groups favoring private development and a 'state's rights' ideology to gain a strategic advantage over groups allied with New Deal policies."[84] The upper basin states, such as Montana and Idaho, which had a history of private power development and Republican governors in office, supported a compact as a means to promote private power interests.

The compact negotiations proceeded through four relatively distinct phases. The first phase, from 1950 to 1952, involved preliminary meetings to determine whether a compact was necessary, what procedures should be followed, and whether and how to obtain congressional consent. The second phase extended from 1952, when federal consent legislation was obtained, to December 1954, when the first compact was signed by the commissioners. Thirteen meetings were held during this period. Beginning with the failure of the Washington and Oregon legislatures to ratify the compact in 1955 and lasting until 1963, the third phase involved continuing efforts to make the compact more acceptable and to resubmit it for ratification. Passage by Washington State was critical, but the compact was defeated by its legislature in 1955, 1957, 1961, and 1963. The fourth phase was characterized by growing futility, increasingly infrequent meetings of the commission, and one last defeat by the Washington legislature in 1965.[85]

The proposed compact would have created a commission consisting of two members each from Idaho, Montana, Oregon, Washington, and Wyoming; one member each from Nevada and Utah; and a federal chairman without a vote.[86] The general powers of the commission would have included data collection and the review of plans for proposed projects "undertaken pursuant to the laws of the United States" if the project had the capacity of diverting more than 200 cfs or storing more than 25,000 ac-ft. The commission would have had limited authority over water quality, fish and wildlife, and recreation issues.

The core of the compact consisted of a trade of upper basin storage for a share of future hydropower. The upper basin states would have allowed large reservoirs to be constructed in their area to provide flood control and stable flows for the lower basin. In return, the upper basin states would have been guaranteed "a major part" of the hydropower for future needs. The compact did not apportion the waters of the basin, but it did provide a limited subordination of lower basin nonconsumptive uses to upper basin consumptive uses. The compact would have prohibited out-of-basin transfers unless all the signatory states agreed.

The Columbia River Compact negotiations again illustrate the time necessary to conclude multistate agreements. Even though the compact ultimately was not ratified, the commissioners were able to reach agreement; the downfall of the compact was the inability of one state, Washington, to resolve internal disagreements over the public-private power controversy. One obvious conclusion is that negotiators must have the authority to bargain.

MISSOURI RIVER COMPACT EFFORTS

An effort was made in the early 1950s to conclude an interstate compact among the Missouri River basin states. A Missouri River States Committee was organized with Governor Sigurd Anderson of South Dakota as chair; the Council of State Governments provided staff assistance. A preliminary draft was prepared in 1952 and was reviewed by the committee in December of that year. A revised draft of the Missouri River Basin Compact was prepared in January 1953, but the compact ultimately failed.

The compact would not have apportioned the basin's waters; the emphasis of the proposal was rather to establish a Missouri Basin Commission "tailored to fit the Basin's special needs."[87] Three major purposes were identified for this commission: (1) to assure a high degree of coordination in the basin; (2) to promote effective participation by the states and federal government in the development of a basic, broad policy for the region; and (3) to use existing government agencies in the construction of facilities and operation of programs.[88]

The draft compact contained several peculiarities. For one, the draft was built around the "core" states of Kansas, Missouri, Montana, Nebraska, North Dakota, and South Dakota, whose approval would have been required for the compact to be effective. Iowa, another main stem state, was not considered part of the "core," though along with Colorado and Minnesota, Iowa could upon ratification have become a full member of the compact.

Another peculiarity was the extensive authority given to the federal government. The federal government was allotted three to five members on the commission and "a vote equal to that of the total number of votes of the Commissioners of the party states present."[89] One might suspect that this provision contributed greatly to the downfall of the proposal.

The explanatory notes to the proposal indicated that the commission's powers would have been "recommendatory only" but diffidently added that "the official character of the body as an organic agency of the Basin's states and of the national government will endow its recommendations with considerable weight."[90] The commission's actual responsibilities for comprehensive planning extended to both the land and water resources of the basin, data collection, and coordination of state and federal agencies. Governments or private parties proposing projects that indicated a "substantial effect on interstate relations in the use of water" would have been required to submit their proposals to the commission. The commission, however, could not reject or modify a proposal; its authority would have extended only to making "such recommendations as it deems necessary."[91]

This compact proposal did not wear well. Its enormous breadth authorized sweeping natural resource planning in the basin and even volunteered the commission as the joint agency for administering future agreements on pollution control and regional forests, parks, and preserves.[92] Yet the actual power of the commission to implement the plans was virtually nonexistent. The intention seems to have been to institutionalize, at almost any cost to the states, intergovernmental communications among the basin states and federal agencies with planning as the focal activity. Indian tribes were not to be part of that mix.[93] With the heavy federal presence on the commission (coupled with the likelihood that planning dollars would be federally supplied), the commission's plans would have certainly reflected the federal interest and perspective.

EVALUATION OF WATER RESOURCE COMPACTS

In a report for the National Water Commission, attorney Jerome C. Muys evaluates the four classes of water-related compacts mentioned earlier[94] and concludes that water allocation and flood control agreements have been "generally adequate given their relatively modest objectives."[95] Pollution control compacts have yielded no cleaner rivers than streams without these agreements. By comparison, Muys praises certain comprehensive water management compacts, such as the Delaware River Basin Commission (discussed in Chapter 7).

Muys also examines numerous arguments for and against interstate water compacts. The major advantage of water compacts is their adaptability to the particular needs of a basin "in accordance with [the] particular regional philosophy of appropriate intergovernmental relations."[96] Interstate water compacts also provide an opportunity to manage a river system as a complete ecological system:

> The unification of a natural region with an administrative one is an appealing idea for geographers and other analysts who are concerned with mankind's relationship with its environment. . . . Many of the environmental crises of the twentieth century have resulted from externalities generated by artificial political boundaries. . . . Interstate water compacts ideally aim at eliminating externalities caused by the separation of river basin management into discrete administrative units. Theoretically, compacts permit comprehensive river basin management. Yet, no compacts have truly succeeded in eliminating externalities because regional governments that they establish do not coordinate well with pre-existing governments which create the compacts.[97]

The chief argument against water compacts is that they impose yet another governmental layer, one that usurps state and federal authority over water resources.[98] Dislike of such an addition is expressed in the limited authority granted to compact commissions and their "anemic" funding.[99] "The irony of this approach," says Muys, "is that the more successful the states have been in hobbling compact agencies in order to protect their sovereign prerogatives, the more likely it has become that regional water problems will be dealt with by federal programs wholly superseding state or local authority."[100]

Another major criticism of interstate water compacts is the long period generally required to negotiate and obtain ratification.[101] With many states and the federal government involved, and with numerous approval points within each state, there are numerous opportunities for delay or rejection. Muys argues, however, that the creation of a compact "is not inherently more cumbersome and time-consuming . . . than other institutional approaches" such as federal legislation or litigation.[102]

A third criticism of water compacts is that the states themselves have been only nominally committed to regional problem solving and water management. As so vividly portrayed in the 1985 Missouri River negotiations, state "participation has been cautious and hesitant, concerned primarily with preservation or promotion of their individual interests."[103]

A final criticism of the interstate compact concerns the ambiguity of the federal role. Although federal representatives are often involved in compact negotiations and often serve as the chairs of compact commissions, the compacts have generally not afforded the federal government a meaningful decision-making role. Nor has the federal government pledged to conform its actions to the purposes of the compacts. Thus, state and federal governments have frequently gone their separate ways, failing "to achieve meaningful coordination of federal and nonfederal water resources plans and actions."[104] Interstate compacts, when submitted to Congress, have also resulted in undue congressional meddling in local affairs.

Application of the Law of the Union Doctrine, in particular, has resulted in harsh criticism. In *Pennsylvania v. Wheeling & Belmont Bridge Co.*,[105] the U.S. Supreme Court held that when congressional consent is given to an interstate agreement, the agreement becomes federal law or the "Law of the Union." Thus, congressional approval results in these agreements being interpreted as federal law. The doctrine indicates that after congressional approval of a compact, a state may not amend or withdraw without congressional consent. West Virginia tested this interpretation of the doctrine after entering into a compact with seven other states to control pollution in the Ohio River basin. Although Congress had consented to the compact, the West Virginia Supreme Court declared participation a violation of the state constitution. On appeal, the U.S. Supreme Court held that West Virginia could not unilaterally decide that the compact violated state law and withdraw from the compact. "A State," the Court indicated, "cannot be its own ultimate judge in a controversy with a sister State."[106]

Since the doctrine was recognized in the *Wheeling* decision and upheld in the West Virginia case, "this peculiar proposition has been alternatively repudiated and reaffirmed in successive Supreme Court opinions."[107] In the case of *Cuyler v. Adams* (1981),[108] the Supreme Court

> gave this doctrine the most extravagant application in its history when they transmuted into federal law an interstate agreement for which Congress' consent certainly was not required . . . , for which consent never was sought by any state, and the purported "consent" to which consisted only of a few words in a federal statute enacted a quarter century prior to the interstate agreement, encouraging in the vaguest and most general of hortatory terms unspecified measures of cooperation among states for law enforcement and crime prevention.[109]

Yet the Supreme Court has held that a commission or administrative body created by a congressionally approved interstate agreement is not thereby transformed into a federal agency.[110] As one observer concludes:

> This bizarre doctrine does indeed have disruptive and debilitating consequences for intergovernmental relations. The consequences would be even more severe if the doctrine really were taken seriously and applied consistently; but it is not. Its most troubling consequence at the present time, therefore, is that it renders the law of interstate agreements inconsistent and unstable, making the consequences of cooperation substantially unpredictable, and thus unnecessarily discouraging creative efforts to deal with modern problems.[111]

In summary, states must be highly motivated to attempt a water resources compact, which often requires that events and conditions coincide to put a group of states in the necessary frame of mind. The states must have a strong sense of urgency, uncertainty, or potential advantage. In the Colorado River basin, the promise of large-scale, federally subsidized water development and the fear of preemptive water appropriations within rival states brought the states to the table. Maintenance of the status quo is generally quite appealing to powerful interests. By comparison, change brings risk and uncertain consequences. Uncertainty and risk are present in all compact negotiations. Finally, the availability and quality of technical information are important to the speed and success of negotiations and the implementation of the resulting agreements.

Compacts do not solve all problems. Some issues are impossible to resolve during negotiations; others are left intentionally ambiguous. In the compacts examined in this chapter, for example, reserved rights, water quality, groundwater, evaporation and seepage losses, fish and wildlife protection, and interstate water exporting and marketing are issues that have usually not been addressed. All interested parties must ask themselves, Will negotiations and the structure and processes of a compact make it easier or harder to resolve problems?

Although efforts to negotiate a compact for the Missouri River basin have previously failed, several advantages might result from another attempt. The negotiations themselves would put all states on notice that a real problem exists in the basin; in fact, an attempt at negotiations may be required before the U.S. Supreme Court will even take an equitable apportionment case.[112] If negotiations were successful, many persistent problems among the states could be solved, and the states would enjoy greater certainty about their water rights. Furthermore, a compact could be concluded without lengthy and costly equitable apportionment litigation before the U.S. Supreme Court.

Conversely, there could be many disadvantages as well. Negotiators might not be able to resolve all important issues; vague or incompletely resolved topics could provoke later debate over interpretation. A river system as complex as the Missouri presents difficult technical problems, and the data necessary to reach an agreement might not be available. The firm and settled expectations of upper and lower basin states might leave little room to negotiate. Upper basin states, for example, "see the Missouri as a resource to be used for power and consumed for irrigation . . . [and] downstream states . . . see the Missouri as a source to be contained to prevent downstream flooding and to be delivered . . . in a polite but regular flow for navigation . . . and to dilute effluent."[113]

Finally, the question of reserved water rights of tribes may be a divisive force. Upper basin states are likely to see this obligation as a basinwide responsibility; lower basin states are likely to argue that these rights must be charged against upper basin allocations of water. Many of the states—both from the upper and lower basins—would likely oppose tribal participation in the negotiations.

The Compact Clause offers the only explicit constitutional means for states to resolve regional natural resource problems short of litigation. Occasionally, the federal government forms part of the compacting process, but if the past is any guide, the tribal governments never do.

CHAPTER SEVEN

New Patterns of Federalism in River Management

The U.S. Constitution was not drafted with river basin management in mind. Few examples exist of states and federal agencies collaborating in water management decisions in a hydrologically defined watershed that is indifferent to political boundaries. Even fewer are the examples of states, federal agencies, and tribes cooperating in the management of the water resources of a river basin.

Yet the need for regional, intergovernmental resource management institutions is becoming ever more pronounced. Most resource and environmental problems have geographic and intergovernmental implications. For water management, the need for such institutions is underscored by the increasing water scarcity in western states, the heightened concerns about water quality, and the growing interest of tribes in their water resources.

Although governments can still effectively use interstate compacts to order their relations, new patterns of American federalism may be more promising for intergovernmental river basin management. These new patterns are found in innovative experiments under way in different parts of the United States.[1]

The federal-interstate compact is one such experiment. With roots in the water resource compacts discussed previously, the federal-interstate compact, as illustrated by the Delaware River Basin Compact, reflects a river basin institution with extensive management authority. Two other intergovernment agreements, the Fort Peck–Montana Compact and the North Pacific Salmon Agreements, show how tribal governments can participate as sovereigns with states and the federal government in the management of water and other aquarian resources. Finally, at the frontier of successful interstate cooperation are the Northwest Power Planning Council and the Great Lakes Charter (see Map 7.1).

FEDERAL-INTERSTATE COMPACT: THE DELAWARE RIVER COMPACT

The Delaware River Basin Compact[2] and the Susquehanna River Basin Compact[3] are examples of comprehensive regulatory and project devel-

Map 7.1. Selected transboundary resource areas. (Map by Leslee Unser)

opment compacts. These compacts set forth ambitious agendas for basinwide water planning and coordinated development and management
of water resources.[4] They also provide for an administrative entity with
state and federal representation and are therefore known as "federal-interstate compacts."

The Delaware River Basin Compact, the first federal-interstate water
compact, was approved in 1961 (after three earlier attempts) by Delaware, New Jersey, New York, Pennsylvania, and the United States. The
330-mile Delaware River originates in New York and flows along the borders of the other three states to the Atlantic Ocean. The upper reaches of
this 13,000 square-mile basin are sparsely populated, but the lower basin
is heavily populated. Approximately 20 million people, including 7 million within the basin, depend on the Delaware River, its tributaries, and
groundwater for their supplies.[5]

The Delaware River Basin Compact is unusual in that the impetus
for its formation came from outside the basin. In the 1920s, New York
City attempted to divert water near the Delaware's headwaters to supple-
ment its water supplies, and the ensuing dispute led to litigation before
the U.S. Supreme Court. In a 1931 decree[6] (amended in 1954),[7] the Court
allowed New York City's diversion on the condition that it mitigate the
effects of low flows downstream. Among other reasons for the formation

of the compact were a 1955 flood that resulted in the death of ninety-seven people and the threat of pollution to the river's estuaries.[8]

Gubernatorial leadership, especially on the part of Nelson Rockefeller of New York, was important to the adoption of the compact.[9] Federal approval was subsequently obtained, and "this was the first interstate water compact not merely consented to by the Congress, but one in which the Congress joined the United States to the compact."[10] Federal joinder, however, did not come easily. Seven federal agencies, including the Departments of Interior and Justice, opposed federal participation, and before congressional assent was obtained, two modifications were made to the compact. First, Congress retained the right to amend or repeal portions of the agreement, and second, the president was given the power to suspend elements of the comprehensive plan that, if applied to federal agencies, would violate federal law or otherwise not be in the national interest.

The commission established by the compact consists of four governors and one representative of the federal government who is appointed by the president. The commission meets monthly during most of the year and has a staff of forty individuals, including twenty-five professionals. The burden of the annual budget of $2.7 million is shared: 25 percent each by Pennsylvania and Delaware, 20 percent each by New York and the United States, and 10 percent by New Jersey. The commission operates by majority vote except when determining dues or when modifying the rights and obligations under the 1954 U.S. Supreme Court decree (which requires unanimous voting). One observer believes this voting requirement has been important in avoiding deadlock and in reaching practical, compromise decisions.[11]

The requirement of a comprehensive basin plan is a major feature of the compact. To assure that development projects conform with this plan, the compact gives the commission licensing authority by providing that "no project having a substantial effect on the water resources of the basin shall hereafter be undertaken by any person, corporation or governmental authority unless it shall have been first submitted to and approved by the Commission."[12] The commission is bound to approve a proposed project if it "would not substantially impair or conflict with the comprehensive plan." A project not satisfying that standard may be either rejected or approved subject to conditions. Unless the president disaffirms portions of the plan as not being in the national interest, the plan can also be binding on the federal government:

> Whenever a comprehensive plan, or any part or version thereof, has been adopted with the concurrence of the member appointed by the President, the exercise of any powers . . . of the United States with

regard to water and related land resources in the . . . Basin shall not substantially conflict with any such portion of such comprehensive plan.[13]

After final congressional approval in 1961, the commission began developing its comprehensive plan. The first phase, a project-oriented plan based largely on work done by the U.S. Army Corps of Engineers, was approved in 1962. A key component was construction of Tocks Island Dam, a multiuse project. Public opposition to the dam increased during the 1970s, and by 1975, a majority of the basin's governors (and subsequently the commission itself) had decided not to request federal construction funds. With the cancellation of the Tocks Island project, the 1962 plan was no longer valid. In 1976, a detailed level-B planning study[14] was undertaken to look fifteen to twenty years into the future. The study took five years to complete and cost $1.5 million.

The Delaware River Compact vests the commission with the authority to construct and manage projects determined to be "necessary, convenient or useful for the purposes of [this] compact."[15] The commission has the power to equitably apportion the water resources among the basin states, as long as the apportionment does not run contrary to the 1954 U.S. Supreme Court decree (unless the decree is modified by unanimous agreement, which has been done twelve times, usually as the result of drought conditions).[16] The commission also must approve diversions and discharges beyond certain threshold amounts. In 1978, as a result of Pennsylvania's dissatisfaction with certain features of the compact, the signatories commenced "good faith" negotiations to recommend changes in commission policies. In 1983, these changes were approved by the basin state governors and the mayor of New York and sent to the commission.[17]

Jerome Muys has been one of many observers to praise the Delaware River Compact and the Delaware River Basin Commission. "It was, and is, my enthusiastic conclusion," Muys has said, "that the Delaware River Basin Commission (DRBC) has compiled an impressive record of accomplishments, much of which . . . would not have resulted but for the existence and efforts of DRBC."[18] As of 1976, Muys found the accomplishments of the compact and the commission to be

- an important contribution in alleviating the 1965–1966 northeastern drought;
- review of 2,500 proposed projects for their conformance with the comprehensive plan;
- development of a basin water quality program, including regional sewage collection and treatment works;

- imposition of fees for consumptive use of water in excess of 1961 levels;
- assumption of nonfederal cost-sharing on certain projects within the basin;
- completion of water supply and demand studies, as well as a master power plant siting study; and
- facilitation of public comment and participation.[19]

More recently, drought management, toxic substances, estuarial water quality, groundwater overdrafts, and flood losses have been issues of high priority within the basin.[20] The regulations of the commission are set forth in a basinwide water code that emphasizes water conservation requirements and water quality standards.[21]

A study by the U.S. Comptroller General concluded that equitable and adequate funding of the commission is crucial to its future.[22] In the past, New York officials have questioned the need for the commission, believing that "it duplicates State efforts, infringes on State rights,"[23] and "is dominated by the downstream States who receive most of the benefits."[24]

The commission's executive director believes the commission has been very successful in forging cooperative working relationships among the signatories. The commission has avoided bureaucratization (such as that afflicting the Tennessee Valley Authority, which receives approximately $100 million per year from the federal government), for the compact requires, "to the fullest extent feasible and desirable," that the commission use other agencies to assist in its work. The commission has been able to promptly address problems, such as drought, and has been able to mediate interstate disputes.[25]

Muys argues that western states should consider federal-interstate compacts like the Delaware agreement, basing his argument on the extensive federal land holdings in the region, the role of the federal government as the trustee for tribes asserting their reserved water rights,[26] and the growing regulatory importance of federal water quality legislation.

It is meaningless to talk of comprehensive planning and management of water and land resources in the West if the federal government is not to be an integral part of the effort. Effective water and land use planning requires a fully cooperative, coordinated effort among the federal government, the states and, perhaps most important, the Indian tribes who are probably holding the biggest and most secure water rights in the West.

What is needed is a Congressionally approved regional institutional arrangement which will mandate cooperative, coordinated action by federal agencies in conformity with the views of the affected basin states, while necessarily reserving the federal government's right to assert the paramount national prerogative in appropriate situations.[27]

AGREEMENTS INVOLVING TRIBAL GOVERNMENTS

Two important agreements significantly involve tribal governments: the Fort Peck–Montana Compact, the first approved water apportionment agreement between a state and tribes that was secured without federal legislation, and a set of institutional arrangements collectively known as the North Pacific Salmon Agreements. The salmon case study is included here because it illustrates how positive actions to protect one resource, fish, can be orchestrated through a variety of coordinated forums and how tribes can participate meaningfully with states, the U.S. government, and the Canadian government.

Fort Peck–Montana Compact

Ratification of the Fort Peck–Montana Compact[28] in spring 1985 represented the largest Indian water rights settlement in history.[29] The recent origins of this compact date from 1973 when Montana passed a comprehensive Water Use Act[30] that for the first time required permits for new water rights and for changes to existing water rights. Yet because the permit system would not ultimately work without knowledge and consideration of pre-1973 water rights, a statewide water adjudication process was initiated.[31]

Some tribes believed the Water Use Act would result in impermissible state jurisdiction over their water rights. In 1975, the United States filed suit in federal court to adjudicate the reserved rights of the Northern Cheyenne and the Crow Indian reservations,[32] but in 1976, the U.S. Supreme Court ruled in *Colorado River Conservation District v. United States (Akin)*[33] that the McCarran Amendment enables state courts to adjudicate Indian, as well as federal, reserved rights as part of a comprehensive statewide adjudication process.

Encouraged by the *Akin* decision, Montana revised its Water Use Act in 1979 to create a state court adjudication process for the comprehensive adjudication of water rights—including federal and Indian reserved rights.[34] Also, in an attempt to resolve the problem of reserved rights, the state legislature created the Montana Reserved Water Rights Commission.[35] The commission has the authority to negotiate on behalf of the state and submit for legislative approval compacts with federal agencies and Indian tribes.

The commission has nine appointed members: four of the appointments are made by the governor, two by the senate, two by the house of representatives, and one by the attorney general. Influential members of the senate and house were chosen to keep the state legislature informed of the commission's work and to assist in the ratification by the legislature of compacts concluded between the commission and tribes or federal agencies. The commission has its own staff but draws upon the resources of the Department of Natural Resources and Conservation and other state executive agencies.

After the commission was formed in 1979, invitations to negotiate were sent to the seven tribes and three federal agencies claiming reserved water rights. As soon as the tribes and federal agencies assigned representatives, informal talks began. By 1980, formal negotiations had begun with the Northern Cheyenne tribe, the Confederated Salish and Kootenai tribes of the Flathead Reservation (located in the Columbia River system), the Sioux and Assiniboine tribes of the Fort Peck Reservation, the U.S. Department of Agriculture, and the U.S. Department of the the Interior. Approximately one year after negotiations began, the Flathead tribes terminated negotiations with the commission. Since 1981, the Assiniboine and Gros Ventre tribes of the Fort Belknap Reservation, the Crow, the Rocky Boys' Chippewa-Cree tribe, and the Turtle Mountain Chippewa tribe of North Dakota have joined in negotiations. Informal negotiations are also under way with the Department of Defense.

By fall 1982, a compact had been negotiated with the Fort Peck tribes. Although the parties had agreed to submit the compact to the 1983 Montana legislature, the commission notified the Fort Peck Tribal Council in April 1983 that the proposed compact would not be submitted for ratification. In part, this decision arose from state agencies' concerns about the jurisdictional, administrative, and enforcement terms of the agreement. In part, the decision was urged by the attorney general who was awaiting the U.S. Supreme Court's decision in *Northern Cheyenne Tribe v. Adsit* (companion to *San Carlos Apache Tribe v. Arizona*),[36] which raised the issue of whether state courts in so-called "disclaimer states"[37] are an appropriate forum for the litigation of reserved water rights.

Montana's victory in the litigation (the Court decided that Montana's state courts *are* an appropriate forum to consider reserved water rights) no doubt was an incentive for all tribes to consider negotiating with the compact commission. Yet the failure to submit the Fort Peck Compact for legislative ratification raised questions about the commission's good faith (even though the tribal council itself had not ratified the agreement). Negotiations therefore broke down with the Fort Peck tribes, as well as the other tribes, and were not resumed until October 1984. This second round of negotiations extended into the ninety-day 1985 session of the Montana legislature. An agreement was reached during the last weeks of the session, and the compact was submitted to the legislature for approval. After thorough briefings, the compact was rapidly approved by wide margins in both houses. The compact was also approved by the tribal council.

The agreement was structured in such a way that congressional approval was required only for the tribes to market water. Montana feared that downstream Missouri River states, concerned about the implications of the settlement for their future water supply, would withhold consent. The compact was formally approved by the U.S. attorney general and the secretary of the interior. When the water marketing provision was finally submitted to Congress in 1991 for approval, the tribe's attorney requested that congressional ratification of the entire compact be secured at the same time. Unfortunately, earlier fears were realized when Senator John Danforth of Missouri placed a "hold" on the bill, preventing Senate approval of the compact. Although the bill died when Congress adjourned in 1992, the state and tribes continue to assume that the compact is effective.

The most important provision of the compact is the quantification of the tribal water rights. The tribes are given the annual right to divert from the Missouri, the tributaries that flow through or adjacent to the reservation, and groundwater the lesser of either 1,050,472 ac-ft/yr of water or the amount of water necessary to supply a consumptive use of 525,236 ac-ft/yr. In either case, no more than 90 percent of the water can come from surface sources. The water right has a priority right of May 1, 1888. A few existing uses, both by Indians and non-Indians, are protected and not subordinated by the agreement.

Water uses by the following persons or entities constitute a charge against the compact award: the tribes, whether water is used within or outside the reservation; individual Indians on the reservation; non-Indians who have succeeded to an Indian allotment; persons receiving water from the Fort Peck Irrigation Project; the United States as trustee for the tribes or their members; and other persons authorized to use water either on or off the reservation. On the reservation, the tribal water can be used for any purpose; off the reservation, it must be used for a beneficial purpose. If water is moved out of state, the transfer must be pursuant to state law. The compact provides a limited procedure for the state or other interested persons to object to a diversion of water or use of water outside the reservation.

Water can also be transferred (with or without consideration) to non-Indians, either on or off the reservation, but the transfer can only be of the right to use the water. The tribes may not alienate or permanently transfer the water awarded under the compact. The tribes are guaranteed the right to transfer 50,000 ac-ft/yr for consumptive and nonconsumptive uses off the reservation. In the event that the state's own marketing authority (presently at 50,000 ac-ft) is increased, the tribes are authorized to transfer an additional 50 percent of any state authority over 50,000 ac-ft. The compact requires tribes to give the state an opportunity to share as an equal partner in water transfers.

The tribes were authorized during the first five years of the compact to establish instream flows for fish and wildlife resources on the Missouri tributaries, which flows also have an 1888 priority date (senior to most other water uses in the upper basin). Approximately 58,000 ac-ft/yr were selected for instream flows. These rights are to be counted as consumptive uses of water. Any subsequent change in the use of instream flows must have the state's consent.

The tribes were given a year to adopt a water code that must be approved by the secretary of the interior. Upon approval, the tribes have "final and exclusive jurisdiction" to administer the tribal water right. The tribes have adopted a code, but the secretary has placed a moratorium on the approval of such codes. The tribes are also required to provide the state quarterly with detailed information about the use of the tribal water right. Administration of the Fort Peck Irrigation Project remains with the U.S. government.

The state retains authority to administer nontribal water rights whether within or outside the reservation. The compact also requires the state to provide the tribes quarterly with detailed information about groundwater and surface water uses under state law that occur on or appurtenant to the reservation.

A special Fort Peck–Montana Compact Board of three people resolves conflicts over the use of groundwater, surface water (with some exceptions), and interpretation of the compact between the tribes (or any person claiming the right to use the tribal water rights) and persons claiming a right to use water under state law. One member of the board is selected by the tribes, the second by the governor, and the third by the other two. The state and tribes readily agreed upon the naming of the initial third person to the board. Since its creation, the board has received only one formal complaint, from a non-Indian claiming tribal interference with her water rights, but the complaint was dismissed prior to a full hearing.

The Fort Peck–Montana Compact has significant advantages for both the state and the tribes. The tribes have received a huge amount of water—more than any other western tribe. The settlement allows them to manage their water and to transfer water off the reservation with little federal or state interference. The tribes participated as sovereigns in the negotiations, and the agreement is truly of their own choice. The tribes received no financial assistance in putting their water to work, perhaps the principal weakness of the agreement. Although they still can approach the federal government or the state for assistance, the tribes lost their leverage when their reserved rights were quantified. For its part, Montana has attempted to ensure that a half-million ac-ft/yr of Missouri River water can be developed in the state for the benefit of its Indian and non-Indian residents.

The settlement does institutionalize ongoing communication and problem solving by the creation of the compact board. It is certainly fortunate that the board has not been called upon to settle many disputes, but it could take a stronger role in encouraging dialogue and undertaking preventive problem solving.

North Pacific Salmon Agreements

The North Pacific Salmon Agreements, though not pertaining directly to water, represent innovative intergovernmental efforts to manage an important aquatic resource.

Indians in the Pacific Northwest have depended on the Pacific salmon for 11,000 years, according to some estimates, and the fish is part of Indian culture, religion, and commerce.[38] With the arrival of non-Indians to the region in the nineteenth century, competition for the salmon began. Under an 1855 treaty with the United States, the rights to fish, hunt, and gather berries were reserved to the tribes, yet almost immediately, these rights came under attack or were ignored.

After the construction of main stem dams on the Columbia River during the depression and World War II, the salmon's migratory patterns were seriously altered. This development, in conjunction with Indian and non-Indian fishing, resulted in the endangerment of the resource itself. Litigation on behalf of the tribes of Washington and Oregon was brought by the federal government. During the 1970s, the case of *United States v. Washington*[39] made its way repeatedly up and down the federal court system. Ultimately, the courts affirmed certain principles. As a result of the treaty, the tribes have the right to fish and to have fish available. They also have the exclusive right to manage the fish on their reservations and the right, off the reservation, to manage the fishery resource cooperatively with state officials.

Many state officials and non-Indians believed the Indians could not responsibly manage the salmon and that the resource would be destroyed. Bitter feelings remained between Indians and non-Indians, and no vehicle for cooperation was available to help state and tribal officials begin to manage the resource.

In the early 1980s, however, two developments enabled state and tribal officials to overcome their differences. The first was the passage of the Pacific Northwest Electric Power Planning and Conservation Act,[40] discussed in the next section, which all parties realized would affect the fisheries resource of the Northwest. While the legislation was pending, state and tribal officials met on an informal, ad hoc basis to develop needed amendments. The second development was the threat to the salmon resource, as salmon migration was being affected by unregulated Canadian catches in the North Pacific. Negotiations between the United States and Canada over this issue had been ongoing since 1976, but after judicial decisions about tribal management authority in the early 1980s, the tribes were allowed to participate as full members of the U.S. delegation to the international negotiations. Over the next few years, representatives from twenty-four tribes became involved in all aspects of these negotiations, including the technical work.

As a result of the negotiations, the Pacific Salmon Treaty was concluded in 1984 and ratified by the governments of Canada and the United States in 1985.[41] The Pacific Salmon Treaty Coalition, consisting of representatives of four states, twenty-four tribes, and forty non-Indian organizations (representing over 8,000 individuals) developed grassroots political support for ratification of the treaty. The treaty grants each country four commissioners. The U.S. delegation is composed of one commissioner from Alaska, one commissioner representing the states of Washington and Oregon, one commissioner representing the twenty-four tribes, and one nonvoting federal commissioner.

Although the salmon fishery remains stressed, cooperation among the tribes, states, and national governments has mitigated the decline of some species and brought a slight improvement in others. These cooperative efforts have had other benefits as well. The tribes have created the Columbia River Inter-Tribal Fish Commission to gather the technical information necessary to exercise their management responsibilities. The Columbia River Basin Fish and Wildlife Authority has been created by thirteen tribes, four states, and the federal government to develop consensus policies for managing fish and wildlife resources. Disputes concerning private forestry practices (which have an effect on fisheries habitat) have funneled through the Timber-Fish-Wildlife Forum. This consensus process has yielded a timber management agreement that is now being implemented.

Although the resource issues differ from those in the Missouri River basin, this case does offer some lessons. Significantly, litigation was ultimately an unsuccessful strategy for conflict resolution here. Moreover, a single, unified organization may not be necessary for responsible natural resource management if several coordinated institutions share the same goal. In the Northwest, the parties have built organizations through which they may both resolve conflicts and cooperate in attempting to protect salmon. The tribes are full, responsible partners in these institutions.

INTERSTATE COOPERATION

Two recent intergovernmental agreements are truly on the cutting edge of interstate cooperation and dispute resolution. The first case study concerns the Northwest Power Act and the Northwest Power Planning Council created by the act. This complex and novel institution formalizes cooperation and direction among four northwestern states and federal agencies and attempts to integrate planning for energy, fish, and, implicitly, water. The second case study, the Great Lakes Charter, affords a relatively informal, flexible method for coordinating the water resource policies of the states and provinces surrounding the Great Lakes.

Northwest Power Planning Council

The Pacific Northwest Electric Power Planning and Conservation Act[42] was signed by President Jimmy Carter on December 5, 1980.[43] Designed to ensure that the electricity needs of Idaho, Montana, Oregon, and Washington are met, the act affects the entire 259,000-square-mile Columbia River basin, including its thirty subbasins. It provides for public participation in northwestern energy decisions and the protection of the Columbia River's fish and wildlife habitat. The statute's goals are entrusted to the Northwest Power Planning Council (NWPPC), made up of commissioners from the four northwestern states. Drafting the complex legislation did not begin until 1976, but it was passed after only four years of intensive work and compromise.

Hydropower development has fundamentally altered the Columbia River system and threatens the survival of salmon and other anadromous fish. Starting with Rock Island Dam in Washington in 1933, 130 dams with hydroelectric generating capacity have been constructed in the Columbia River system. The thirty-one federal dams alone generate 20,000 megawatts of electricity and store 20 million ac-ft of water. The dams have blocked fish migration routes, changed water flows and temperatures, and flooded the natural habitats of both fish and wildlife. As a result of the dams and other causes, the annual production of adult salmon and steelhead trout in the basin is perhaps 20 percent of what it was in the early 1800s.[44] This troubling relationship between hydroelectric power and anadromous fish provided the context for congressional action that resulted in the Northwest Power Act.

The act resulted from a number of specific factors. First, the Bonneville Power Administration (BPA), the region's federal power marketing agency, had forecast a major energy shortage for the 1980s. The forecast was based on projected population growth, and the BPA issued a "Notice of Insufficiency" to its customers in 1976. The notice said that by 1983 the agency would no longer guarantee power for all users in the Northwest. Second, power costs were unequal in the region. Public power customers were paying far less than those buying private power because public utilities had a superior right to BPA's cheaper hydropower. Investor-owned utilities increased the discrepancy by building expensive coal and nuclear plants to offset Bonneville's decision not to renew its private utility contracts in 1973. Third, the Northwest's governors felt a need for regional energy decision-making authority. They did not want the Northwest's energy future to be determined by the BPA or in Washington, D.C.

The first comprehensive Northwest power planning bill was introduced by Washington's Senator Henry Jackson. The bill, drafted by the Pacific Northwest Utilities Conference Committee, was an attempt to bring planning authority to the Northwest. According to the bill, utilities would determine the amount of conservation, coal, and other energy resources needed in the region. The bill did not pass, but its idea of a regional council with the authority to determine whether utilities should build power plants was supported by the governors of Montana and Idaho.

In 1979, the Northwest Electric Power Planning and Conservation Act was introduced by senators from Washington, Oregon, and Idaho. The bill was controversial. It established, among other things, a regional planning council made up of gubernatorial appointees and guaranteed funding for all needed power projects. The bill was opposed by both the BPA and environmentalists. The BPA did not want to be governed by a political council, and environmentalists were afraid the act would guarantee funding for nuclear plants. The bill was reluctantly supported by the public utilities when they realized that, without it, the BPA would allocate their power supply. The region's governors strongly supported the bill. After an intensive lobbying effort by gubernatorial aides, the majority of the Northwest's congressional delegation voted for the bill. It passed the House of Representatives by a vote of 284–77 and passed the Senate on a voice vote.

The three mandates of the act are to provide electricity to Idaho, Washington, Oregon, and Montana; to provide for public participation;

and to protect and enhance the Columbia River basin's fish and wildlife habitat. The bill also created the Northwest Power Planning Council to administer these mandates. The council consists of two representatives of each basin state. Although funded through BPA revenues, it is an independent federal agency.

The act contains a number of important changes for the Northwest's power planning process. Before passage of the act, the utilities were planning to construct over twenty large coal- and nuclear-fired power plants. Congress was skeptical about the forecasts and whether coal and nuclear plants were the best way to meet growing demands. As a result, the NWPPC is required to prepare a twenty-year Northwest power plan that must be updated every five years.[45] The plan forecasts the region's future electrical energy demands and incorporates new criteria created by the act to determine the best ways to meet these demands. Resources are reviewed for their cost-effectiveness ("least-cost" planning), flexibility, compatibility with the existing hydropower system, and environmental acceptability. Conservation receives the greatest emphasis, followed by renewable resources, high-efficiency resources, and resources that use waste heat. Conservation—defined as improvements in energy efficiency that result in reduced consumption—is now considered an energy resource for the region along with renewable sources, coal, and water. Since these new criteria have been adopted, no new nuclear- or coal-fired plants have been built. Until recently, the region has had a surplus of energy.

The act also addresses the rate disparities that helped lead to its creation. The BPA may buy electricity from private utilities at the average system cost of generating it, and in turn, the investor-owned utilities can buy Bonneville's low-cost electricity at the same rate as public utilities. Most of the difference is paid by the direct service industries (such as aluminum companies). The companies have agreed to the arrangement in order to obtain the long-term contracts and reliable energy supply that the act provides them.

The council also works to provide opportunities for public involvement in its planning process. Meetings are held every three weeks throughout the region, and the public is invited to comment either at the meetings or through written testimony. The meeting agendas are published in the NWPPC's magazine, *Northwest Energy News,* and its newsletter, *Update!* This accessibility has made previously disenfranchised groups such as the Indian tribes reasonably successful in affecting BPA activities.

The fish and wildlife provisions of the act, the first attempts to study the fauna of the entire Columbia River basin, represent another important change. Prepared by the NWPPC's Portland-based staff, the council adopted a fish and wildlife plan in November 1982; it was amended in 1984 and 1987. The plan sets forth strategies to mitigate the effects of dams and reservoirs on animal habitats.[46] To implement the plan, the council works with fish and wildlife agencies, Indian tribes, power system operators, and federal agencies to restore fish and wildlife populations. In 1988, the council placed 44,000 miles of rivers and streams off limits to future hydropower development.

Surprisingly, fish, not an energy crisis, provide NWPPC with its greatest challenge. The council's efforts during the 1980s—fish ladders, increased hatchery production, the screening of water intakes, periodic flows to flush young fish down the river, and the barging of other smolt through the large reservoirs—seemed to have reversed the declining population. The number of chinook salmon returning to the Columbia River from the ocean increased from 79,000 in 1979–1980 to 436,000 in 1988, but further study showed that a majority of these fish originated in hatcheries and that the natural stock continues to decline.

Snake River sockeye has now been listed as endangered under the Endangered Species Act,[47] and three species of Snake River chinook have been listed as threatened. In an effort to avoid serious disruptions to the Northwest's energy system that might result from federal agency or court actions to protect the fish, the NWPPC is redoubling its efforts to protect salmon. A four-phase program, a Strategy for Salmon, has been initiated by the council. The first phase, completed in August 1991, focused on immediate steps that could be taken to rebuild fish runs. Phase two, completed in December 1991, addressed fish passage improvements at dams, increased river flows during the annual juvenile fish migration, and harvest reductions. The protection and restoration of fish habitat was emphasized in the third phase, which was completed in September 1992. The fourth phase aims to protect resident fish that do not migrate into the ocean and other wildlife.[48] However, the National Marine Fisheries Service, the federal agency primarily responsible for salmon listed under the Endangered Species Act, is developing its own restoration plan, which may have serious implications for the council and its work.

The Northwest Power Planning Act has created an innovative organization that draws on the character of river basin commissions and valley authorities of the past. What is distinctive about the act is that it places the energy, fish, and, to a certain extent, the water of the region in the hands of state-appointed commissioners who give direction to state and federal agencies. The council takes a more integrated watershed perspective than agencies or utilities of the past. The council has been able to use some of the basin's hydropower revenues to complete long-range planning and address long-ignored basin needs such as the damage to fish and aquatic systems. Unfortunately, the council's future depends on its ability to restore the salmon in a manner that does not significantly disrupt the energy system of the Northwest. If this challenge is not met, the council's other significant achievements will be jeopardized or forgotten.

Great Lakes Charter

The Great Lakes Charter,[49] a nonbinding "statement of principles," has created a permanent organization for encouraging cooperation in the management of the Great Lakes. A statement of principles, negotiated but not adopted in 1986 by representatives of the Missouri River basin states, followed this informal, nonbinding approach. The Great Lakes Charter was signed by the governors of eight Great Lakes states[50] and the premiers of Ontario and Quebec on February 11, 1985. The goal is the cooperative management of the Great Lakes, "founded upon the integrity of the natural resources and ecosystem of the Great Lakes Basin."[51]

Several factors attracted support for the charter.[52] Growing consumptive uses of Great Lakes basin water increased competition for the resource. Forty million people live within the basin, and 28 million people rely upon the lakes for drinking water. A study completed in 1985 by the International Joint Commission suggested that consumptive use may double over the next thirty-five years.

Great Lakes opinion makers became concerned about the possibility of out-of-basin transfers.[53] For example, a 1981 study identified the Great Lakes as a possible water source for a coal slurry pipeline from Wyoming, and the U.S. Supreme Court's 1982 decision in *Sporhase v. Nebraska*[54] cast doubt on the ability of states to bar such interstate transfers. Thus, in November 1983, the six governors who compose the Council of Great Lakes Governors passed a resolution against out-of-state water transfers and established a task force to draft an agreement among the basin's governments. Two other states and two provinces were invited to participate. The task force was told to examine a wide range of alternatives to enable the region to resist interbasin diversions.

In its report, the task force recommended a charter which "would be a framework based on institutional arrangements which are flexible and tailored to specific tasks . . . draw[ing] upon the strengths and resources of existing institutions and agencies."[55] The proposed charter was adopted by the governors and premiers in February 1985—after three years of meetings and one year of formal negotiations.

As a nonbinding agreement, the charter depends on the good faith of the signatories for its effectiveness. The five principles contained in the charter stress the integrity of the Great Lakes basin, cooperation among jurisdictions, protection of the water resources, prior notice and consultation, and cooperative programs and practices. Furthermore, the governors and premiers pledge not to increase diversions or consumptive uses of basin water without first seeking the consent of all states and provinces. Perhaps the most important provision is the promise to create common data bases to facilitate the exchange of water use information. A water resources committee was created to oversee the data management function. The charter also commits the states and provinces to enacting legislation that will "ensure appropriate management and conservation of the basin's water resources."[56]

Quite surprisingly, the factors that brought about the Great Lakes Charter are similar to those that have caused conflict in the Missouri River basin. The principal motivating factor for the agreement was a proposal similar to ETSI: the possible use of Great Lakes water for a coal slurry pipeline from the Powder River coalfields.[57] There are other similarities as well. The states had varying capacities to document water supply and demand; as a result, the states have identified the gathering of water data as a high priority.

One might ask, therefore, why the Great Lakes states have been able to achieve harmony while the Missouri River basin states have not. An important reason may be that the Great Lakes states are not ranged into two camps of "haves" and "have nots," whereas the Missouri basin states are divided by virtue of the inequities of the Pick-Sloan Plan. Moreover, there was a shared perception that all the Great Lakes states and provinces would lose if out of basin water exports commenced.

The Great Lakes states and provinces have realized a significant achievement, and their efforts should be a model for Missouri basin decision makers. The charter was negotiated in a short period of time with the assistance of government and nongovernment experts. A flexible though principled document that can support a more comprehensive water management policy, the charter enjoys the support of the basin's businesses and foundations. The charter is a simple, nonbinding document, but it has the commitment of the basin's governors and premiers.

Decision makers in the Missouri River basin have an impressive array of intergovernmental resource management institutions from which to choose. The Delaware River Basin Commission reveals that the Constitution's Compact Clause provides enough flexibility for integrated, regional resource management and that the federal government can be an active participant. The Fort Peck–Montana Compact and the North Pacific Salmon Agreements indicate that tribes can be full partners in these institutional arrangements.

The Northwest Power Planning Council and the Great Lakes Charter represent different approaches, but they both show that states—in particular, governors—can lead the natural resource policies of a region. These arrangements, however, rely greatly on consensus and persuasion and result in broad policies that are left to the existing federal and state agencies to implement.

A region's governors must lead in establishing these intergovernmental, resource management institutions. Although many governors have been deeply involved in Missouri River issues, none has emerged from the fray to serve as a basin statesman and provide the sustained leadership necessary to create an effective, lasting institution.

With the exception of the Fort Peck–Montana agreement, these arrangements came into being either as the result of a threat from outside the region or significant discord among the governments of the region. Prolonged drought in the Missouri River basin may offer a crisis of sufficient proportions to force agreement on a river management institution.

CHAPTER EIGHT

Federalism and New Policies for the Missouri River Basin

Intergovernmental affairs in the Missouri River basin were at an all-time low in 1987 and 1988 after the ten-state negotiations collapsed, the Missouri Basin States Association closed its offices, and litigation continued. Matters could only improve, and they have. The major participants have attempted to restore basin relationships and build a firmer foundation for intergovernmental cooperation and river management. Initiatives have come from a public interest group, the states, the tribes, and the federal government. None of these efforts has resulted in a comprehensive solution to the basin's problems, and every step of the way is perilous.

MISSOURI RIVER MANAGEMENT PROJECT

The public interest group initiative was the Missouri River Management Project, sponsored with foundation support by the Northern Lights Institute.[1] From 1985 to 1990, Northern Lights sought to improve public understanding of Missouri River issues, increase communications among basin decision makers, and present alternative river management institutions and policies. In the last phase of the project, Northern Lights attempted to found the Missouri River Assembly, a forum consisting of the three types of sovereign government in the basin—state, tribal, and federal.

The Northern Lights Institute is a research and education center located in Missoula, Montana, serving the residents of the northern Rockies and northern Great Plains—particularly the states of Idaho, Montana, and Wyoming. Formed in 1981 with a National Science Foundation planning grant, Northern Lights was to examine and influence the major issues that affect the region's economy, environment, and culture. The institute has addressed these issues through policy analysis, an ambitious publication program that includes the quarterly magazine *Northern Lights*, public education events, and artistic and cultural events based on themes concerning life in the region.

The staff of the Missouri River Management Project adopted an approach that was grounded in their prior experience in community development activities, political campaigns, grassroots conservation activities, and river basin projects elsewhere in North America. They emphasized the need to involve the important decision makers, to make the process widely available to the public, to provide well-written explanatory publications, and to use other media (e.g., video, literature, poetry) in project activities.

Although the initial organization of the project was assisted by the writings of noted conflict-management theorists such as Roger Fisher, William Ury,[2] Lawrence Susskind, and Jeffrey Cruikshank,[3] the project staff eventually concluded that these popular approaches to dispute resolution were too procedurally sterile to apply in the Missouri River basin. Project managers were greatly influenced by the thought of John Wesley Powell, one of the original proponents of western reclamation, who believed that political organizations and economic units in the West should organize around natural watersheds.[4] Powell's watershed approach provides a basis for contemporary thought concerning bioregionalism and ecosystem management such as that represented in the legal scholarship of Charles Wilkinson[5] and in Charles Foster's studies of regional organizations.[6]

Much of the theoretical base for the Missouri River Management Project evolved with the project. Eventually, Daniel Kemmis, the former speaker of the Montana House of Representatives and a senior fellow at Northern Lights, provided the foundation with a more substantive, value-laden negotiation process designed for community building (discussed in Chapter 9). As project managers learned more about the basin and the desires of its people, they attempted to build understanding and cooperation among the basin's residents.

Upper Basin Emphasis (1985–1987)

Beginning in 1985, the first phase of the Missouri River Management Project emphasized public education in the upper basin. A ten-member project steering committee, composed of representatives from the four upper basin states (Montana, Wyoming, North Dakota, and South Dakota) and two observers from the Missouri Basin States Association, was established to define the precise goals, provide overall guidance, and communicate the purposes and activities of the project to the broader public. In November 1985, Northern Lights published a special Missouri River issue of *Northern Lights*. Titled "The Wet and Wild Missouri," this publication attracted the interest of individuals and organizations throughout the region, and 9,000 copies were distributed.

The steering committee requested that Northern Lights staff prepare a detailed analysis of water management and policy in the upper Missouri basin. In the analysis paper, *Boundaries Carved in Water,*[7] a historical narrative is used to answer three fundamental questions: Why is there no interstate agreement or apportionment of the river? How do state water policies and management strategies affect the potential to achieve such an agreement? If interstate agreement were to occur, how would the individual states respond, given their management philosophies and histories in water matters?

Institute staff consulted with University of Montana journalist Jyl Hoyt to produce two half-hour radio features called "Reflections on the Missouri." These programs traced early uses of the Missouri and outlined current management issues facing the river and its major tributaries. Public radio stations in Montana broadcast the full features to a listening audience of 80,000. Shortened versions were syndicated and broadcast to a commercial AM-FM radio audience of over 200,000 in eastern Montana, northern Wyoming, and the western Dakotas.

The premiere activity during this phase of the project, however, was a two-day symposium in Billings, Montana, in October 1986. About 150 people attended, including many reporters from print and electronic media. The symposium began with a thirty-minute, six-projector slide-tape program, "Images of the Missouri—The Multitudinous River," that examined the contemporary uses and the background for conflict by showing what the Missouri River has meant to artists, settlers, engineers, the New Dealers, and Indian people. Twenty-five speakers addressed the past, present, and future management of the Missouri. Most speakers acknowledged past attempts to achieve intergovernmental cooperation, noted the general failure of these efforts, and called for new forms of cooperation from an audience composed primarily of agency personnel from state and federal governments, tribal members, academics, and leaders of public interest groups. Keynote speakers included then-Governor William Janklow of South Dakota; law professor Charles Wilkinson; Edward Weinberg, former Department of the Interior solicitor; and Donald Worster, author of *Rivers of Empire* and other books on natural resource history.

At the conclusion of the symposium, participants called for the continuation of the project. Because twenty-five Indian tribes are located in the basin and many have major claims to the water of the Missouri and its tributaries, participants emphasized the need to involve the tribes more actively in future discussions and decisions.

Basinwide Emphasis (1987–1988)

The second phase of the Missouri River Management Project was designed to bring Indian tribes into Missouri River management discussions and to allow tribal members to express their needs and expectations for the water resource. Project managers expected that tribal involvement would also help non-Indians understand the nature and extent of Indian water rights and the sovereign stature of tribal governments.

During this phase, the steering committee was enlarged to fifteen to include representatives from the lower basin states and from several of the basin's Indian tribes. Also, a series of sixteen *Missouri River Briefs* was published to help the public better understand the major water issues on the Missouri and appreciate the status of the tribes in the basin and their interest in Missouri River water.[8] Copies or excerpts of the briefs were sent to a large mailing list that included over two hundred newspapers in the basin.

The focal event for the second phase was the Symposium on the Future of the Missouri River, held in May 1988 in Billings. Approximately 150 people attended, representing states, tribes, federal agencies, and private interests, to discuss long-term management of the Missouri River. Successful case studies from around the country were presented to show how conflicts over shared natural resources can be resolved and how states, tribes, and federal agencies can work together to develop environmentally sound management policies for the natural resources they share.

Participants first attended one of three refresher courses on Missouri River issues: Indian water rights, the Pick-Sloan Plan, and current management policies for the river. Then, through panel presentations and discussions, participants examined the successes and failures of Missouri River management, heard a series of case studies that presented alternative methods of river management, and then developed possible approaches for future management. The participants discussed the issues and alternatives both in small groups and in plenary sessions.

At the concluding session, symposium participants offered recommendations for future project activities, including the following:

- A forum, composed of senior state, tribal, and federal representatives should be created to continue the basinwide dialogue. Special efforts must be made to involve the tribes and representatives of the lower basin states. The forum should be structured as an intersovereign organization, although the way to accommodate the basin's numerous tribes is unclear. The intersovereign organization might be created by Congress or by informal agreement among the sovereigns. Northern Lights should provide support for the creation of such a forum.

- More informal communication is needed to develop trust and an understanding of the different needs and perspectives in the basin. A forum would be a place where trust could grow, and where conflicts could be mediated. Nonconfrontational processes should be utilized. The organization's proceedings should be open to the public.
- Participants saw the need for states and Indian tribes to have their own caucuses. In particular, a coalition of Missouri River basin tribes should be established to coordinate activities and positions, and to share technical information.
- Regardless of how it is created, the intersovereign forum should begin addressing the distribution of benefits in the basin, their role in regional economic development, and the basin account of revenues from hydropower and other sources. Computer-assisted negotiations and simulations should be used to experiment with new policies for the Missouri River Basin.
- Such an intersovereign organization should have political clout, especially with Congress, and should be able to cut through the water bureaucracy. The organization should also stress communication with, and the involvement of, basin residents.[9]

From this set of recommendations, the Missouri River Assembly was born.

FORMATION OF THE MISSOURI RIVER ASSEMBLY (1988–1990)

Project managers and members of the steering committee recognized that the Symposium on the Future of the Missouri River marked an important transition in the project. Before May 1988, the project had been primarily educational and directed at a loosely defined audience. After the symposium, project proponents recognized that they had broad, if somewhat tentative, support to create a new institution for the basin. The unique, important predicate for the institution was that it would be an intersovereign forum with state, tribal, and federal participation.

In a series of staff and steering committee meetings, a specific plan was developed to create the Missouri River Assembly, which would be this intersovereign organization. The assembly was conceived as an organization of approximately 100 members representing the three sovereign groups of the basin: the ten states, the twenty-five Indian tribes, and several important federal water management agencies.

Although their efforts were delayed pending foundation grant renewals, project staff made hundreds of telephone calls throughout the winter and spring of 1989 to identify crucial state, tribal, and federal decision makers to be considered for membership. A matrix of more than 200 of these individuals was developed to ensure a balance of perspectives.

In August 1989, letters were sent to the following:

Invited to be Delegates (76)
State governments:
    Governors (ten states; MBSA directors expected to be appointed)
    State senators (ten states)
    State representatives (nine states; Nebraska excepted)
    Missouri Basin Fish and Wildlife Committee (one representative)
Federal government:
    Corps of Engineers
    Bureau of Reclamation
    Western Area Power Administration
    Bureau of Indian Affairs (Billings Area)
    Bureau of Indian Affairs (Aberdeen Area)
Tribal governments (twenty-five reservations; tribal chair or representative)
Other basin interests:
    Agricultural interests (four individuals)
    Environmental interests (four individuals)
    Public power interests (four individuals)
    Navigation interests (four individuals)
Invited to be Observers (148)
Basinwide observers (65):
    Project steering committee
    Project staff
    Federal agencies (Departments of Agriculture, Commerce, and Interior; Environmental Protection Agency; Federal Energy Regulatory Commission)
    Congressional committee staff (Indian Affairs, Interior, Energy, Environment)
    State governmental organizations (Western Governors Association, Western States Water Council)
    Other regional organizations

International representatives (Canada, International Joint
    Commission)
Financial institutions
Individuals
Individual state observers (83):
    Personal staff from each state's congressional delegation
    Media from each state

Eventually, seventy-two delegates were appointed, including representatives of the governors of eight states, legislators from nine states, representatives of twenty-three reservations, and representatives from six federal agencies. More than thirty other people accepted invitations to become observers and many other people, including the press, informally attended assembly meetings.

After most of the appointments had been made, project staff members telephoned the assembly delegates to welcome them, explain in more detail the purpose of the assembly, and help them identify and receive reference material for individual study. Using a standard questionnaire, staff members interviewed the delegates concerning their perceptions of basin conflict, their expectations for the assembly, and their suggestions for the agenda for the first meeting. The survey results were tabulated and presented in oral and written form at the first assembly meeting.

The May symposium had recommended that states and tribes organize separate caucuses in order to better share information and coordinate their positions. Before the assembly's first meeting, Northern Lights worked with the Missouri Basin States Association, the organization of the chief water managers for the basin states, and with a caucus of basin tribes. In August and November 1988, in Seattle and St. Louis, respectively, a project staff member and a consultant facilitated two planning retreats for the MBSA. The association had been weakened by years of internal divisiveness, and the outcome of the retreat was a candid exchange of perspectives and a work plan for the organization.

In March 1989, Northern Lights, in conjunction with the American Indian Resources Institute of Oakland, California, facilitated a meeting in Billings of fourteen Missouri basin tribes. The meeting consisted of presentations on Indian sovereignty and water issues in the basin and discussions among the seventy participants on how the tribes could better cooperate. This meeting assisted the efforts of the tribes to create the permanent basinwide organization discussed later in this chapter.

Another recommendation of the 1988 symposium was "to identify the data upon which the governments agree, to isolate the [water resource] data upon which they disagree, to define data needs, and to make data more usable to all parties."[10] In early 1989, Northern Lights commissioned an initial survey of water data users and providers in the basin. In October 1989, Northern Lights and MBSA jointly sponsored a workshop in Omaha, Nebraska, for water data managers from state, federal, and tribal agencies to discuss water data problems, new technologies, and strategies for improvement. A report of this water data project was submitted by Northern Lights and MBSA to the participants.

Convening of the Missouri River Assembly

The first meeting of the Missouri River Assembly was held November 12–14, 1989, at Laclede's Landing in St. Louis—the original embarkation point for exploration and navigation of the Missouri River. Approximately seventy delegates and eighty observers attended.

The agenda, prepared by the steering committee and project staff after interviewing many of the delegates by phone, set rather modest goals: to let the delegates and observers become acquainted with one another, to allow the participants to hear different perspectives concerning basin water management, and to reach consensus on the need for further assembly meetings and a plan to guide the assembly's work.

The meeting was preceded by a series of workshops offering delegates and observers an opportunity to learn more about different aspects of the Missouri. These presessions covered Indian water rights, the Pick-Sloan Plan, the main stem management policies of the Corps of Engineers, and alternative river management institutions. The first plenary session consisted of a physical and social overview of the Missouri River basin and presentations by four delegates with different perspectives on Missouri River issues (federal, tribal, lower basin, upper basin).

Delegates and observers were preassigned to ten balanced, small groups, and these groups were asked to identify (1) the "essential interests" in the basin, (2) critical Missouri River water issues facing decision makers, and (3) possible solutions. In a later plenary session, each small group presented its responses to these topics. A work-plan drafting committee, with representatives from each type of government, was appointed to meet while the other assembly participants took a dinner cruise up the Mississippi to the mouth of the Missouri. Meeting past midnight, the committee, using the small groups' reports (particularly the comments on critical issues and possible next steps), developed a proposed work plan for the assembly.

In a laborious three-hour plenary session the next day, the drafting committee presented the draft and answered questions. Assembly delegates (with input from observers) reached consensus on a work plan that included the participants' expectations for the assembly, the significant issues in the basin (sixteen in all), and the suggested processes for addressing these issues.[11]

Some of the more important issues included the impacts of drought, conflicts over the distribution of benefits and costs under the Pick-Sloan Plan, the failure of residents to maintain a basinwide perspective, and the lack of communication among basin residents and between residents and their leaders. The delegates called for a second meeting of the assembly, requested additional educational activities from Northern Lights, and supported the Corps of Engineers' review of the master manual controlling reservoir operations.

With the assembly's consent, the members of the work-plan drafting committee became the interim management committee for the assembly. The Missouri Basin States Association agreed to help support the second meeting of the assembly, and several MBSA directors participated on the interim management committee to plan the next meeting.

The second assembly meeting was held in Bismarck, North Dakota, on June 3–5, 1990. Although attendance was lower and there had been some turnover of delegates and observers, the second meeting was much more substantive than the first. Before the meeting began, delegates and observers toured Garrison Dam and the Fort Berthold Reservation to see the impact of Missouri River development on the Arikara, Hidatsa, and Mandan tribes.

The first plenary session began with a photographic tour of the basin and its tributaries, followed by panel presentations on eight main benefits derived from the Missouri River (flood control, navigation, irrigation, power generation, municipal water use, tribal rural water development, tourism and recreation, and fish and wildlife). Case studies of different regional approaches to river basin management were then discussed. Participants heard about the New England River Basin Commission, the Delaware River Basin Commission, the Northwest Power Planning Council, and the Great Lakes Charter. The first day concluded with a "pitch-fork fondue" on the banks of the Missouri highlighted by dances by members of the Three Affiliated Tribes of the Fort Berthold Reservation.

Assembly participants spent the next day in preassigned small groups discussing the advantages and disadvantages of the different water management institutions presented the preceding day, attempting to reach consensus on "the characteristics of a model framework or organization to manage or facilitate water management in the Missouri River basin,"[12] and identifying the steps that could be followed to implement such a framework or organization. On the final afternoon, the small groups reported on their work to the assembly during a plenary session. An effort was then made to reach consensus on one or more organizational models for Missouri River management that could be explored and developed in more detail. The so-called gang-of-four proposal (discussed in Chapter 9) emerged as a leading candidate. The assembly then adjourned with participants requesting a third meeting later in 1990, sponsored by Northern Lights and MBSA, to continue the search for improved Missouri River management policies and institutions.

The Missouri River Assembly never met again. The Northern Lights Institute was unable to secure sufficient foundation funding to reconvene the assembly, and several project staff members departed. Although MBSA considered for a while sponsoring the third assembly meeting under its auspices, its members began concentrating on rebuilding their organization, addressing drought-related problems, and participating in the Corps of Engineers' review of the master manual for Missouri River reservoir operations.

MISSOURI BASIN STATES ASSOCIATION/MISSOURI RIVER BASIN ASSOCIATION

After the meetings of the Missouri River Assembly, the members of the Missouri Basin States Association (MBSA) were forced to confront the problems and future of their organization. Indeed, their evaluation of the organization had started in late 1988 in the two retreats facilitated by the Northern Lights Institute. The review was continued in 1990 in response to the organizational models developed by Missouri River Assembly participants and a bill introduced by Congressman Byron Dorgan of North Dakota to create a Missouri River Council, composed of state and tribal representatives and the secretary of the army, empowered to govern the Missouri River dams.

With a new executive director in place (the former executive director of Northern Lights), the MBSA directors began evaluating different organizational models, including several that had been presented at the last meeting of the Missouri River Assembly. They soon discussed creating their own version of a Missouri River Council composed of ten state representatives, a tribal representative, and nonvoting federal members.[13]

Even though federal legislation would be necessary to implement the plan, the proposed council would supplant the Corps of Engineers as the principal policymaker for the river. Through an innovative system of conflict resolution and voting, power would be shifted to the states when they could agree and to an independent arbitrator when they could not. If a majority of council members agreed on a recommendation, the corps would be bound to follow the policy unless it notified the council of its disapproval within five days and provided an explanation.

If 70 percent or more of the council membership agreed on a proposal, the corps would be required to implement the policy unless it could convince an independent special master by "substantial credible evidence that the recommendation is technically infeasible or in violation of the law."[14] The corps would be required to implement a policy supported by all council members unless it could demonstrate to a special master by clear and convincing evidence that the policy was infeasible or unlawful.

When a hearing on Congressman Dorgan's bill was held in March 1991, MBSA representatives urged delay in congressional action until they had completed their review of organizational alternatives (the bill died without further action). Shortly thereafter, the MBSA membership rejected the Missouri River Council concept and other major structural changes. The association explained its decision as follows:

> First, consensus cannot be legislated, and no amount of congressional authority will guarantee agreement among the basin's states and tribes on how to manage the Missouri River. Therefore, establishing a new basin entity—one which in all likelihood would involve the same people serving on MBSA's board—would probably not improve the basin's ability to resolve basin-wide conflicts. Second, our members recognized that consensus among the representatives of the basin's states and tribes will carry a considerable amount of political authority, even if the organization making the recommendation is purely advisory.[15]

By this time, the need to respond to continuing drought conditions had surpassed the need for structural reform. In spring 1991, MBSA and General Eugene S. Witherspoon of the corps agreed to cooperate in developing the 1992 annual operating plan for the Missouri River reservoirs, and throughout the summer, an MBSA technical group met with the corps to review operating options. In August, MBSA recommended that winter releases from the dams be as low as possible, that releases during the navigation season (navigation service levels) be as specified in the master manual for reservoir operations, and that the navigation season, which normally extends eight months, be closed up to five weeks early depending on runoff. In November, the corps finalized the 1992 annual operating plan and incorporated MBSA's recommendations. The association itself noted that "the result of this seemingly minor change was an historic agreement among the basin's state and tribal representatives on how to operate the River system. The process was unifying rather than divisive, and its [sic] contributed to improved relations among and between the basin's states, tribes, and the Corps of Engineers."[16]

This pattern of MBSA–Corps of Engineers collaboration continued in the development of the 1993 and 1994 annual operating plans. The 1993 plan was almost identical to the previous plan, and the 1994 plan provided for a two-week curtailment of the navigation season if drought returned to the basin. The Missouri River Natural Resources Committee (MRNRC), consisting of representatives of state and federal fish and wildlife agencies, also participated in the development of these plans. In order to restore native fish populations, MRNRC members sought an operating plan that mimicked the natural flows or hydrograph of the river before the dams were built.

The basin states have reached agreement in other areas as well. In fall 1992, the directors of MBSA agreed to change the organization's name to the Missouri River Basin Association (MRBA) in order to formally recognize that the organization now included a voting tribal member. In 1992 and 1993, the MRBA directors unanimously agreed to support increased federal appropriations for the U.S. Geological Survey and its cooperative program with the states, technical planning assistance to the states and tribes, prevention of stream bank erosion, funding of a biodiversity trust fund, and mitigation of fish and wildlife damage caused by river development. Dave Sprynczynatyk, the association's chair, testified on these recommendations before congressional subcommittees in March 1993.[17] Iowa, Kansas, Missouri, Nebraska, South Dakota, along with the Corps of Engineers, the Environmental Protection Agency, the Coast Guard, and the Fish and Wildlife Service, have also formed the Lower Missouri River Hazardous Materials Coordination Group to develop plans to respond to spills of hazardous substances in the river.[18]

MNI SOSE TRIBAL WATER RIGHTS COALITION

Since the final meeting of the Missouri River Assembly, the basin's Indian tribes have significantly improved their capacity to participate in Missouri River decision making. Representatives of thirteen tribes met in September 1990 to discuss the formation of a Missouri tribal coalition. They asked for voting representation on the Missouri Basin States Association, a request that was granted when MBSA added a tribal representative as a director of the association. Brenda Schilf of the Three Affiliated Tribes of the Fort Berthold Reservation initially served in this position.

Tribal leaders met again in April 1991 to discuss their organization and to work with the Corps of Engineers in developing a policy statement formalizing the corps' commitment to work closely, fairly, and impartially with tribes. The corps later established a new position of Native American Affairs Coordinator with an office in Omaha.

In 1992, the tribes continued their efforts to organize a permanent coalition. Finally, in October, the Mni Sose Tribal Water Rights Coalition was incorporated under "the inherent sovereignty and lawful authority of each of the member tribes"[19] with initial financial support from the federal government and the member tribes. The primary purpose of the nonprofit corporation is "to assist member tribes, bands and/or communities in the development, assertion, enhancement and protection of their water rights as recognized under treaty, federal law, tribal law, international law and/or other local law."[20] Shortly after its formation, the coalition hired Daryl Wright, a Chippewa-Cree from the Rocky Boys Reservation in Montana, as executive director, and Wright replaced Brenda Schilf on the MBSA board of directors. Mni Sose has its offices in Rapid City, South Dakota.

Since its formation, Mni Sose has sought to enlarge its membership of Indian tribes (twenty-two of the basin tribes have joined) and has held a series of conferences. The coalition has emphasized several major themes, particularly state efforts to quantify their reserved or aboriginal water rights by litigation or settlement. The coalition has been critical of the lack of federal support given to the tribes in litigation and negotiation processes; it also faults the Justice Department for coercing tribes into settlements and the Department of the Interior for failing to approve tribal water codes.[21]

Tribal leaders seek a greater role in Missouri River decision making. Executive Director Wright has noted that

> The tribes located in the Missouri River Basin represent over one-third of the total land base in Indian Country and have a vast amount of undetermined water interests. There is strength in numbers. And membership in the coalition will give tribes a Big Voice in determining water policy and management practices in the basin. . . . in time, the coalition will become a major player in the determination of tribal water resources in the . . . basin.[22]

The coalition has criticized the master manual review process that is being conducted by the corps. In testimony to the U.S. Senate Committee on Environment and Public Works, Wright noted that the review process has not considered the reserved water rights of the tribes and has not addressed how reservoir operations will be modified once tribal water rights are developed. In closing, the Mni Sose spokesman observed that "the bottom line is that American Indian families continue to haul drinking water while the corps releases water from its massive reservoirs in order to enhance navigation."[23]

THE CORPS' MASTER MANUAL REVIEW

Drought conditions began in spring 1987 and continued until severe flooding occurred during the spring and summer of 1993. This six-year drought resulted in river flows only slightly higher than the Dust Bowl period of 1930 to 1933, and by April 1991, total storage behind the main stem dams was at an all-time low of 42.1 million ac-ft. Diminished Missouri River flows affected all uses of water in the basin. Navigation flows were reduced and the navigation season shortened. Hydropower production, normally 10 billion kwh, dropped in some years to 70 percent of normal production, forcing the Western Area Power Administration to secure alternative sources of power for its contractors. Whereas the hydropower system usually produces $45 million in surplus power, $33 million had to be purchased by WAPA in 1992.

In the upper basin, recreational use of the reservoirs diminished as water levels left boat marinas and other commercial developments high and dry. In the lower basin, municipal and industrial water intakes had to be lower or extended and the diluting capacity of the river was reduced. In both the upper and lower basins, fish and other aquatic animals were stressed by the lower reservoir and river levels and the increasing temperature of the water.

By October 1989, North Dakota's Quentin Burdick, chair of the powerful U.S. Senate Environment and Public Works Committee, had had enough. In a letter to President Bush that reverberated through the command structure of the Corps of Engineers, Burdick bluntly stated:

> I am writing . . . to advise you of my extreme displeasure with the Army Corps of Engineers in its management of the Missouri River during a prolonged and severe drought.
>
> The upper Missouri River Basin is entering its third straight year of drought. Yet the military commanders in charge of river management intend to release more water next year than they did this year or last for the questionable purpose of keeping Missouri River navigation operational. . . . The decision to release this water was made by the Corps of Engineers AFTER a meeting I attended with the Division Commanding General, Governor Sinner of North Dakota, and Governor Mickelson of South Dakota; AFTER a private meeting on the subject which I had with the Chief of Engineers; and AFTER I waited for three months to receive an answer from the Chief of Engineers as to why he was permitting the system to be operated in a manner contrary to basic economic and environmental criteria.[24]

Within two days, Brigadier General Patrick J. Kelly, Director of Civil Works, announced that the corps would undertake a review of the master water control manual, which was first released in 1960 and had not been updated since 1979. The corps gave numerous reasons for the review: the ten-year period since the last review, the failure to develop federally sponsored irrigation, the growth in private irrigation, increased importance of lake and river recreation, the growing number of municipal and industrial water intakes, the lack of growth in commercial navigation, changes in the navigation channel and its capacity, more strenuous water quality standards, and the listing of threatened and endangered species.

The master manual is a seven-volume document that establishes the policies for managing the main stem reservoirs "as a hydraulically and electrically integrated system."[25] The manual sets forth critical criteria, such as when to make cuts in the length of the navigation season or in the level of flows supporting navigation.

Since the amount of water coming into the Missouri is beyond the corps' control, the agency must operate the system by varying the amount of water held in the main stem reservoirs and the timing and amount of water released from the reservoirs. The total reservoir storage of 73.5 million ac-ft is divided into four zones: a permanent pool of 18.1 million ac-ft (25 percent); carryover multiple use zone of 39 million ac-ft (53 percent); annual flood control and multiple use zone of 11.7 million ac-ft (16 percent); and the exclusive flood control zone of 4.7 million ac-ft (6 percent).

The permanent pool provides storage for sediment inflows; a minimal pool for recreation, fish, and wildlife; and minimum heads for hydropower production. The carryover multiple use zone is "an intermediate zone [that] provides a storage reservoir for irrigation, navigation, power production, and other beneficial conservation uses."[26] This zone would be completely used if the drought of the 1930s were repeated. The exclusive flood zone and the annual flood control and multiple use zone are evacuated by March 1 of each year to accommodate spring and summer runoff. The master manual calls for a full eight-month navigation season if 41 million ac-ft are in storage on July 1.

The corps outlined four activities for the master manual review: (1) technical evaluations; (2) development of possible alternatives and the assessment of the economic, environmental and social impacts of those alternatives; (3) preparation, review, revision, and publication of a draft environmental statement (EIS); and (4) preparation and filing of the final EIS. A Phase 1 report completed in May 1990 identified a range of alternatives and sufficient analysis of their potential economic, social, and environmental impacts to allow the selection of fewer alternatives to study more thoroughly during Phase 2.[27]

Almost immediately, other forces began to shape the course of the master manual review. Asked by an upper basin congressman to investigate the corps' management of the river during 1988, the U.S. General Accounting Office (GAO) in turn requested the corps' legal opinion on its authority to manage the Missouri River system. The corps' general counsel responded that the agency has authority to consider recreational values in setting the releases from the upper basin reservoirs but must primarily consider the original Pick-Sloan Plan purposes of flood control, navigation, irrigation, and hydropower production. Any change in the primary purposes of Missouri River operations must be made by Congress based on a consensus, best manifested in a compact, among the states and tribes.[28]

The legal opinion concluded that the upper basin preference embodied in the O'Mahoney-Milliken Amendment protects only traditional diversions of water, not instream and nonconsumptive uses of water like recreation. The corps' chief attorney conceded that "any proposition to operate the Missouri River main stem reservoirs solely to benefit Mississippi River interests would thus concern extraordinary circumstances and considerations of extraordinary authority."[29]

In early 1991, South Dakota, North Dakota, and Montana challenged this opinion in a Billings federal court.[30] The upper basin states sought a declaratory judgment that the 1944 Flood Control Act establishes only flood control and upper basin consumptive uses as primary purposes, leaving the corps with discretion to revise other priorities in order to provide greatest economic benefit to the entire basin. Iowa and Missouri intervened in the litigation to support the corps. The upper basin states asked tribes to join their position but received no formal response.

A report by the U.S. General Accounting Office issued on January 27, 1992, changed the corps' approach to the master manual review and the posture of the litigation pending in federal court. The GAO concluded, among other things, that the corps, not Congress, had established the operating priorities for the Missouri River main stem reservoirs and that the corps did not need congressional approval to change the priorities.[31] Thus, newer upper basin water uses, such as recreation, could be considered equally with other uses in the master manual review process.

After the GAO report, the corps attempted to end the federal court litigation—both by negotiation and by summary court proceedings. In March 1992, the U.S. Department of Justice, which represents federal agencies in such lawsuits, offered to settle the litigation based on the principles set forth in the GAO report: that Congress did not establish operating priorities for reservoirs and that project purposes could be changed by the corps to account for environmental and economic conditions in the basin. This settlement offer was immediately opposed by the lower basin. Twenty-two U.S. senators from lower Missouri and Mississippi basin states sent a letter to Nancy Dorn, assistant secretary for the army (Civil Works), demanding that the corps continue to protect downstream flows for commercial navigation.

The corps filed a motion in April 1992 asking the federal district court to dismiss the upper basin states' suit, asserting that the states lacked standing, that there was no final agency action ripe for review, and that operation of the main stem reservoirs fell under the corps' discretion. After several settlement conferences with the parties, the court dismissed the litigation in February 1993, holding that the case was moot since the corps was undertaking the master manual review, considering all uses of water, and giving them equal consideration. The dismissal notwithstanding, the upper basin states claimed victory, pointing to the fact that the corps was now giving important consideration to contemporary upper basin water uses.[32]

In early 1993, the administration of President Clinton assumed power, and both the upper and lower basin jockeyed for influence over the master manual review. In February, seventy-one members of Congress from lower Missouri and Mississippi basin states asked Clinton to elevate the review to a special cabinet-level task force "consisting of at least the Secretaries of Defense, Transportation, and Agriculture."[33] Nine congressional members from the upper basin responded in their own letter to the president, asking to let the corps complete the master manual review process.

The work was delayed by these developments and the extensive comments received on earlier documents, but the corps finally released its *Preliminary Draft Environmental Impact Statement (EIS)* during the summer of 1993. This document thoroughly reviewed the corps' work to date and previewed the operational changes likely to be made in the system. In its work, the corps looked at two primary features of the master manual: (1) the amount of system storage set aside for the permanent pool and the resulting size of the carryover multiple use zone and (2) releases of water for various needs including water supply, flood control, power production, water quality, irrigation, navigation, recreation, and environmental quality.

The corps then developed and analyzed two groups of alternatives that presented variations of reservoir storage and water releases (flow series). A total of 277 alternatives (called National Economic Development, or NED, alternatives) were examined that would maximize total economic benefits from the system. Thirty alternatives (called Environmental Quality, or EQ, alternatives) that would maximize environmental values in the system were also studied. Eventually, the corps studied seven alternatives in even more detail by using a ninety-three-year simulation period. The corps indicated that most scenarios have little effect on hydropower production or water supply; these uses vastly exceed the economic value of such uses as navigation and recreation.

The preliminary EIS has implications for permanent pool storage and releases from the reservoirs, particularly during drought conditions. Increasing the size of the permanent pool has little total economic impact. The economic benefits of hydropower and upper basin recreation are slightly increased, but navigation benefits are sharply reduced. Raising the permanent pool does appear to improve environmental values—especially the nesting habitat of terns and plovers. With one exception, variations in flows to the lower basin also have minor total economic impact. The EQ flow alternatives that have the highest economic returns produce benefits of approximately $20 million per year below the best performing NED alternatives. If the navigation season is split to mimic the natural flows of the river to benefit fish, thereby providing no navigation support in August or September, that activity is severely affected by economic losses of between 39 and 62 percent.

The preliminary EIS concludes that by reducing navigation flow and cutting off the navigation season length earlier in the drought, water is conserved for future use. This conservation leads to economic and environmental benefits for the system, though navigation is affected. As the preliminary EIS notes, "No alternatives have been identified that substantially improve physical habitat for native riverine fish species without shifting the effects of drought to navigation."[34]

The revised draft environmental impact statement and the corps' preferred management alternative were not expected until summer 1994. Colonel John Schaufelberger, the corps' division commander, predicted that because of the polarization of the basins and the politicization of the issues, the final decisions probably would be made at the corps' headquarters.

Clearly, major changes will be made in how the corps operates the Missouri River system. Because the corps is considering a broader range of economic and environmental values than heretofore, the importance of navigation will diminish and the system will likely be operated to serve multiple uses. Navigation will be further harmed if system operations must be further modified to protect threatened and endangered species—especially in times of drought.

During the spring and summer of 1993, however, drought was far from anyone's mind. From April 1 to July 25, the Midwest averaged more than eighteen inches of rain, with many areas receiving thirty inches. Even heavier rains came in July and July. The summer was the wettest in a century in parts of Montana and all of North Dakota, South Dakota, Minnesota, and Iowa. Nebraska, Kansas, Missouri, and Wyoming also received near-record precipitation. Consequently, storage in the main stem reservoirs increased by 12 million ac-ft over the previous year.

Although the Mississippi River basin was much harder hit by these storms, there was also flood damage throughout the Missouri River basin. Flood damage in South Dakota alone was estimated at almost $600 million, and the commercial navigation season was suspended when dam releases were reduced to slow the water flowing into the lower basin. The Western Area Power Administration had to purchase electricity to make up for its lost production. On October 1, 1993, storage in the Missouri River main stem reservoirs was 56.9 million ac-ft—the average for the 1967–1992 period.[35] All reservoirs but Fort Peck and Gavins Point were full. The great flood of 1993 appeared to have replaced the great drought of the 1980s.

CHAPTER NINE

Of Rivers, Fish, and Men

Since the 1940s, numerous efforts have been made to create a lasting institution to manage the Missouri River, but none of these efforts has succeeded. While tensions among the jurisdictions within the basin have continued to mount, the few cooperative structures that existed have been terminated or seriously weakened. With President Reagan's repeal of earlier executive orders, the Missouri River Basin Commission and the Old West Regional Commission (Title V) were dismantled in the early 1980s. In 1987, the states of the Missouri Basin States Association (MBSA), discouraged by a round of inconclusive negotiations, dismissed the MBSA staff, closed the association's Omaha office, and gave the association's extensive library and water accounting model to the Corps of Engineers. The transfer was symbolic; in the absence of an effective state presence in the basin, the Missouri River had become a federal river—the domain of the corps. Interjurisdictional cooperation in the basin had reached its lowest ebb.

In part, this situation resulted from the "commodity" orientation that parties have generally taken toward the Missouri River. Water management policies have not been based on the river as an integrated ecological system. Rather than recognizing that the Missouri binds the basin together "with a thousand invisible cords,"[1] policymakers have allowed its waters to be fractured into multiple units of kilowatt hours of electricity and acre-feet of water, agricultural outputs, and barge tonnage. The river is most frequently experienced by basin residents as a commercial product line.

This commodity orientation reflects the engineering imperative that has characterized water development in the twentieth century, that is, the notion that there is a technical solution to any problem. Because a river exists, so the logic goes, it should be diverted, dammed, or otherwise manipulated. Human achievement is measured by the grandeur of the plan and the amount of concrete that is poured. The culture and economy of indigenous people who happen to live on the sites of proposed dams and reservoirs should not be a barrier to progress.

The problems of the Missouri River basin have also resulted from the ongoing efforts of the federal government to nationalize the river. To be sure, this effort was authorized by the congressional commerce and navigation powers. Certainly, it was undertaken with the best of intentions to prevent flooding and assist in the region's economic develop-ment. And, granted, the federal government attempted to "coordinate" with other governments in the basin—albeit from the top down and in a way that rarely included the tribes.

Pick-Sloan originated during a time when action by the federal gov-ernment was desired and warranted. As the years passed, the resulting organizations and policies may not have been the choice of the states, but the appeal of "ultimate development" and federal expenditures pur-chased their acquiescence.

POSSIBILITIES FOR CHANGE

The Pick-Sloan Plan is fifty years old, and the vision of comprehensive Missouri River basin development has faded. With the overall decline in the agricultural sector, many farmers have forgotten that there ever was a dream of extensive irrigated agriculture in the upper basin, and until the floods of 1993, lower basin residents had forgotten the stake they have in the flood storage capacity of the upper basin reservoirs. Residents in Minneapolis or Denver turn on their lights and do not know or care whether the electricity was produced at Garrison Dam or at a coal-fired power plant. The generation of leaders who developed the vision of inte-grated basin development has gone. Can there be a new vision for the basin?

Factors Favoring the Status Quo

Inertia in the Missouri River basin is great, and the incentives to main-tain the status quo strong. The lower basin states, especially, are satisfied enough to oppose most major changes. The states of Missouri, Iowa, and Kansas, for example, have their flood prevention, and they enjoy a navigation potential far exceeding their commercial capacity. Nebraska has done particularly well: it has the largest amount of acreage and greatest percentage of land irrigated under the Pick-Sloan Plan, one of the largest shares of Pick-Sloan hydropower, and navigation and flood control benefits. These lower basin states are generally content as long as water levels are sufficiently high for eight months of navigation, the elec-tricity keeps coming, and it doesn't rain too much.

The states of Colorado and Minnesota, both on an edge of the basin, are equally satisfied with the status quo. They were not promised much under Pick-Sloan, nor did they lose land to reservoirs as did the upper basin states. What they have received under Pick-Sloan has probably ex-ceeded their private expectations. Minnesota receives more cheap hydroelectric power that any other any basin state, and because of its reliance on Mississippi River navigation, it has also benefited from the continual flows of the Missouri—undiminished by significant upper basin irrigation. Colorado has not seen any of its promised irrigation developed, but the promised amount was but modest (103,000 acres), and the state has received a small amount of the basin's cheap hydropower, supplemented by hydropower from other parts of WAPA's electrical grid.

Thus, five of the basin states are content with current circumstances. Even the relatively new interests of these states' residents in recreation, water quality, and riparian values are usually served by flows that are undiminished by upper basin agricultural diversions.

Federal natural resource and fiscal policies have also contributed to the inertia. The national will to complete water development projects has dissipated, and the Bureau of Reclamation is transforming itself into a water management and engineering services agency. The Reagan administration emphasized state primacy over water resources and, by abolishing the Missouri River Basin Commission, eliminated the one agency that was still planning for the completion of Pick-Sloan. The Corps of Engineers is happy to manage the dams, maintain the navigation channel, and use its authority over the reservoirs for water marketing and other purposes. Certainly, environmental organizations do not want to see more water development.

Even some upper basin states have acquiesced in this inertia. Wyoming, which has received virtually nothing from the Pick-Sloan Plan, has chosen to rely on its own funds to pay for water development. Montana, which lost 590,000 acres to Fort Peck, received only 76,200 acres of irrigation, and gets about two-thirds of the hydropower it produces, has been rather quiet on the topic of Pick-Sloan. Only North Dakota, with its incomplete Garrison Diversion Project, and South Dakota, with its ETSI, Cost Recovery Authority, and rural domestic water initiatives, have been the "squeaky wheels" in the basin.

Factors Favoring Further Divisiveness in the Basin

Nevertheless, there may be forces powerful enough to disrupt the inertia in the basin. Factors such as the severe drought of 1987–1993 may produce conflict of a magnitude that no state can avoid. During the drought, upper basin reservoirs were drawn down, diminishing recreation and tourism, and lower basin states experienced disruptions to navigation, municipal water supplies, and waste water treatment.

Drought may recur, or these periods of prolonged dryness could indicate permanent climatic change with even more devastating consequences. With reduced runoff from the Rockies, which produces about half of the entire flow of the Missouri, upper basin agricultural diversions (although only a fraction of the irrigation originally promised) would take a greater percentage of the water. Relationships among states over tributary streams would deteriorate (e.g., Montana and Wyoming could wrangle over the Yellowstone River; Colorado, Kansas, and Nebraska over the Republican River; Wyoming and South Dakota over the Belle Fourche River; Nebraska and Wyoming over the Niobrara basin; Kansas and Nebraska over the Big Blue River).

The real fight, however, could result from the competition among those wanting water for hydropower production, navigation, and threatened or endangered species. These uses all benefit from instream flows, and the timing of the flows can be critical. Navigation interests want water released between March and October; the corps and WAPA want sufficient water in the reservoirs for midwinter hydropower production; the fish want high flows in the spring and early summer and reduced flows during late summer. Mississippi River navigators would be damaged by continuing low flows from the Missouri and might renew their calls for diversions of water from the Great Lakes to the Mississippi. Such drought conditions could lead to a major reformulation of how the Missouri River is managed.

Missouri River flows could also be reduced by events unrelated to drought. For instance, an ETSI-type of contract for an out-of-basin diversion could be approved by the Corps of Engineers.[2] Or an energy crisis precipitated by another Middle East conflict could lead to reduced flows if coal and synthetic fuel plants were constructed in the upper basin. In either case, upper/lower basin conflict would result.

In the case of an out-of-basin diversion, lower basin states would be concerned, as they were in the case of the ETSI proposal, with a precedent being established and would want to share in any compensation for the water. Litigation such as arose from ETSI would be likely to reemerge over such issues as the authority granted federal agencies under the 1944 Flood Control Act, the meaning of the O'Mahoney-Millikin Amendment, and the adequacy of the environmental impact statement. In the case of energy development, lower basin states would be concerned about noticeable reductions of flows through the turbines and through the navigation channel. A basinwide equitable apportionment action before the U.S. Supreme Court might result.

The assertion by the basin's tribes of their reserved water rights could also create conflict. Indeed, the Mni Sose Tribal Water Rights Coalition stipulates the recognition of these rights as its primary goal. If reserved rights settlements are reached between the upper basin states and tribes, they may be held up by lower basin congressmen if the agreements require congressional approval (lower basin senators have already placed a "hold" on the approval of the Fort Peck–Montana Compact). The tribes' authority to lease water rights established by a decree or compact for off-reservation purposes (such as for energy development) may be challenged by lower basin states if flows are reduced. In an equitable apportionment action, the amount of tribal water rights, whether established by compact or state court decree, will be an issue, as will the question of whether the reserved rights are charged against the basin or against the states in which the reservations are located.

Hydroelectric power production and the distribution of the accompanying revenues may become divisive issues. Firm power production is marketed under preference contracts to state agencies, municipalities, rural electric cooperatives, and other government entities. With rates as low as one-sixth of commercial wholesale rates, current contract holders have a tremendous financial advantage. Most of these contracts, however, come up for renewal around the year 2000, when entities not presently served by the system will demand that the benefits of public power be spread more broadly. Meanwhile, several of the North Dakota and South Dakota tribes have submitted or are developing proposals for additional compensation for the loss of their lands, economies, and culture to the main stem Missouri reservoirs. These tribes are targeting both preference power and hydropower revenues as potential sources of compensation.

The authority given to the U.S. Fish and Wildlife Service under the Endangered Species Act may be another source of conflict in the basin. The agency's plans to protect threatened or endangered fish and other species will strongly influence decisions about reservoir levels and the amount and timing of flows from the reservoirs. Indeed, the river may ultimately be run primarily to protect the fish, with severe consequences for future upper basin consumptive uses and lower basin navigation.

Finally, the most probable cause of further conflict in the basin will be litigation over the corps' final management decisions, which will be based on the master manual review. The parties hurt by the review—whether upper or lower basin states or the tribes—are expected to seek judicial review of the review process and the results.

Factors Favoring Cooperation in the Basin

A harmonious future in the basin seems unlikely. If cooperation is to be achieved, it may result from outside threats, the ability to increase the "pot" of existing benefits, or both. An outside raid on basin resources could solidify basin opposition. If, for instance, a proposal were made to divert large amounts of water to the Southwest, basin states could be expected to look beyond the immediate financial incentives and line up in opposition (as the Great Lakes states have done), but such a massive interbasin diversion is unlikely these days. Southwestern cities have determined that conservation measures and the purchase of surrounding agricultural water rights will meet their water needs—probably for the next forty years.

A more likely national raid will be on the basin's hydroelectric power resource. This will not be a diversion of the actual power but of revenues from the power sales. A close but failing vote in the House of Representatives in 1984 on a proposal to charge market rates for the hydropower produced by the Colorado River projects (sponsored by Representative Barbara Boxer of California) indicates that many national leaders are dissatisfied with preference power rates. Although this "Boxer rebellion" was hastily beaten back, there are many reasons to believe it will reemerge—especially with chronic federal deficits. A proposal to increase power rates in the Missouri River basin to benefit the national treasury may unify opposition (although the efforts of some upper basin states may be lukewarm in view of the lack of support for irrigation development they received from other basin states).

Basin cooperation may result from efforts to increase the "pot" of benefits available for distribution among the basin governments.[3] The governments may be able to develop methods to share information and data on water and water-related resources. Additional investments in hydropower capacity may provide more power for distribution among the governments. Tribes and states may cooperate in developing linked proposals for quantifying reserved rights and investing state and federal money in water development projects (similar to the Animas–La Plata–Southern Ute proposal in southwestern Colorado).

Perhaps the most promising basis for cooperation, and certainly the riskiest venture, is for the basin states and tribes to obtain—for their shared benefit—the basin's hydropower revenues. This coup could be accomplished by the states and tribes actually purchasing the hydropower generation facilities, by the states and tribes obtaining federal legislation to allow revenues to stay in the basin, or by a compact allowing the states and tribes to impose a surcharge on hydropower produced in the basin. Existing hydropower rates are now set to repay the power investment and irrigation aid, and any of these proposals would therefore require rate increases. Yet if the revenues were distributed equitably among basin governments, the proposal might engender wide support. For example, money could be made available for habitat improvements in the lower basin, for water development or broader social purposes on reservations, and for investments in drought-proofing and water conservation measures in the upper basin. Throughout the basin, investments could be made in fish and wildlife restoration and recreation.

The major risk, of course, is that the hydropower system will not be able to maintain moderate rates while still paying for itself and producing revenues for other basin purposes. During both the drought of 1987–1993 and the flood of 1993, WAPA was forced to buy electricity from other sources in order to supply its customers. Also, it may be difficult to communicate successfully this proposal to basin residents and federal decision makers. Without support from basin residents, the proposal will deteriorate into a contentious debate with current public power beneficiaries. If the members of Congress fail to grasp the vision of basin investments and improvements, they may approach these discussions with the idea that these proposals can be turned into an opportunity to benefit the national treasury by increasing hydropower rates.

A realist cannot be optimistic about the future of intergovernmental relationships in the Missouri River basin. There are, however, two factors that occasionally make a difference in the ordering of human affairs. One is the goodwill that is a fundamental part of the American character; the other is individual leadership. One must not underestimate the ability of basin residents to understand the inequities that have resulted from the Pick-Sloan Plan or their potential support of public policies to correct these inequities. Leaders may yet come forward who will be able to touch that goodwill and communicate a vision for a just, progressive future.

INSTITUTIONS AND POLICIES FOR THE MISSOURI RIVER

An institution is an organization fused with values, "a natural product of social needs and pressures—a responsive, adaptive organism."[4] A new institution is necessary for Missouri River management. A new set of values, perhaps a new Pick-Sloan Plan supported by basin residents, is needed to affirm how the river system will be managed. A stable, broadly representative organization, such as the Missouri River Assembly, is needed to implement these policies and to resolve conflicts along the way. Values and organization are inseparable in charting the future of the Missouri.

The states, the tribes, and the Corps of Engineers have each taken notable steps since 1990 to improve Missouri River management and to improve relations with one another, but their efforts are not yet sufficient. The states have added a tribal representative to the Missouri River Basin Association, have reestablished an office with an executive director, and have undertaken very practical steps to influence the development of the corps' annual operating plan and to support federal appropriations. The tribes have created a formal organization including most of the basin tribes; they can now articulate tribal perspectives whenever Missouri River issues are taken up. For its part, the corps is undertaking the master manual review, which will present many management options to decision makers. The corps has also improved communications with the states and tribes through annual consultations over the annual operating plan and the appointment of a Native American Affairs Coordinator.

Still, the states, tribes, and federal agencies continue to pursue their narrow interests. A basinwide perspective is lacking, and the basin is always just a filing fee away from another round of basinwide litigation. A social judgment, setting forth basic values, has not been reached about how the Missouri River should be managed.

New Pick-Sloan Plan

The original Pick-Sloan Plan embodied a set of public values and policies that seemed appropriate for the needs of basin residents in the post–World War II decade when, in fact, it was insensitive to many main stem tribes and to the Missouri River's ecology. Many of the plan's goals have been unfulfilled or distorted, leaving an inequitable distribution of benefits and costs and significant environmental damage.

Where do we look for a new set of values—a social judgment—for managing the Missouri River? A recent report by the University of Colorado's Natural Resources Law Center, *Searching Out the Headwaters*, provides "a principled foundation for making water policy: a water ethic rooted in basic values of our society."[5] The result of the Western Water Policy Project, a multiyear effort supported by the Ford Foundation, *Searching Out the Headwaters* formulates this water ethic as three basic principles:

- The principle of conservation: water should be used with care;
- The principle of equity: the whole community should be treated fairly; and
- The principle of ecology: nature should be respected.[6]

Most of the problems now facing Missouri River decision makers stem from violations of these principles during the fifty-year history of the Pick-Sloan Plan. The tribes and upper basin states have not received their share of the benefits of the system. The tribes are still waiting for fair compensation for the lands taken, as well as water and electricity for homes on the reservations, and the upper basin states are waiting for a fair share of the hydropower produced at the reservoirs within their states and the opportunity to make new uses of the stored water that will never be used for irrigation. The ecology of the entire river has been significantly disrupted by the dams and navigation channels, with adverse impacts on fish, wildlife, and riparian vegetation. And, while there is a relative abundance of water in the basin, water has been wasted: evaporation from the reservoirs is one of the largest "uses" of water in the system.

A new Pick-Sloan Plan should be developed for the Missouri River basin, one firmly based on the principles of conservation, equity, and ecology. Hydropower revenues could make such a plan possible by providing funding for rural domestic water development, species protection, and ecological restoration. More important, every natural resource policy decision in the basin should be evaluated with these principles in mind.

Institutional Possibilities

The goal of institution-building is to develop an organization that embodies distinct values, has character, and has distinctive competence. The organization provides something needed in the world and provides it better than other organizations.[7] Institution-building is "concerned with innovations that imply qualitative changes in norms, in behavior patterns, in individual and group relations, in new perceptions of goals as well as means. It is not concerned with reproducing familiar patterns, with marginal deviation from previous practices. . . . The dominant theme is innovation."[8]

The process of institution-building requires the performance of several important functions:

- leadership, frequently by a change-oriented elite;
- strategic planning and monitoring;
- the development of doctrine, "a series of themes which project, both within the organization itself and in its external environment, a set of images and expectations of institutional goals and styles of action";[9]
- the adoption of a program, "the translation of doctrine into concrete patterns of action";[10]
- the deployment of resources; and
- the development of linkages "with a limited number of organizations . . . [to] engage in transactions for the purpose of gaining support, overcoming resistance, exchanging re-

sources, structuring the environment, and transferring norms and values."[11]

Individuals attempting to build an institution must avoid two pitfalls. The first danger is that of utopianism, the unrealistic formation of great dreams that lead to an overgeneralized, unexamined sense of purpose. The second trap is that of opportunism, accepting short-term payoffs when more fundamental change is necessary.[12]

Charles H. W. Foster has studied regional water management institutions in the New England states, and he offers many insights relevant to the Missouri River basin. For Foster, defining the region is the first important step in creating a regional institution. A region has at least four dimensions:

> A distinctive *spatial* dimension is usually helpful—hopefully one with a high degree of geographic and ecological integrity. A *social* dimension is also important. People must feel that they belong to a region. A *functional* dimension is a third organizing element. Here economic self-sufficiency or economic interdependency, or a common set of services required by the region, can provide support of the institution. A common *political* dimension must be present too. The institution must contain a majority of the key leadership elements of the region, both formal and informal, individual and organizational. Although the jurisdictional representation can and will be varied, there must be approximate power parity among them.[13]

Against this template, the Missouri River basin may be too large a region. Although the basin is an ecological system, few residents readily identify with the watershed. Moreover, equivalence of power does not prevail among the basin governments. Yet the functional dimension is satisfied; it is becoming more apparent to tribes, upper basin states, and lower basin states that much of their economic vitality depends on the river.

Foster also observes that the regional institution must have something specific to do: "regions don't have truth—only utility."[14] The regional organization must not lose touch with its constituents or become too much a power of its own. He cautions organizers to "avoid giving your regional organization much of any direct power, but provide it ready access to those who exercise such authority. The objective should be to attain a condition of de facto power. Keep the organization small so that it functions in non-competitive and non-threatening ways."[15] Foster also notes how crucial timing is to the creation and success of a regional organization.

Northern Lights' efforts to create the Missouri River Assembly relied upon many of these tenets of institution-building. Funded by the Ford Foundation and others for the express purpose of initiating change, the goals of Northern Lights were to offer broader participation (especially by the tribes) in Missouri River decision making, be sensitive to the watershed's ecological systems, and be committed to the development of improved policies for river management. The aim was to create a forum in which citizens and decision makers in the basin could reach a social judgment about river management and provide for its implementation.

If reestablished, a Missouri River Assembly could be the basin institution that incorporates the values of a new Pick-Sloan Plan.[16] With representation from the states, tribes, and federal agencies, the assembly could provide opportunities for basin decision makers to share their perspectives, improve mutual understanding, agree on basic values about river management, and thereby develop new policies for the river. The assembly begins as a process for these discussions. It is to be hoped that it will become an institution that embodies new understandings among the governments of the basin and new policies for the river.

This approach is not unprecedented. As we have seen, leaders in other parts of the country have forged innovative interjurisdictional agreements concerning natural resources, for example, the Great Lakes Charter, the Northwest Power Planning Council, and the Pacific Salmon Agreements.[17]

At the last meeting of the Missouri River Assembly, participants offered a more refined version of a permanent structure for the assembly. The proposal is a potential avenue to balanced participation by the three types of sovereigns in the basin. Composed of delegates from each of the basin states, tribes, and important federal water management agencies, the assembly would meet several times a year to develop broad recommendations. Its first tasks would be to write a charter to govern its operations and to develop a broad statement of water management principles. In addition, the upper basin states, the lower basin states, the tribes, and the federal agencies would each select one co-chair who would serve on the executive committee of the assembly (a "gang of four"). This committee would meet regularly and would have authority to implement the assembly's statement of principles and other policies, to mediate disputes among the governments, to develop recommendations to the assembly and the member governments, and to advise the Corps of Engineers on river operations. Action by the executive committee would require three affirmative votes. The assembly or the executive committee could appoint committees to address specific problems such as water data issues. A formula would be developed to allocate the assembly's funding among the member governments. An interstate agreement or federal legislation might eventually be developed to require the basin's governments to adhere to the policies of the assembly and its executive committee—much like the federal agencies in the Pacific Northwest conform to the policies of the Northwest Power Planning Council or the individual state members of the Delaware River Compact comply with the water code of the basin commission.

In addition to its emphasis on institution-building, the Missouri River Management Project, culminating in the assembly, was also an attempt to restore federalism to water management in the basin. The unfettered federal dominance in the management of the Missouri is no longer effective or desirable. Tribal governments have not been adequately involved in river decision making, and the states have often had little influence. Whereas the U.S. Constitution affords few formal opportunities for states, federal agencies, and tribes to work together to manage a river system, the project explored new opportunities for intergovernmental relations that might take place in the margins of the Constitution.

The search was instructive. The Delaware River Basin Compact demonstrates that an agreement developed under the Constitution's Compact Clause can result in basinwide water resource management. The Fort Peck–Montana Compact and the North Pacific Salmon Agreements indicate that tribes can participate as sovereigns along with states and the federal government. The Northwest Power Planning Council represents a holistic approach to managing the region's energy and aquatic resources with a body of state representatives providing effective guidance to federal agencies. The Great Lakes Charter is an example of a relatively informal, nonbinding, flexible agreement that has resulted in successful coordination among many government agencies and successful adaptation to problems ranging from drought to high lake levels. These are new patterns of American federalism, and several of them have added tribes as a new dimension of this federalism. These case studies offer compelling precedents for citizens and decision makers in the Missouri River basin.

Finally, the Northern Lights' effort was also one of community-building in the Missouri River basin, and in one sense, the need to build and revitalize communities is a requirement of our time. In the 1820s, Georg Wilhelm Friedrich Hegel predicted that when the American frontier had vanished, Americans would be forced to confront one another and jointly solve their social problems.[18] Only then would America have the opportunity to prove the richness of its civic life. Because we can no longer escape to the open West, we must finally learn to solve our problems within our communities—whether that community is Bismarck or the Missouri River valley.

Sociologist Amitai Etzioni has published a book called *The Spirit of Community* in which he discusses the tenets and agenda of a movement he calls communitarianism. Etzioni presents a succinct diagnosis of contemporary American civic culture: "a strong sense of entitlement—that is, a demand that the community provide more services and strongly uphold rights—coupled with a rather weak sense of obligation to the local and national community."[19] As an example, he cites a recent study indicating that Americans expect to be tried before a jury of their peers but are reluctant to serve on one. Etzioni's prescription is that truly *"free individuals require a community,* which backs them up against encroachment by the state and sustains morality by drawing on the gentle prodding of kin, friends, neighbors, and other community members, rather than building on government controls or fear or authorities."[20]

Michael Lerner, editor of the monthly magazine *Tikkun,* has developed similar ideas in his concept of the "politics of meaning." Lerner argues that "we need to be part of loving families and ethically and spiritually grounded communities that provide a meaning for our lives that transcends the individualism and me-firstism of the competitive market."[21]

The concept of community-building developed by Dan Kemmis, mayor of Missoula, Montana, is perhaps most relevant here. In *Community and the Politics of Place* (1990), this former speaker of the Montana House of Representatives develops a concept of community and civic life that may be of special interest to people interested in western natural resources. Kemmis argues that communities are relationships among individuals gathered around a place. The place gathers people together by simultaneously relating and separating them. Public life in America, he says, "can only be reclaimed by understanding, and then practicing, its connection to real, identifiable places"[22] such as mountains and rivers. When people constitute themselves as a community or a public, they create something different and greater than themselves. That which they create is the res publica—the "public thing." The res publica includes the place (the mountains, the plains, the coast, the river) around which people unite.

Building communities in a city or in a watershed, according to Kemmis, is "first, last, and always, a matter of engagement—engagement with each other, with the place we inhabit, with its (and our) strengths and limitations. No one can build a barn alone, or get all the calves branded." But in the American West, "at any one of these activities, absolutely everyone, no matter how ungifted they might have felt, was put to work at something."[23] No one has the whole answer to any problem, but everyone has part of the answer.

Water can be an organizing principle in our communities. The citizens of western Montana are developing at the grassroots level a water plan for the Clark Fork River; in the state of Washington, the Chelan Agreement is both a social judgment of the importance of that state's waters and a forum for community development of subbasin plans; and California's droughts have resulted in unprecedented examples of local cooperation. When entire watersheds are considered, the community-building process can extend into several states—as evidenced by the Great Lakes Charter and the Northwest Power Planning Council. The Missouri River could be the res publica for all basin residents.

The Missouri River Management Project, culminating in the ill-fated Missouri River Assembly, was an ambitious effort to convene state, tribal, and federal, and private sector representatives to discuss their problems and to chart the future of the Missouri, including necessary policy changes and new institutions. As an educational project, Northern Lights' work succeeded in disseminating excellent educational materials to basin decision makers, providing opportunities for Missouri River basin residents to share and debate their different perspectives, and introducing examples of policies and institutions that could be tried in the basin. As a social change project, Northern Lights was less successful. The project was a catalyst for greater recognition of the basin tribes and their stake in Missouri River issues, which led in turn to the formation of Mni Sose, a permanent coalition of basin tribes and tribal representation on the Missouri River Basin Association.

The Missouri River Management Project failed, however, in its efforts to help basin residents agree on solutions to their conflicts. Bold new policies have not been adopted, an innovative river management institution remains elusive, and incremental approaches continue to predominate. The Missouri River Assembly, because it proposed changes in basin decision making, constituted a threat to federal and state agencies and to those groups that have been able to achieve their interests through the existing political system. Albeit representative of more basin interests, the size of the assembly was unwieldy. Ultimately, Northern Lights was unable to secure the direct, personal leadership of one or more governors, senators, or members of Congress whose involvement could have elevated the visibility and impact of the project and the assembly's anticipated work. The institute was also unable to attract local grassroots support that could have provided another basis for political support. For most basin residents, the Missouri River system is an abstraction; local problems of crime, education, and environment appear more real and pressing.

Yet without the Missouri River Assembly, or something like it, water policies will continue to be made with important stakeholders absent. Litigation will persist as the dominate mode of conflict resolution. The basin's destiny will be determined more by federal engineers and Office of Management and Budget analysts than by citizens in local town halls or tribal council chambers.

The dams on the main stem and tributaries of the Missouri River embody the values of their creators. They are also burdened by the values that time and circumstances have grafted upon them. Originally synonymous with progressive notions of employment, mastery of the hazards of nature, regional development, and federal assistance, these Missouri River dams have come to symbolize regional divisiveness, the excesses of federal supremacy, insensitivity to native people, and indifference to ecological systems.

We cannot begin anew in the Missouri River basin. We cannot substitute a new canvas for the one that Colonel Lewis Pick, William Glenn Sloan, and their followers have so significantly altered, but perhaps we can redeem their work and perhaps we can overlay new values, new policies, and new institutions on their canvas. Perhaps we can still paint a portrait of promise, rather than one of peril, for the Missouri River and for all who live in its basin.

Abbreviations

ac	acre of land
ac-ft	acre-foot of water (a quantity of water sufficient to cover one acre of land with one foot of water or 325,851 gallons; an amount sufficient to meet the annual domestic needs of a family of five)
maf	million acre-feet of water
ac-ft/yr	acre-foot of water per year
cfs	cubic-foot per second (a flow rate of 448.8 gallons per minute)
gpm	gallons per minute
gpd	gallons per day
kw	kilowatt
kwh	kilowatt hour
mw	megawatt
mwh	megawatt hour

Glossary

Adjudication: the judicial procedure used to determine the ownership, nature, and extent of water rights. In a general stream adjudication, all the water rights to a river system are joined in the same judicial proceeding.

Appropriation: the legal right established under the prior appropriation doctrine to use water for a beneficial use.

Beneficial use: those uses recognized by statute or common law as appropriate uses of water. Under the prior appropriation doctrine, beneficial uses usually include domestic, agricultural, industrial and municipal, stock watering, and sometimes fish and wildlife uses.

Compact Clause: the authority granted by ARTICLE 1, SECTION 9 of the U.S. Constitution authorizing states to enter into interstate agreements but requiring congressional approval of those agreements.

Consumptive use: the use of water in a manner that prevents it from being returned to the body of water from which it was extracted. The term includes the use of water for domestic, agricultural, municipal, or industrial purposes but can also denote loss of water to evaporation or movement outside the watershed.

Diversion: (1) water withdrawn from its source (lake, river, stream) or (2) the act of withdrawing water from its source.

Equitable apportionment: the legal proceeding before the U.S. Supreme Court in which a body of water (lake or river) is divided among states according to equitable principles that have been established by the Court.

Groundwater: water under the surface of the earth. Groundwater may be tributary if it is hydrologically related to surface water or nontributary if it is found in underground formations without a hydrologic relationship to surface water.

Junior water rights: rights to use water under the prior appropriation doctrine that were established later in time than senior water rights. In times of water shortage on a stream, junior uses must be curtailed ("called") in inverse seniority.

Law of the Union doctrine: the holdings of the U.S. Supreme Court that once an interstate agreement has been approved by Congress, it becomes federal law and is subject to interpretation under federal law.

Nonconsumptive use: the use of water in a manner that allows it to remain in its source or allows it to be returned undiminished in quantity to its source. The term includes the use of water for hydroelectric power generation, navigation, fish and wildlife, and recreational purposes.

Percolating groundwater: groundwater that seeps or filters through underground soils without a defined channel.

Practicably irrigable acreage (PIA): the judicially established method for determining the amount of water to which an Indian reservation is entitled for agricultural purposes under the reserved water rights doctrine. The method is based upon how much land can be used efficiently and economically for agricultural purposes if irrigation water is made available.

Prior appropriation doctrine: the legal system for allocating water that developed in the arid western states. Under the doctrine, a person can establish a water right by putting the water to beneficial use. Water can be transported far away from the source from which it is withdrawn. The most important aspects of the water right are the priority date, the date when the diversion was originally established to allow beneficial use of the water, and the amount of water that can be used.

Public trust doctrine: the judicial doctrine that governments hold important natural resources, such as shorelines and the beds of navigable lakes and streams, in trust for their citizens. Thus, government officials must exercise a high duty of care in the management and protection of these resources. The public trust doctrine has been codified in the constitutions and statutes of some states.

Reserved water rights: water rights impliedly created by Congress when it sets aside land for the creation of Indian reservations, national parks, national forests, or other purposes. When such reservations have been created, Congress has, by implication, reserved sufficient water to serve the primary purposes of the reservation. The priority date of the water right is generally the date the reservation was established. Water reserved for Indian reservations are called Winters rights after the U.S. Supreme Court case of *Winters v. United States*, the 1908 decision that established the doctrine.

Riparian doctrine: the legal system for allocating water that developed in the water-abundant, eastern states. Under this doctrine, property owners next to a waterway (riparians) are entitled to use the water but must return the water to the waterway undiminished in quantity or quality. Some states allow riparian owners to reasonably diminish the quantity and quality of the water.

Senior water rights: rights to use water under the prior appropriation doctrine that were established earlier in time than junior water rights. In times of water shortage on a stream, senior uses can curtail ("call") junior uses in inverse seniority.

Surface water: fresh water on the surface of the earth including lakes, streams, and rivers. The term can also include runoff.

Trust doctrine: the fiduciary obligation of the federal government, as holder of legal title to tribal land and resources, to exercise a high degree of care in the management of those lands and resources for the benefit of a tribe and its members.

Indian Reservations in the Missouri River Basin

In the following material, "trust" indicates lands held by the United States as trustee for the tribe, which may not include all lands composing a reservation. Population figures are from the 1990 U.S. Census, the Bureau of Indian Affairs, or the tribe. All of this material can be found in Bob Anderson, "Indian Reservations and Tribes of the Missouri River Basin," in *Boundaries Carved in Water: The Missouri River Brief Series*, no. 11 (Missoula, Mont.: Northern Lights Institute, June 1988).

Reservation/ Date Established	Tribe	Linguistic Group	Land (acres)	Population
MONTANA				
Blackfeet (1855)	Blackfeet	Algonkian	1,500,000 total 960,000 trust	13,000 enrolled 6,900 on reservation
Crow (1851)	Crow	Siouan	2,300,000 trust	6,900 enrolled 4,724 on reservation
Fort Belknap (1888)	Assiniboine Arapahoe (Gros Ventre)	Siouan Algonkian	654,000 total 622,000 trust	4,300 enrolled 2,338 on reservation
Fort Peck (1871, 1888)	Assiniboine Sioux	Siouan Siouan	2,000,000 total 900,000 trust	8,600 enrolled 5,782 on reservation
Northern Cheyenne (1884)	Northern Cheyenne	Algonkian	445,000 total 439,000 trust	5,100 enrolled 3,542 on reservation
Rocky Boys (1921)	Cree Chippewa	Algonkian Algonkian	108,000 trust	3,600 enrolled 1,882 on reservation
Turtle Mountain (main reservation in N. Dakota, outside basin)	Chippewa	Algonkian	Allotments in Montana	16,100 enrolled 4,746 on N.Dak. reservation
NORTH DAKOTA				
Fort Berthold (1851)	Arikara Hidatsa Mandan	Caddoan Siouan Siouan	981,000 total 419,000 trust	8,000 enrolled 2,999 on reservation
Standing Rock (1868)	Teton Sioux (Hunkpapa, Blackfeet) Middle Sioux (Upper Yanktonais) (Lower Yanktonais)	Siouan Siouan	2,300,000 total 850,000 trust	4,870 on reservation
(Sisseton-Wahpeton under South Dakota)				

Reservation/ Date Established	Tribe	Linguistic Group	Land (acres)	Population
SOUTH DAKOTA				
Crow Creek (1868)	Middle Sioux (Lower Yanktonais)	Siouan	250,000 total 130,000 trust	2,800
Cheyenne River (1889)	Teton Sioux (Miniconjou, Two Kettle, Sans Arcs, Blackfeet)	Siouan	2,800,000 total 1,300,000 trust	9,673 enrolled 5,100 on reservation
Flandreau Santee (1866)	Santee Sioux	Siouan	2,360 total 2,360 trust	600
Lower Brule (1863, 1889)	Teton Sioux	Siouan	230,000 total 133,000 trust	994 on reservation
Pine Ridge (1887)	Teton Sioux	Siouan	1,800,000 total 928,000 trust	18,000 enrolled 11,182 on reservation
Rosebud	Teton Sioux	Siouan	957,000 total 434,441 allotted	8,043 on reservation
Sisseton-Wahpeton (1867)	Santee Sioux	Siouan	108,000 total	7,977 enrolled 3,527 on reservation
(Standing Rock under North Dakota)				
Yankton	Sioux	Siouan	40,000 total 40,000 trust	1,994 on reservation

Reservation/ Date Established	Tribe	Linguistic Group	Land (acres)	Population
NEBRASKA				
(Iowa under Kansas)				
Omaha (1854)	Omaha	Siouan	30,000 total 30,000 trust	3,000 enrolled 2,000 on reservation
(Sac & Fox under Kansas)				
Santee (1866)	Santee Sioux	Siouan	5,800 total 2,200 allotted	425 on reservation
Winnebago (1865)	Winnebago	Siouan	27,000	3,100
KANSAS				
Iowa (1861)	Iowa	Siouan	985 total	588 on or near reservation
Kickapoo (1854)	Kickapoo	Algonkian	10,600 total 7,000 trust	370 on reservation
Sac & Fox (1861)	Sac and Fox	Algonkian		300 enrolled 612 on reservation
Potawatomi (1837)	Potawatomi	Algonkian	77,000 total 77,000 trust	4,000 enrolled 502 on reservation
WYOMING				
Wind River (1863, 1868)	Shoshone Arapahoe	Shoshonean Algonkian	1,800,000 total 1,800,000 trust (approx)	5,676 on reservation

Provisions of the Flood Control Act of 1944

The following are abstracts of the minor features of the Flood Control Act of 1944. A description of the major features of the statute is provided in Chapter 3.

SECTION 3: LOCAL CONTRIBUTION OF LANDS, EASEMENTS, RIGHTS-OF-WAY

By making reference to a 1936 statute (as modified by a 1938 law),[1] Section 3 simply incorporates the provisions of earlier law requiring states or localities to provide the land, easements, and rights-of-way necessary for the corps' construction of dams and reservoirs. These provisions require states and localities to indemnify the United States from damages caused by the construction works. These incorporated provisions also require states and localities to operate the completed works in accordance with regulations issued by the secretary of the army.

SECTION 4: PUBLIC USE OF RESERVOIR FACILITIES

This section of the act gives the chief of engineers broad authority to develop reservoirs for park and recreational purposes. Implicit in this section is Congress's acknowledgment of the primary authority of the corps to regulate activities on reservoirs behind the dams it operates.

The corps can develop and operate such facilities on its own or it can license others to do so. Federal, state, and local agencies have preference to obtain these licenses and can do so for no monetary consideration. Subsequent amendments have authorized licenses to nonprofit organizations for reduced or nominal consideration. Revenues from these license agreements are deposited in the U.S. Treasury as miscellaneous receipts.

This section also establishes a strong policy of public access to the waters of corps-operated reservoirs. The waters are to be open for public use, without charge, and the shores of the reservoirs are to be available for "ready access to and exit from" the water. The application of state fish and game laws to these reservoirs, however, is recognized.

Later amendments to this section[2] have authorized licensees of the corps to cut timber and grow and harvest crops as activities incidental to wildlife management. The present law also establishes criminal liability for unauthorized dumping in a reservoir.

SECTION 11: AUTHORIZATION OF PRELIMINARY EXAMINATIONS

This section of the act simply authorizes preliminary examinations and surveys for flood control, navigation improvement, and runoff and soil-erosion-prevention projects in two dozen states. Some of these investigations were authorized for the states of Minnesota, Missouri, Kansas, and Nebraska.[3]

SECTION 12: ADDITIONAL AUTHORIZATIONS

A total of $962 million was authorized in Section 12 for the construction of the projects contained in the legislation, as well as surveys, investigations, and stabilization projects. The vast majority of this money ($950 million) was an authorization to the Corps of Engineers. This section is not codified.

SECTION 13: AUTHORIZATION OF RUNOFF AND SOIL EROSION CONTROL PROGRAMS

Eleven runoff and soil erosion control projects are authorized by Section 13 of the act (which has not been codified). Only one of these, the Little Sioux River watershed, is within the Missouri River basin (for which $4.3 million was authorized). These projects were also authorized to provide for the "national security" and a postwar public works program, with actual construction to begin once materials and labor became available or when the war ended. The legislature of any concerned state would have to approve the acquisition of land by the federal government for any of these projects. This section also provides for the payment in lieu of taxes of 1 percent of the purchase price or value of any property acquired by the federal government for these projects.

SECTION 14: REAUTHORIZATION OF FUNDS FOR RUNOFF AND SOIL EROSION PROJECTS

The balance of $10 million that had been previously authorized in 1938 for watershed improvement projects was reauthorized under Section 14 of the act. The money, however, was redirected to the projects enumerated in Section 13, with the proviso that no more than 20 percent of the authorization be spent on any one project. This section has not been codified.

SECTION 15: EMERGENCY MEASURES TO RUNOFF AND SOIL EROSION

Section 15 is actually an amendment to the 1938 Flood Control Act,[4] which authorizes the secretary of agriculture to undertake measures to retard runoff and prevent soil erosion in those watersheds in which the Corps of Engineers is constructing flood control or navigation projects.[5] Section 15 adds to this earlier version by authorizing the secretary of agriculture to undertake these runoff and soil erosion control measures on an emergency basis if fire or other natural calamity has suddenly impaired the ground cover in a watershed. The secretary is authorized to spend $100,000 a year (now raised to $300,000) on such emergency measures.

SECTION 10: ADDITIONAL AUTHORIZED PROJECTS

The projects composing the general comprehensive plan for flood control and navigation on the Missouri were not the only projects authorized by the 1944 legislation. In Section 10, specific projects in thirty-eight basins, plus the territory of Hawaii, were also authorized. Ten of these projects were in the Missouri River basin, and the money authorized for these projects totaled almost $18.4 million. A Kansas City flood control project and a project on Cherry Creek in Colorado accounted for $16 million of this total.

These projects were authorized to provide for the "national security" and a postwar public works program. Although only detailed plans were to be developed while World War II continued, actual construction was to begin once materials and labor became available or when the war ended. Upon the recommendation of the chief of engineers and the Federal Power Commission, the secretary of war was given final authority to approve the installation of penstocks in dams for the production of hydroelectric power.

Statement of Principles for the Management of Missouri River Basin Water Resources: Final Proposed Draft, November 20, 1986

PURPOSE

The purpose of this Statement is to establish principles which will allow the Missouri Basin States to cooperatively manage the water resources of the Basin. These principles will allow each state to use its water resources independently but openly and in harmony with the other basin states. These principles will provide a common basis for the states to work cooperatively with the federal government in managing the basin's resources. Honoring these principles will allow our states to manage the waters of the Missouri River Basin. This is not a legally binding agreement, but is instead intended to set forth a statement of principles which the States can currently agree upon and which, if implemented in good faith, could result in resolution of our differences.

PRINCIPLES

To achieve the purpose set forth in this Statement, we subscribe to the following principles and implementing actions.

PRINCIPLE I: SHARING OF INFORMATION

We will share information about current and planned uses of water in the Missouri River Basin, as well as information about significant developments or changes in our states' water laws, policies, and practices.

Implementing Actions

A. On or before July 15, 1987, and every year thereafter, the Missouri Basin States Association (MBSA) will compile and maintain, by state, records of current consumptive use and planned consumptive use of water in the Missouri River Basin based on the best available information provided by each state. The MBSA will report annually these current and planned uses, as well as information about significant developments or changes in state laws or policies. Each state agrees to seek improvements in its reporting system to meet the MBSA system requirements.

B. Each state receiving a permit request or otherwise becoming aware of a proposal for (1) an out of state diversion of Missouri Basin water from a basin state of more than 2,500 acre-feet per year and 3.5 cubic feet per second or (2) any new or increased consumptive use or diversion of basin water greater than 10,000 acre-feet per year and 14 cubic feet per second will notify the MBSA, which in turn will notify each subscribing state. This information exchange is intended to provide information to the Missouri River Basin states on a timely basis so as to facilitate discussion prior to final decision consistent with the laws of the state. These reporting requirements may be adjusted as experience dictates.

PRINCIPLE II: REASONABLE USE OF WATER (KANSAS VERSION)

We will not interfere with the efforts of any basin State to develop a reasonable amount of water for new consumptive uses.

Implementing Actions

A. We recognize that the legal and physical availability of water in the Missouri River and its tributaries allows each state to put additional water to consumptive use. New consumptive uses that are reasonable and in accordance with law should proceed without judicial challenge from any other state.

B. The MBSA will, when approved by the Board of Directors, conduct studies of the environmental and economic costs and benefits of various levels and types of consumptive use. These studies can be utilized in formulating new management principles.

C. Until December 31, 1991, new consumptive uses of water developed by the following states from the Missouri River and its tributaries on or after January 1, 1987, not exceeding the amounts set forth in the following schedule, are deemed to be reasonable by us.

Iowa	300,000 acre-feet per year
Kansas	300,000 acre-feet per year
Missouri	300,000 acre-feet per year
Montana	600,000 acre-feet per year
Nebraska	300,000 acre-feet per year
North Dakota	600,000 acre-feet per year
South Dakota	600,000 acre-feet per year

Option 1. Change all amounts to 600,000.
Option 2. Delete "and its tributaries" and do not change amounts.

The above amounts are not additive from year to year.

D. We recognize that various views exist on the acceptability of out of basin water transfers. Until December 31, 1991, cumulative totals of transfers of Missouri River Basin water out of a basin state not exceeding 10 percent of the amounts set forth in the above schedule should proceed without judicial challenge.

PRINCIPLE II: REASONABLE USE OF WATER (MONTANA VERSION)

We will not interfere with the efforts of any basin State to develop a reasonable amount of water for new consumptive uses.

Implementing Actions

A. We recognize that the legal and physical availability of water in the Missouri River Basin allows each state to put additional water to consumptive use. New consumptive uses of Missouri River water that are reasonable and in accordance with law should proceed without judicial challenge from any other state.

B. During the period January 1, 1987, through December 31, 1989, new consumptive uses of water from the Missouri River that are developed by the following states and do not exceed the amounts set forth in the following schedule are deemed to be reasonable:

Iowa	125,000 acre-feet per year
Kansas	125,000 acre-feet per year
Missouri	125,000 acre-feet per year
Montana	250,000 acre-feet per year
Nebraska	125,000 acre-feet per year
North Dakota	250,000 acre-feet per year
South Dakota	250,000 acre-feet per year

The above amounts are exclusive of any new uses of water resulting from projects constructed after this date and expressly authorized and funded by Congress after 1964.

If prior to December 31, 1989, new consumptive use from the Missouri River in any of the above states reaches 80 percent of the amount set forth in this schedule, the MBSA will, within 180 days, develop a proposed modification to this schedule as needed to provide for anticipated new consumptive use by the above states. This modified schedule will be based on all available information, including that developed in accordance with Principle III. The proposed schedule will, in turn, be submitted to the governors of the signatory states for ratification as an amendment to this principle.

C. On or before December 31, 1989, the MBSA may, on the basis of available information, develop revised levels of new consumptive use from the Missouri River as set forth in Paragraph B. Consumptive use associated with Indian and non-Indian federal reserved water rights will be included in those determinations. (Editor's note: Principle III[C] should be deleted if this paragraph is adopted.)

D. The amounts set forth in Paragraph B are in addition to any Missouri River Basin water awarded to a state under a compact, treaty, or court decree in effect on January 1, 1987. These amounts are also in addition to any Missouri River Basin water awarded to an Indian tribe or federal agency in quantification of its reserved rights, by act of Congress, court decree, executive order, treaty, compact, or other agreement.

PRINCIPLE III: ANTICIPATORY PROBLEM SOLVING

We will work to obtain information and needed analysis for further management policies which will allow us to continue discussions to reach agreement on water resource issues that have the potential to divide us.

Implementing Actions

A. We recognize the adoption of this Statement of Principles has commenced an important and productive dialogue among our States. We also recognize that these principles do not encompass all of the potentially divisive issues that may arise between or among our states. Discussions among our states should continue through senior officials appointed by the Governors to the Board of Directors of the MBSA. When it is deemed necessary or appropriate amendments to this statement may be proposed to the Governors of the basin states.

B. In addition to work required elsewhere in this Statement, during the first five years following the execution of this statement, the states will undertake the following:

1. (a) The quantification of current consumptive and nonconsumptive uses; (b) the development of an improved water accounting system; (c) the development of a simulation model; (d) the establishment of a verifiable hydrologic data base for the Missouri River and its tributaries.

2. The MBSA staff, with policy direction from the MBSA Board of Directors, shall communicate on a continuous basis with agencies of the Federal Government to assure that operation of the mainstem reservoirs can provide for future consumptive uses with a minimum effect on current uses.

3. Develop a means by which states can further benefit from hydroelectric power generation (or revenues therefrom) in the basin.

4. Petition the Congress to authorize the Corps of Engineers to correct or mitigate to the extent possible those channel problems caused by features of the Pick-Sloan Missouri Basin Program as part of the ongoing development and maintenance of the Program.

C. On or before December 31, 1991, the states will develop, on the basis of new information, revised levels of consumptive use for the states as expressed in Principle II. Consumptive use associated with federal reserved and Indian water rights will be included in those determinations.

D. The MBSA may undertake other studies which will further the purpose and principles of this Statement. These studies may be utilized in formulating new management principles.

PRINCIPLE IV: CONFLICT RESOLUTION

We will attempt to resolve water resource conflicts by means other than litigation.

Implementing Actions

A. We believe that informal and formal dispute resolution procedures are preferable alternatives to litigation in resolving conflicts. If disputes or conflicts arise, their resolution should be first attempted through a non-litigative process developed by MBSA or mutually agreed upon by the concerned states.

B. These procedures may be utilized whenever one state has a reasonable belief that one or more states has violated the principles contained in this Statement or threatened any legal right of the complaining state to basin waters. These procedures will also be available to resolve disputes concerning the basin waters which states signatory to this statement, signatory states and other states, or signatory states and federal agencies agree to resolve thereunder.

C. Within one year of the effective date of this Statement, the MBSA will adopt procedures to implement this dispute resolution process.

PRINCIPLE V: THE MISSOURI BASIN STATES ASSOCIATION

The states will utilize the Missouri Basin States Association as a means to implement the principles contained in this document.

Implementing Actions

A. We agree that a reorganized MBSA with procedures to insure all states' interests are protected is necessary. The states will strive to reach consensus on decisions taken to implement this Statement. The Board of Directors of MBSA will consist of one senior official from each state who is appointed by the Governor of that state.

B. To further the implementation of these principles, the Board of Directors will meet at least semi-annually to continue and improve communication among our states; to identify potentially divisive issues; to identify opportunities for mutual cooperation which will benefit the states; to develop plans, principles, or other means to resolve conflicts or to realize opportunities; and to undertake other duties incident to the organization's purpose.

C. An annual report of MBSA programs, activities, and finances will be made available to the Governors, legislatures and congressional delegations of the states.

D. The subscribing states should undertake within one year of the effective date of this Statement the steps necessary to make the organization, finances and programs of MBSA consistent with this Statement.

PRINCIPLE VI: FEDERAL INVOLVEMENT

We will cooperate with, and seek the cooperation of the federal government in managing the basin's water resources.

Implementing Actions

A. We acknowledge that implementation of these principles will be undertaken through cooperation of the federal government. The states will use their best efforts to secure the necessary cooperation of the federal government.

B. The states will seek to ensure all federal actions concerning the Missouri

River and its tributaries are in compliance with applicable state laws, policies, plans and these principles.

C. The states will mutually seek federal funding to assist in implementing the principles contained in this Statement.

RECOGNITION OF RIGHTS

A. This Statement of Principles is not intended to nor does it in fact apportion the waters of the basin among the basin states. Nothing in this Statement shall act to reduce, enlarge, limit or otherwise modify current consumptive use in any of the states.

B. Each Missouri River Basin state reserves and retains all rights and authority to seek, in any state, federal, or other appropriate court or forum, adjudication or protection of its respective rights in and to Basin water resources, in such manner as may now or hereafter be provided by law.

C. No existing interstate water compact, court decree, international treaty or individual state water right is in any way changed or affected by this Statement.

D. This Statement does not affect or diminish the laws of any state, the federal government or other jurisdiction concerning water resources, nor does it affect or govern the reserved rights of any Indian tribe or federal agency to the waters of the Missouri River Basin.

DEFINITIONS

This Statement of Principles is to be interpreted and understood in accordance with the following definitions:

A. "Annual" or "annually" mean the period January 1 to December 31.

B. "Consumptive use" means a volume of surface water and interconnected ground water removed from the Missouri River Basin due to human activities and no longer available for use or storage within the Basin. For purposes of this Statement, evaporation from the mainstem reservoirs is excluded from this definition.

C. "Current consumptive use" means a consumptive use, as recognized by the laws of the respective states, originating or occurring within a state prior to January 1, 1987, regardless of the ultimate place of use.

D. "Diversion" means the act of taking water from a stream or other body of water into a canal, pipeline or other conduit.

E. "Mainstem reservoirs" means the water bodies formed by Fort Peck, Garrison, Oahe, Big Bend, Fort Randall, and Gavins Point dams.

F. "Missouri Basin States Association" or "MBSA" mean that organization established by the ten Missouri River Basin states on September 18, 1981 under the laws of the State of Nebraska.

G. "Missouri River Basin" or "Basin" mean the area within the United States from which surface water runoff is drained by the Missouri River and its tributaries.

H. "Missouri River" or "Mainstem" mean the watercourse of the Missouri River from the confluence of the Gallatin, Jefferson, and Madison Rivers in Montana to its confluence with the Mississippi River.

I. "New consumptive use" means a consumptive use of water originating or

occurring within a state begun on or after January 1987, regardless of the ultimate place of use.

J. "Permit request" means any form being used by a state for an application
to use water.

K. "Planned consumptive use" means any federal, state, local or private
plan to withdraw water from the Missouri River and its tributaries.

L. "States," "Basin states," "subscribing states" or "signatory states" mean
the States of Colorado, Iowa, Kansas, Minnesota, Missouri, Montana, Nebraska,
North Dakota, South Dakota, and Wyoming.

APPROVAL AND EFFECTIVE DATE

This Statement of Principles is signed and subscribed to on the dates specified by
the following Governors:

GOVERNOR
State of Colorado

GOVERNOR
State of Iowa

GOVERNOR
State of Kansas

GOVERNOR
State of Minnesota

GOVERNOR
State of Missouri

GOVERNOR
State of Montana

GOVERNOR
State of Nebraska

GOVERNOR
State of North Dakota

GOVERNOR
State of South Dakota

GOVERNOR
State of Wyoming

Great Lakes Charter: Principles for the Management of Great Lakes Water Resources

FINDINGS

The Governors and Premiers of the Great Lakes States and Provinces jointly find and declare that:

The water resources of the Great Lakes Basin are precious public natural resources, shared and held in trust by the Great Lakes States and Provinces.

The Great Lakes are valuable regional, national and international resources for which the federal governments of the United States and Canada and the International Joint Commission have, in partnership with the States and Provinces, an important, continuing and abiding role and responsibility.

The waters of the Great Lakes are interconnected and part of a single hydrologic system. The multiple uses of these resources for municipal, industrial and agricultural water supply; mining; navigation; hydroelectric power and energy production; recreation; and the maintenance of fish and wildlife and a balanced ecosystem are interdependent.

Studies conducted by the International Joint Commission, the Great Lakes States and Provinces, and other agencies have found that without careful and prudent management, the future development of diversions and consumptive uses of the water resources of the Great Lakes Basin may have significant adverse impacts on the environment, economy, and welfare of the Great Lakes region.

As trustees of the Basin's natural resources, the Great Lakes States and Provinces have a shared duty to protect, conserve, and manage the renewable but finite waters of the Great Lakes Basin for the use, benefit, and enjoyment of all their citizens, including generations yet to come. The most effective means of protecting, conserving and managing the water resources of the Great Lakes is through the joint pursuit of unified and cooperative principles, policies and programs mutually agreed upon, enacted and adhered to by each and every Great Lakes State and Province.

Management of the water resources of the Basin is subject to the jurisdiction, rights and responsibilities of the signatory States and Provinces. Effective management of the water resources of the Great Lakes requires the exercise of such jurisdiction, rights, and responsibilities in the interest of all people of the Great Lakes region, acting in a continuing spirit of comity and mutual cooperation. The Great Lakes States and Provinces reaffirm the mutual rights and obligations of all Basin jurisdictions to use, conserve, and protect Basin water resources, as expressed in the Boundary Waters Treaty of 1909, the Great Lakes Water Quality Agreement of 1978, and the principles of other applicable international agreements.

217

PURPOSE

The purposes of this Charter are to conserve the levels and flows of the Great Lakes and their tributary and connecting waters, to protect and conserve the environmental balance of the Great Lakes Basin ecosystem; to provide for cooperative programs and management of the water resources of the Great Lakes Basin by the signatory States and Provinces; to make secure and protect present developments within the region; and to provide a secure foundation for future investments and development within the region.

PRINCIPLES FOR THE MANAGEMENT OF GREAT LAKES
WATER RESOURCES

In order to achieve the purposes of this Charter, the Governors and Premiers of the Great Lakes States and Provinces agree to the following principles:

Principle I: Integrity of the Great Lakes Basin

The planning and management of the water resources of the Great Lakes Basin should recognize and be founded upon the integrity of the natural resources and ecosystem of the Great Lakes Basin. The water resources of the Basin transcend political boundaries within the Basin and should be recognized and treated as a single hydrologic system. In managing Great Lakes Basin waters, the natural resources and ecosystem of the Basin should be considered as a unified whole.

Principle II: Cooperation among Jurisdictions

The signatory States and Provinces recognize and commit to a spirit of cooperation among local, state, and provincial agencies, the Federal governments of Canada and the United States, and the International Joint Commission in the study, monitoring, planning, and conservation of the water resources of the Great Lakes Basin.

Principle III: Protection of the Water Resources of the Great Lakes

The signatory States and Provinces agree that new or increased diversions and consumptive uses of Great Lakes Basin water resources are of serious concern. In recognition of their shared responsibility to conserve and protect the water resources of the Great Lakes Basin for the use, benefit, and enjoyment of all their citizens, the States and Provinces agree to seek (where necessary) and to implement legislation establishing programs to manage and regulate the diversion and consumptive use of Basin water resources. It is the intent of the signatory states and provinces that diversions of Basin water resources will not be allowed if individually or cumulatively they would have any significant adverse impacts on lake levels, in-basin uses, and the Great Lakes Ecosystem.

Principle IV: Prior Notice and Consultation

It is the intent of the signatory States and Provinces that no Great Lakes State or Province will approve or permit any major new or increased diversion or consumptive use of the water resources of the Great Lakes Basin without notifying and consulting with and seeking the consent and concurrence of all affected Great Lakes States and Provinces.

Principle V: Cooperative Programs and Practices

The Governors and Premiers of the Great Lakes and Provinces commit to pursue the development and maintenance of a common base of data and information regarding the use and management of Basin water resources, to the establishment of systematic arrangements for the exchange of water data and information, to the creation of a Water Resources Management Committee, to the development of a Great Lakes Basin Water Resources Management Program, and to additional and concerted and coordinated research efforts to provide improved information for future water planning and management decisions.

IMPLEMENTATION OF PRINCIPLES

Common Base of Data

The Great Lakes States and Provinces will pursue the development and maintenance of a common base of data and information regarding the use and management of Basin water resources and the establishment of systematic arrangements for the exchange of water data and information. The common base of data will include the following:
    1. Each State and Province will collect and maintain in comparable form data regarding the location, type, and quantities of water use, diversions, and consumptive uses, and information regarding projections of current and future needs.
    2. In order to provide accurate information as a basis for future water resources planning and management, each State and Province will establish and maintain a system for the collection of data on major water uses, diversions, and consumptive uses in the Basin. The States and Provinces, in cooperation with the Federal Governments of Canada and the United States and the International Joint Commission, will seek appropriate vehicles and institutions to assure responsibility for coordinated collation, analysis, and dissemination of data and information.
    3. The Great Lakes States and Provinces will exchange on a regular basis plans, data, and other information on water use, conservation, and development, and will consult with each other in the development of programs and plans to carry out these provisions.

Water Resources Management Committee

A Water Resources Management Committee will be formed, composed of representatives appointed by the Governors and Premiers of each of the Great Lakes States and Provinces. Appropriate agencies of the federal governments, the International Joint Commission, and other interested and expert organizations will be invited to participate in the discussion of the Committee.
    The Committee will be charged with responsibility to identify specific common water data needs; to develop and design a system for the collection and ex-

change of comparable water resources management data; to recommend institutional arrangements to facilitate the exchange and maintenance of such information; and to develop procedures to implement the prior notice and consultation process established in this Charter. The Committee will report its findings to the Governors and Premiers of the Great Lakes States and Provinces within 15 months of the appointment of the Committee.

Consultation Procedures

The principle of prior notice and consultation will apply to any new or increased diversion or consumptive use of the water resources of the Great Lakes Basin which exceeds 5,000,000 gallons (19 million liters) per day average in any 30-day period [7.78 cfs, 463 ac-ft per month, or 5,555 ac-ft/yr].

The consultation process will include the following procedures:

1. The State or Province with responsibility for issuing the approval or permit, after receiving an application for such diversion or consumptive use, will notify the Offices of the Governors and Premiers of the respective Great Lakes States and Provinces, the appropriate water management agencies of the Great Lakes States and Provinces and, where appropriate, the International Joint Commission.

2. The permitting State or Province will solicit and carefully consider the comments and concerns of the other Great Lakes States and Provinces, and where applicable, the International Joint Commission, prior to rendering a decision on an application.

3. Any State or Province which believes itself to be affected may file a written objection to the proposed diversion or consumptive use. Notice of such objection stating the reason therefore will be given to the permitting State or Province and all other Great Lakes States or Provinces.

4. In the event of an objection to a proposed diversion or consumptive use, the permitting State or Province will convene a consultation process of the affected Great Lakes States and Provinces to investigate and consider the issues involved, and to seek and provide mutually agreeable recommendations to the permitting State or Province.

5. The permitting State or Province will carefully consider the concerns and objections expressed by other Great Lakes States and Provinces, and the recommendations of any consultation process convened under this Charter.

6. The permitting State or Province will have lead responsibility for resolution of water management permit issues. The permitting State or Province will notify each affected Great Lakes State or Province of its final decision to issue, issue with conditions, or deny a permit.

The prior notice and consultation process will be formally initiated following the development of procedures by the Water Resources Management Committee and approval of those procedures by the Governors and Premiers. During the interim period prior to approval of formal procedures, any State or Province may voluntarily undertake the notice and consultation procedure as it deems appropriate.

Basin Water Resources Management Program

In order to guide the future development, management, and conservation of the water resources of the Great Lakes Basin, the signatory States and Provinces commit to the development of a cooperative water resources management program for the Great Lakes Basin.

Such a program should include consideration of the following elements:

1. An inventory of the Basin's surface and groundwater resources;
2. An identification and assessment of existing and future demands for diversions, into as well as out of the Basin, withdrawals, and consumptive uses for municipal, domestic, agricultural, manufacturing, mining, navigation, power production, fish and wildlife, and other uses and ecological considerations;
3. The development of cooperative policies and practices to minimize the consumptive use of the Basin's water resources; and
4. Recommended policies to guide the coordinated conservation, development, protection, use, and management of the water resources of the Great Lakes Basin.

Research Program

The Great Lakes States and Provinces recognize the need for and support additional research in the area of flows and lake levels required to protect fisheries and wildlife, a balanced aquatic environment, navigation, important recreational uses, and the assimilative capacity of the Great Lakes system. Through appropriate state, provincial, federal and international agencies and other institutions, the Great Lakes States and Provinces will encourage coordinated and concerted research efforts in these areas, in order to provide improved information for future water planning and management decisions.

PROGRESS TOWARD IMPLEMENTATION

The Governors and Premiers of the Great Lakes States and Provinces commit to the coordinated implementation of this charter. To this end, the Governors and Premiers shall, no less than once per year, review progress toward implementation of this Charter and advise one another on actions taken to carry out the principles of the Charter together with recommendations for further action or improvements to the management of the Great Lakes Basin water resources.

The signatory States and Provinces consider each of the principles and implementing provisions of this Charter to be material and interdependent. The rights of each State and Province under this Charter are mutually dependent upon the good faith performance by each State and Province of their respective commitments and obligations under the Charter.

The following sequence will be adhered to by the Great Lakes States and Provinces in implementing the provisions of this Charter:

1. The Water Resources Management Committee will be appointed by the Governors and Premiers within 60 days of the effective date of this Charter and will submit its recommendations to the Governors and Premiers of the Great Lakes States and Provinces within 15 months of the appointment of the Committee.

2. Upon the signing of the Charter, and concurrent with the activities of the Water Resources Management Committee, the Great Lakes States and Provinces will commence collecting and assembling existing Great Lakes water use data

and information. The water use data collected and assembled by the States and Provinces will include, but not be limited to, the data and information specified under the "Common Base of Data" provisions of the Charter. Copies of the data and information collected and assembled by the States and Provinces will be submitted to the Water Resources Management Committee. The Great Lakes States and Provinces will pursue: the collection of data and information on the use and management of Basin water resources; the establishment of systematic arrangements for the exchange of water data and information on a continuing basis as enabled by existing state and provincial data collection and regulatory programs; and, where necessary, the enactment of water withdrawal registration and diversion and consumptive use management and regulatory programs pursuant to the provisions of the Charter.

3. To assist in the ongoing collection of Great Lakes water use data and information, and in the development of the Basin Water Resources Management Program, States and Provinces will pursue the enactment of legislation where it is needed for the purposes of gathering accurate and comparable information on any new or increased withdrawal of Great Lakes Basin water resources in excess of 100,000 gallons (380,000 liters) [0.3 ac-ft] per day average in any 30-day period.

4. The prior notice and consultation process will be formally initiated following the development of procedures by the Water Resources Management Committee and approval of those procedures by the Governors and Premiers. Any State or Province may voluntarily undertake additional notice and consultation procedures as it deems appropriate. However, the right of any individual State or Province to participate in the prior notice and consultation process, either before or after approval of formal procedures by the Governors and Premiers, is contingent upon its ability to provide accurate and comparable information on water withdrawals in excess of 100,000 gallons (380,000 liters) [0.3 ac-ft] per day average in any 30-day period and its authority to manage water withdrawals involving a total diversion or consumptive use of Great Lakes Basin water resources in excess of 2,000,000 gallons (7,600,000 liters) per day in any 30-day period [6.14 ac-ft per day or 2,244 ac-ft/yr].

5. Development of the Basin Water Resources Management Program will commence upon receipt and formal approval by the Great Lakes Governors and Premiers of the recommendations of the Water Resources Management Committee.

Reservation of Rights

The Great Lakes States and Provinces mutually recognize the rights and standing of all Great Lakes States and Provinces to represent and protect the rights and interests of their respective jurisdictions and citizens in the shared water and other natural resources of the Great Lakes region.

Each Great Lakes State and Province reserves and retains all rights and authority to seek, in any state, provincial, federal, or other appropriate court or forum, adjudication or protection of its rights in and to Basin water resources, in such manner as may now or hereafter be provided by law.

In entering into this Charter, no Great Lakes State or Province shall be deemed to imply its consent to any diversion or consumptive use of Great Lakes Basin water resources now or in the future.

Definitions

For purposes of this Charter:

> Withdrawal means the removal or taking of water from surface or groundwater.
>
> Consumptive use means that portion of water withdrawn or withheld from the Great Lakes Basin and assumed to be lost or otherwise not returned to the Great Lakes Basin due to evaporation, incorporation into products, or other processes.
>
> Diversion means a transfer of water from the Great Lakes Basin into another watershed, or from the watershed of one of the Great Lakes into that of another.
>
> Interbasin diversion means a transfer of water from the Great Lakes Basin into another watershed.
>
> Great Lakes Basin means the watershed of the Great Lakes and the St. Lawrence River upstream from Trois Rivieres, Quebec.
>
> Great Lakes Basin water resources means the Great Lakes and all streams, rivers, lakes, connecting channels, and other bodies of water, including tributary groundwater, within the Great Lakes Basin.
>
> Great Lakes States and Provinces means the States of Illinois, Indiana, Michigan, Minnesota, New York, Ohio, and Wisconsin, the Commonwealth of Pennsylvania, and the Provinces of Ontario and Quebec.
>
> Great Lakes Region means the geographic region comprised of the Great Lakes States and Provinces.

Work Plan of the Missouri River Assembly: As Approved by the Assembly, November 14, 1989, St. Louis, Missouri

PREAMBLE

The Missouri River Assembly is an important convocation of representatives of the three basin sovereigns—the states, Indian tribes, and the federal government—as well as other groups and individuals interested in the management of the Missouri River. The Assembly's purpose is to provide a continuing forum to identify and explore consensual approaches for resolving Missouri River management issues.

The Assembly met in general session for the first time on November 13 and 14, 1989, in St. Louis, Missouri. The Assembly was staffed by the Northern Lights Institute with funding by the Ford Foundation.

At its meeting, the Assembly adopted this work plan as a statement of its activities through the second session of the Assembly scheduled for Spring 1990 in Bismarck, North Dakota. This work plan contains a summary of the critical Missouri River management issues facing the basin and the activities the Assembly will undertake to address these issues.

EXPECTATIONS OF THE ASSEMBLY

Most of the Delegates to the Assembly were interviewed before this meeting of the Assembly to ascertain their expectations of the Assembly. These Delegates identified the following objectives for the Assembly:

1. Through dialogue and listening, gain an understanding of the interests and concerns of the other participants and meet them as individuals;
2. Create a sense of belonging to a river system rather than simply to individual sovereign entities; and
3. Develop a consensus list of basin water-related issues, resolve to address them, and agree on a process for doing so.

Much of the first day was spent sharing perspectives on the Missouri River—both in general sessions and in small groups through face-to-face discussions. These small groups also identified water-related issues and made suggestions for addressing these issues. These issues and suggestions were assimilated by a Work-Plan Drafting Committee. They have been considered, modified, and adopted by the full Assembly meeting on Tuesday morning, November 14th. This document, therefore, is the Work Plan for the Assembly.

SIGNIFICANT ISSUES

The issues identified by the Assembly included the following (but not listed in any priority):

1. *Drought.*   Recent drought conditions have demonstrated the limits of the Missouri River to meet current uses. Drought in the Missouri River Basin has an important effect on the regional and national economy. Sufficient plans need to be developed to operate reservoirs and manage flows during such drought conditions.

2. *Distribution of benefits and impacts of Pick-Sloan to date.*   The implementation of the Pick-Sloan Plan has resulted in upper and lower basin conflicts. There is a need to examine and quantify the benefits, as well as the sacrifices, that resulted from the Pick-Sloan Plan. Such an examination would help people understand the consequences of failing to complete the Pick-Sloan Plan.

3. *Finite resource.*   The Missouri River is a finite resource subject to potentially infinite demand. We must recognize the limits of the resource as we think about management of the river.

4. *Lack of a basin-wide perspective.*   People tend to see the basin narrowly—such as upper or lower basin problems. The need is to develop a more holistic understanding of the basin.

5. *Lack of communication.*   We lack sufficient information about the river, how it is managed, what the trade-off's are, and what the limits of the river are.

6. *Identification of common interests.*   We have not worked hard enough to identify the common interests among the various basin governments and among the citizens represented by those governments. Also, there has been a lack of consensus among the three basin sovereigns—the states, the tribes and the federal agencies—which frustrates the ability of these governments to work with one another.

7. *Lack of implementation of the Pick-Sloan Plan.*   The basin governments have not developed an approach for obtaining the benefits envisioned by the Pick-Sloan Plan. Such an implementation plan would provide new momentum. Basin states remain committed to the concept of "ultimate development" of the basin or equivalent benefits to the basin.

8. *Water quality.*   There has been a failure to appreciate the relationship between water quantity and water quality and between groundwater and surface water.

9. *Water marketing.*   There are uncertainties about the practical and legal ability to market water, as well as the effects of water marketing on the basin. This includes proposals by states or tribes to market water, as well as the exportation of water out-of-basin.

10. *Financing water projects.*   Our basin does not compete successfully for federal funds for water development and other water-related projects.

11. *Indian reserved water rights.*   Indian reserved water rights potentially affect all water uses in the basin.

12. *Flow management plan.*   The basin plan for managing the flows of the river—the Master Manual—has not been recently reviewed nor its implementation monitored annually.

13. *Losses to fish, wildlife and habitat.*   Past and present development and uses of the river have adversely affected fish, wildlife, and associated habitat—especially for certain species which are now threatened or endangered. Some of

these impacts have not yet been mitigated, thus leaving unmet replacement needs.

14. *Water data management.*   Water data are important for developing a shared understanding of the river and its uses. Some of the major water data problems in the basin are: (a) inconsistent data, unavailable data, and lack of common standards for collecting data; and (b) the inability to make forecast of the effects of changed uses of the river.

15. *Missouri-Mississippi flows.*   The relationship of the flows of the Missouri River to those of the Mississippi River is an issue in the basin.

16. *Fish, wildlife and recreational enhancement.*   While enhancement of these uses has been accomplished in some areas, these are generally undeveloped authorized purposes that need reviewing.

SUGGESTED PROCESSES TO ADDRESS THESE ISSUES

1. *Master manual review.*   We support and endorse the current review of the Master Manual as a positive step. This review should address the adequacy of the Master Manual as a drought contingency plan for the mainstem.

2. *Improve communication and public education.*   As first steps toward the improvement of communication and public education:

   a. We request MBSA and the Northern Lights Institute to cosponsor the second meeting of the Assembly. The agenda should include discussions of navigation and utilize simulations and methods, such as role-playing, for understanding basin perspectives.

   b. At future meetings of the Assembly, the impact of Indian reserved water rights, drought, and major changes in water supply or demand should be illustrated by the use of simulations and physical models of the basin.

   c. We request MBSA and the Northern Lights Institute to identify common interests in the basin and present them at the second meeting of the Assembly.

   d. We request MBSA, Northern Lights Institute, and the tribes to develop issue papers for presentation at future meetings of the Assembly on topics including Indian reserved water rights, navigation, and preservation of fish and wildlife habitat.

3. *Continuation of future assemblies.*   An inclusive mechanism needs to exist to encourage communication, education and consensus in the basin. MBSA, Northern Lights, and the tribes should explore the feasibility of continuing Assembly meetings to address individual issues and form a more permanent forum for furthering the mutual interests in the basin.

For additional information, please contact the Missouri River Assembly, c/o the Northern Lights Institute, P.O. Box 1185, Missoula, Montana 59807–8084 ([406] 721-7415)

NOTES

INTRODUCTION

1. 484 U.S. 495 (1988).
2. *Missouri v. Andrews*, 586 F. Supp. 1268 (D. Neb. 1984).
3. *Joplin Missouri Globe*, February 27, 1988.
4. *Omaha World Herald*, February 26, 1988, 12.
5. *South Dakota v. Hazen*, CIV. No. A1-90-097 (D.N.D. order dated May 9, 1990).
6. *South Dakota v. Hazen*, no. 90-1750 (8th Cir. order dated May 17, 1990).
7. No. Cv. 91-26-JDS-BLG (February 3, 1993).
8. *Kansas v. Colorado*, 206 U.S. 46 (1907).
9. *New Jersey v. New York*, 283 U.S. 336 (1930).
10. *Nebraska v. Wyoming*, 325 U.S. 589 (1945).
11. *Colorado v. New Mexico*, 459 U.S. 176 (1982); *Colorado v. New Mexico*, 467 U.S. 310 (1984).
12. Boulder Canyon Project Act of 1928, 43 U.S.C. § 617 (1984), recognized as an apportionment in *Arizona v. California*, 373 U.S. 546 (1963).
13. *Illinois v. Milwaukee*, 406 U.S. 91 (1972).
14. U.S. Constitution, Art. 1, sec. 10.
15. Colorado River Compact, Colorado Revised Statutes Annotated § 37-61-101 (1990), approved by Congress in Public Law no. 70-642, § 13, 45 Stat. 1057, 1059 (1928).
16. See Charles Wilkinson, *American Indians, Time and the Law* (New Haven: Yale University Press, 1987).
17. *Winters v. United States*, 207 U.S. 564 (1908); *Arizona v. California*, 376 U.S. 340 (1964).
18. E.g., the Clean Water Act Amendments § 518, 33 U.S.C. § 1377 (1987).
19. Tribes are not the only parties that have been left out of these deliberations. Paradoxically, South Dakota was not even allowed by the federal district court to become a party to the *Missouri v. Andrews* litigation, which, in essence, was a challenge of South Dakota's ability to sell water to the ETSI consortium.

CHAPTER ONE: THE ORIGINAL HIGHWAY WEST

1. Montana, North Dakota, South Dakota, Nebraska, Iowa, Kansas, and Missouri are the main stem states.
2. Colorado, Minnesota, and Wyoming.
3. Walter P. Webb, *The Great Plains* (New York: Grosset and Dunlap, 1931), 3.
4. See generally, Mark D. O'Keefe et al., *Boundaries Carved in Water: An Analysis of River and Water Management in the Upper Missouri Basin* (Missoula, Mont.: Northern Lights Institute, 1986), 2–5.
5. President's Water Resources Policy Commission, *Ten Rivers in America's Future* (1950), 166.

6. Ibid., 168.

7. U.S. Geological Survey, *National Water Summary 1985* (1986), 506.

8. Missouri River Basin Commission, *Missouri River Basin Water Resources Management Plan* (May 1980), 26.

9. Water is also imported from the St. Mary's River (Hudson Bay drainage) into the Milk River in Montana.

10. Water is diverted from the Big Hole River to Butte, Montana, in the Columbia River drainage and from the Little Sac River near Springfield, Missouri.

11. John Guhin, "The Law of the Missouri," *South Dakota Law Review* 30 (1985): 346, 354–55.

12. President's Water Resources Policy Commission, *Ten Rivers,* 172.

13. Act of December 22, 1944, Public Law no. 78-534, 58 Stat. 887 (codified in scattered sections of 16 U.S.C., 33 U.S.C. and 43 U.S.C.). Not part of Pick-Sloan, Canyon Ferry (near Helena, Montana) is the seventh main stem dam.

14. U.S. Army Corps of Engineers, Missouri River Division, *1987–1988 Annual Operating Plan* (January 1988), plate 11.

15. See Missouri Basin States Association, *Missouri River Basin Hydrology Final Report* (May 1983). This report sets forth the water accounting system developed by the Missouri River Basin Commission and the Missouri Basin States Association. Because of the scale of development that has been undertaken on the Missouri, the needs for water data and the means of satisfying those needs have also been ambitious. In the 1940s, for instance, the Corps of Engineers started construction of a miniature reservoir operation model for the entire Mississippi and Missouri system. With the labor of prisoners of war, work was started near Jackson, Mississippi, on a 4,500- by 3,500-foot model, covering about 200 acres. The model, however, was never completed. See Committee on Flood Control, H.R. Rep. no. 1309, 78th Cong., 2d sess. (March 29, 1944), reported in *U.S. Code Congressional Service* (1944), 1349.

16. This observation does not ignore the uneven distribution of water resources throughout the basin. Without a dam and conveyance system, reasonably high flows do little good for upper basin farmers.

17. Missouri Basin States Association, *Missouri River Basin,* 1–8.

CHAPTER TWO: WE WHO LIVE BESIDE THE RIVER

1. See, e.g., Arthur Maass, *Muddy Waters: The Army Engineers and the Nation's Rivers* (New York: De Capo Press, 1974); Barbara T. Andrews and Marie Sansone, *Who Runs the Rivers? Dams and Decisions in the New West* (Stanford, Calif.: Stanford Environmental Society, 1983).

2. U.S. Department of Commerce, Bureau of the Census, *Statistical Abstract of the United States 1992,* table 26.

3. Defined by the U.S. Bureau of Census as the gross value of goods and services attributable to labor and property located in each state.

4. *Statistical Abstract,* table 701.

5. Ibid., table 723.

6. U.S. Department of Commerce, Bureau of Census, *1987 Census of Agriculture,* vol. 1.

7. David Getches, *Water Law in a Nutshell* (St. Paul, Minn.: West Publishing Company, 1984), 78–82.

8. Ibid., 52–53.

9. Information for these state surveys came from a variety of sources: Robert E.

Beck, ed., *Water & Water Rights* (Charlottesville, Va.: Michie Company, 1991), vol. 6; U.S. Geological Survey, *National Water Summary 1985* (1986); Mark D. O'Keefe et al., *Boundaries Carved in Water: An Analysis of River and Water Management in the Upper Missouri Basin* (Missoula, Mont.: Northern Lights Institute, 1986); Larry Morandi, *Water Allocation Capacity: A Description of State Planning and Management Authority* (Denver: National Conference of State Legislature, 1986); Neal R. Peirce and Jerry Hagstrom, *The Book of America: Inside Fifty States Today* (New York: Warner Books, 1984); Missouri Basin States Association, "Proceedings: Missouri River Basin State Water Resources Planning Seminar" (January 1983).

10. *Montana Coalition for Stream Access v. Curran*, 682 P.2d 163 (Mont. 1984); *Montana Coalition for Stream Access v. Hildreth*, 684 P.2d 1088 (Mont. 1984).

11. Montana Code Annotated § 85-2-101 et seq. (1993).

12. Peirce and Hagstrom, *The Book of America*, 555.

13. Ibid., 560.

14. Minnesota Statutes ch. 105; Minnesota Rules 6115.0600 et seq.

15. Minnesota Environmental Quality Board, *Protecting Minnesota's Waters: An Agenda for Action in the 1987–1989 Biennium* (1987).

16. 1985 Minnesota Laws chaps. 110B, 112, 473.

17. S.F. 163, 1985 Iowa Acts.

18. Iowa Department of Water, Air and Water Management, *The Iowa State Water Plan* (January 1985), 31.

19. See generally, Nebraska Revised Statutes ch. 46.

20. Leg. Bill 1106 (Neb. 1984).

21. Leg. Bill 1058 (Neb. 1984).

22. Leg. Bill 705 (Neb. 1985).

23. Kansas Statutes Annotated §§ 82a-701 to -732 (1987).

24. Ibid. at § 82a-903.

25. U.S. Statutes, art. 4, 1 Stat. 52 (1789).

26. 5 Missouri Revised Statutes § 5968.

27. Jerry Vineyard, "Water Planning in Missouri," State Water Resources Planning Seminar Proceedings (November 1, 1983), 34, 38.

28. Missouri Revised Statutes §§ 256.500 to -.410.

29. H.B. 1470 (Mo. 1986).

30. Vineyard, "Water Planning in Missouri," 36.

31. See generally, A. M. Gibson, *The American Indian* (Lexington, Mass.: D. C. Heath, 1980).

32. Ibid., 123.

33. Ibid., 353–54.

34. 24 Stat. 388.

35. Gibson, *American Indian*, 506.

36. 25 U.S.C. §§ 461 to 479 (1988).

37. See generally, Bob Anderson, "Indian Reservations and Tribes of the Missouri River Basin," in *Boundaries Carved in Water: The Missouri River Brief Series*, no. 11 (Missoula, Mont.: Northern Lights Institute, June 1988).

38. Information adapted from Anderson, "Indian Reservations."

39. See generally, American Indian Lawyer Training Program, *Indian Tribes as Sovereign Governments* (Oakland, Calif., 1988); Charles Wilkinson, *American Indians, Time and the Law* (New Haven: Yale University Press, 1987).

40. Karen Lewotsky, "Tribal Sovereignty," in *Boundaries Carved in Water: The Missouri River Brief Series*, no. 9 (Missoula, Mont.: Northern Lights Institute, April 1988).

41. U.S. Constitution, Art 1, § 8, cl. 3; Art. 2, § 2, cl. 2.

42. *Johnson v. M'Intosh,* 21 U.S. 543 (1823); *Cherokee Nation v. Georgia,* 30 U.S. 1 (1831); *Worcester v. Georgia,* 31 U.S. 515 (1832).

43. Lewotsky, "Tribal Sovereignty," 3.

44. Ibid., 4.

45. William C. Canby, Jr., *American Indian Law* (St. Paul, Minn.: West Publishing Company, 1981), 21.

46. 25 U.S.C. §§ 461 to 479 (1988).

47. H.R. Con. Res. 108, 83d Cong., 1st sess., 67 Stat. B132 (1953).

48. C. Wilkinson and E. Biggs, "The Evolution of the Termination Policy," *American Indian Law Review* 5 (1977): 139, 151.

49. 358 U.S. 217 (1959).

50. Lewotsky, "Tribal Sovereignty," 6.

51. 411 U.S. 164 (1973).

52. Ibid., 172.

53. Canby, *American Indian Law,* 66.

54. 207 U.S. 564 (1908).

55. Montana Code Annotated § 85-20-201 (1993).

56. Ibid., § 85-20-202.

57. *In re General Adjudication of All Rights to Use Water in the Big Horn System and All Other Sources,* 753 P.2d 76 (Wyoming 1988).

58. *Wyoming v. United States,* 492 U.S. 406 (1989).

59. John E. Thorson, "Resolving Conflicts through Intergovernmental Agreements: The Pros and Cons of Negotiated Settlements," in *Indian Water 1985* (Oakland, Calif.: American Indian Lawyer Training Program/American Indian Resources Institute, 1986), 25, 27.

60. Missouri Basin States Association, *Missouri Basin River Hydrology Final Report* (May 1983), 1–8.

61. See references cited in note 1 of this chapter.

62. See Chapters 3 and 4 for a discussion of the Flood Control Act of 1944 and the Pick-Sloan Plan.

63. Act of August 4, 1977, Public Law. 95-91, § 302, 91 Stat. 578.

64. Western Area Power Administration, *1992 Annual Report* (1992).

65. Ibid.

66. Ibid.

CHAPTER THREE: THE CONSERVATION ERA

1. Act of December 22, 1944, Public Law no. 78-534, 58 Stat. 887 (codified in scattered sections of 16 U.S.C., 33 U.S.C., and 43 U.S.C.).

2. See generally, Marian E. Ridgeway, *The Missouri Basin's Pick-Sloan Plan: A Case Study in Congressional Policy Determination* (Urbana: University of Illinois Press, 1955), 17–46; this book is the definitive treatment of the development of the Flood Control Act of 1944 and the Pick-Sloan Plan.

3. Act of May 20, 1862, ch. 75, 12 Stat. 392.

4. Act of March 3, 1877, ch. 107, 19 Stat. 377.

5. Act of June 17, 1902, ch. 1093, 32 Stat. 388 (codified in scattered portions of 43 U.S.C.).

6. Samuel P. Hays, *Conservation and the Gospel of Efficiency: The Progressive Conservation Movement* (Cambridge, Mass.: Harvard University Press, 1959), 5.

7. Ludwik A. Teclaff, *The River Basin in History and Law* (The Hague: Martinus Nijhoff, 1967), 114.

8. Hays, *Conservation and the Gospel of Efficiency,* 2–3.

9. Mark D. O'Keefe et al., *Boundaries Carved in Water: An Analysis of River and Water Management in the Upper Missouri Basin* (Missoula, Mont.: Northern Lights Institute, 1986), 10.

10. Veto message, H.R. 15444, 60th Cong., 1st sess., *Congressional Record* 4698 (April 13, 1906).

11. Act of June 10, 1920, ch. 285, 41 Stat. 1063 (codified at 16 U.S.C. §§ 791a-828c [1988]).

12. Ridgeway, *Missouri Basin's Pick-Sloan Plan,* 29.

13. Many people, including Senator George Norris of Nebraska, feared Muscle Shoals would be auctioned off to Henry Ford or American Cyanamid, giving them control of the entire waterpower system of the Tennessee (ibid., 31).

14. Act of May 18, 1933, ch. 32, 48 Stat. 58 (codified at 16 U.S.C. §§ 831–831dd [1988]).

15. Ridgeway, *Missouri Basin's Pick-Sloan Plan,* 32.

16. Address by President Franklin D. Roosevelt (April 10, 1932).

17. O'Keefe et al., *Boundaries Carved in Water,* 12.

18. Act of August 31, 1935, 49 Stat. 1028, 1034.

19. H.R. 11958, 74th Cong., 2d sess. (1936) (Rep. Burdick).

20. S. Rosenman, ed., *The Public Papers and Addresses of Franklin D. Roosevelt* (New York: Random House, 1938), 33.

21. U.S. National Resources Planning Board, *Development of Resources and Stabilization of Employment in the United States,* H.R. Doc. 142, 77th Cong., 1st sess. (1941), 227–29.

22. Missouri Valley Regional Planning Commission, *Report for 1942 on the Missouri Valley* (1942), 13.

23. S. Bill 2089, 78th Cong., 2d sess. (1944).

24. Ridgeway, *Missouri Basin's Pick-Sloan Plan,* 95.

25. Ibid.

26. Miles City (Montana) *Star,* September 3, 1944.

27. S. Bill 555 and H.R. 2203, 79th Cong., 1st. sess. (1945).

28. Library of Congress, Legislative Reference Service, *Missouri Valley Authority: Background and Analysis of Proposal, S. 555, 79th Cong.* (Washington, D.C., 1946), 40–72.

29. Ridgeway, *Missouri Basin's Pick-Sloan Plan,* 280. See Ridgeway's more general discussion of the interests favoring and opposing the MVA at 250–81.

30. Rufus Terral, *The Missouri Valley: Land of Drought, Flood, and Promise* (New Haven: Yale University Press, 1947), 230.

31. Ridgeway, *Missouri Basin's Pick-Sloan Plan,* 50–51.

32. S. Doc. No. 247, 78th Cong., 2d sess. (1944).

33. Act of January 21, 1927, ch. 47, 44 Stat. 1010, 1013, adopting H.R. Doc. No. 1120, 60th Cong. 2d sess. (1908).

34. H.R. Doc. No. 308, 69th Cong., 1st sess., as enacted into law by the Rivers and Harbors Act of January 21, 1927, and Flood Control Act of May 15, 1928; H.R. Doc. No. 238, 73d Cong., 2d sess. (1934).

35. Ibid., 6.

36. 78th Cong., 2d sess.

37. H.R. Doc. No. 214, 78th Cong., 2d sess. (1944).

38. "Flood-Control Plans and New Projects: Hearings on H.R. 4485 before the Commission on Flood Control," House of Representatives, 78th Cong., 1st sess. (1943), 17 (statement of Commissioner Harry Bashore).

39. Act of December 22, 1944, ch. 665, § 1, 58 Stat. 887 (codified at 33 U.S.C. § 701-1 [1986]).

40. Ibid.

41. Ibid. (emphasis added).

42. "Affected State or States" is defined as "those in which the works or any part thereof are proposed to be located; those which in whole or part are both within the drainage basin involved and situated in a State lying wholly or in part west of the ninety-eighth meridian; and such of those [States] which are east of the ninety-eighth meridian as, in the judgment of the Chief of Engineers, will be substantially affected" (ibid.).

43. Act of December 22, 1944, ch. 655, § 1, 58 Stat. 887 (codified at 33 U.S.C. § 701-1 [1986]).

44. Ibid.

45. Act of December 22, 1944, ch. 655, § 2, 58 Stat. 889 (codified at 33 U.S.C. § 701a-1 [1986]).

46. Ibid.

47. 91 Stat. 565, 578 (1977). See *United States v. Northeast Texas Elec. Co-op, Inc.*, 693 F.2d 392 (1982).

48. Act of December 22, 1944, ch. 655, § 5, 58 Stat. 890 (codified at 33 U.S.C. § 825s [1986]).

49. This provision has been determined to be too vague to provide guidance in evaluating the decisions of the secretary. *Santa Clara v. Andrus*, 572 F.2d 660 (9th Cir. 1978), cert. denied, 439 U.S. 859 (1979).

50. 484 U.S. 495 (1988).

51. Ibid.

52. Act of December 22, 1944, ch. 655, § 8, 58 Stat. 891 (codified at 43 U.S.C. § 390 [1986]).

CHAPTER FOUR: IMPLEMENTATION OF THE
PICK-SLOAN PLAN

1. U.S. Army Corps of Engineers, Missouri River Division, *1987–1988 Annual Operating Plan* (January 1988), 67.

2. Western Area Power Administration, *1992 Annual Report* (1992).

3. U.S. Army Corps of Engineers, Missouri River Division, *1992–1993 Annual Operating Plan* (December 1992), 90.

4. Magedanz, "Historical Perspectives on the Pick-Sloan Plan," *Public Affairs* 97 (April 1988): 5.

5. U.S. Army Corps of Engineers, Missouri River Division, *1992–1993 Annual Operating Plan*, 71.

6. Act of August 14, 1964, 78 Stat. 446.

7. M. Lawson, *Dammed Indians*, (Norman: University of Oklahoma Press, 1982), xiv.

8. M. Lawson, "Pick-Sloan and the Tribes," in *Boundaries Carved in Water: The Missouri Brief Series*, no. 10 (Missoula, Mont.: Northern Lights Institute, April 1988).

9. See also Robert Cummings, "Memorandum for Fort Berthold Tribes" (Albuquerque, N.Mex., 1986).

10. *Arizona Republic*, August 13, 1990, B-1, col. 1.

11. Larry W. Hess and J. Schmulbach, "The Missouri River: The Great

Plains' Thread of Life," in *Boundaries Carved in Water: The Missouri River Brief Series*, no. 16 (Missoula, Mont.: Northern Lights Institute, April 1991), 3.

12. Ibid., 5.

13. Ibid., 6.

14. Ibid., 8–9.

15. 458 U.S. 941 (1982).

16. In 1974, the Wyoming legislature had authorized ETSI to use up to 200,000 ac-ft/yr of water from the Madison formation, which also underlies portions of South Dakota, for a 1,700-mile coal slurry pipeline originating in Campbell County, Wyoming.

17. Actually, South Dakota arranged to purchase the water from the Bureau of Reclamation under a renewable five-year contract at $30 per acre-foot.

18. *Yankton Press-Dakotan*, October 30, 1981.

19. Hastings (Nebraska) *Tribune*, September 30, 1981, 24.

20. Emporia (Kansas) *Gazette*, November 13, 1981 (quoting Brig. Gen. Mark J. Sisinyak, Omaha Division Engineer).

21. Randy Moody, manager of business development for SCNO Terminal Corporation (formerly the Sioux City–New Orleans Barge Line), *Yankton Press-Dakotan*, October 2, 1981.

22. *Argus Leader*, October 15, 1981, 3D (statement of Dennis Ickes, tribal lawyer; South Dakota responded that reserved rights are limited to the Indian reservation).

23. *Midland News*, October 28, 1981.

24. *Sioux City Journal*, October 2, 1981.

25. *World Herald*, November 6, 1981. The commission also indicated that "past experience has indicated few serious attempts to make Missouri River management decisions in consideration of all the impacts."

26. "When we have some 7 or 8 million acre-feet of water that flows annually out of the state, it places us in a very poor position to criticize South Dakota for taking 50,000 acre-feet of that water annually, only 15,000 acre-feet of which is to be used to transport coal and the balance of which is to go to help the communities in western South Dakota that are very short of water" (*Omaha World Herald*, December 17, 1981).

27. Upper Midwest Report, September–October 1981. The *Sioux City Journal* responded: "For Janklow to assert that South Dakota 'sacrificed' half a million acres of 'prime' farmland is just not so. In the first place, it was not sacrificed; the owners were paid well for that land. Secondly, it was not prime farmland; rolling grasslands and timber bottoms, yes, but no great agricultural loss. There seems to be enough selfishness to go all the way up and down the Missouri River. . . . It calls for a system-wide approach" (*Sioux City Journal*, November 4, 1981).

28. ETSI *Pipeline Project v. Missouri*, 484 U.S. 495 (1988).

29. *South Dakota v. Nebraska*, no. 103 Original (filed August 16, 1985).

30. *South Dakota v. Kansas City Southern Industries*, 880 F.2d 40 (8th Cir. 1989), cert. denied, 493 U.S. 1023 (1990); ETSI *Pipeline Project v. Burlington Northern, Inc.*, no. B-84-979CA (E.D. Texas).

31. Bill Crews, Missouri River Coordinator for the state of Iowa, feared that South Dakota and other upper basin states would "nickel and dime us to a dry river" (*New York Times*, October 2, 1981).

32. In September 1981, a conference of Colorado government and industry leaders passed a resolution indicating that the importation of Columbia or Mis-

souri River water would be necessary to achieve energy independence (*Umaha World Herald*, September 21, 1981).

33. *Sioux City Journal*, November 11, 1981.

34. High Plains Associates, *Six-State High Plains–Ogallala Aquifer Regional Resources Study* (Austin, Tex., March 1982).

35. Congress was also concerned about the economic impacts of oil and gas depletion in the region.

36. To meet Nebraska's needs alone, a $10-billion alternative was studied. It would have required pumping water 2,500 feet in elevation from Fort Randall by canal into the central and southwestern part of the state. It would have diverted 8,000 to 9,000 cfs from the river, or 25–30 percent of the flow passing Omaha, and would have meant the end of navigation on the lower reaches of the river. The cost was estimated at $350 per ac-ft (of which $100 was energy costs) at a time when farmers could afford to pay only $60–$100 per ac-ft (*New York Times*, October 2, 1981).

37. H. O. Banks, "Future Water Demands in the United States," in *The Interbasin Transfer of Water . . . The Great Lakes Connection* (Milwaukee: Wisconsin Coastal Management Council, 1982), 57.

38. Ibid.

39. U.S. Army Corps of Engineers, Missouri River Division (November 13, 1986).

40. This consensus-building process is described in M. Salkoff and F. Blechman, *Mediation among States in the Missouri River Basin 1984–87* (St. Louis: Conflict Clinic, 1988).

41. Western States Water Council, *Indian Water Rights in the West*, study prepared for the Western Governors' Association (Salt Lake City, 1984).

42. Montana Code Annotated § 85-20-201 (1993).

43. *Wyoming v. United States*, 492 U.S. 406 (1989).

44. Montana Code Annotated § 85-20-301 (1993).

45. G. D. Weatherford and F. Brown, eds., *New Courses for the Colorado* (Albuquerque: University of New Mexico Press, 1986), 18.

46. Participants at the 1988 Symposium on the Future of the Missouri River sponsored by the Northern Lights Institute.

47. Western Area Power Administration, *1992 Annual Report, Statistical Appendix* (Golden, Colo., 1992), 65.

48. *South Dakota v. Hazen*, CIV. No. A1-90-097 (D.N.D. 1990); *South Dakota v. Hazen*, 914 F.2d 147 (8th Cir. 1990).

49. U.S. Army Corps of Engineers, Missouri River Division, "Draft Phase 1 Report for the Review and Update of the Missouri River Main Stem Master Water Control Manual" (Omaha, May 1990).

50. J. Ferrell, "Corps Assesses Flood Damage," 2–3 (undated).

51. None of the four federally maintained levees was damaged, but damages were sustained by 25 of 75 federally constructed but locally maintained levees, 110 of 128 levees built and maintained by local levee districts, and all 884 private levees (ibid., 4).

52. Norman Rosenberg, "Climate Change: A Primer; Part 2," *Resources* 87 (Spring 1987): 8, 13.

53. Ibid.

54. Prior to the floods of 1993, estimates of avoided lower basin flood losses ranged from $1.7 billion to $2.3 billion (see U.S. Army Corps of Engineers, Missouri River Division, *1987–1988 Annual Operating Plan* [Omaha, January 1988],

67). See also Magedanz, "Historical Perspectives on the Pick-Sloan Plan," *Public Affairs* 97 (April 1988), 5.

55. A nine-foot-deep, 300-foot-wide navigation channel has been dredged from Sioux City to the mouth of the river.

56. See Cummings, "Memorandum for Fort Berthold Tribes"; see also Lawson, *Dammed Indians*.

57. Bill Crews, "A Downstream Perspective," in *Boundaries Carved in Water: The Missouri River Brief Series*, no. 12 (Missoula, Mont.: Northern Lights Institute, June 1988), 4.

58. As would be expected, lower basin observers saw things differently: "It strikes us that South Dakota has received as many flood control benefits as its downstream neighbors, so that 'sacrifice' talk is specious. In addition, South Dakota and its citizens received the financial benefits of millions of dollars of federal monies spent in the state during the score of years it took to build the entire Missouri River impoundment system in South Dakota. In further addition, these impoundments have given South Dakota a recreational potential that is the wonder and envy of the nation. What kind of 'sacrifice' is this? No, South Dakota has been paid off for the Missouri impoundments" (*Sioux City Journal*, October 3, 1981).

59. For example, leaders in Sioux City, Iowa, have been concerned that after the corps shortened and straightened the river to improve navigation, the river now runs six feet lower and is estimated to lose another one to three feet by the year 2000 (*Des Moines Register*, September 10, 1981).

60. One lower basin leader commented on the states' inability to cooperate to their mutual advantage: "The Missouri River Basin has not experienced its legitimate share of growth, opportunity and share of federal investments. The states and their congressional representatives should develop a coalition to begin to address the issues of continued growth lag, disparity of defense employment and federal procurement" (D. Meisner, Executive Director, Siouxland Interstate Metropolitan Planning Council, quoted in *Omaha World-Herald*, December 17, 1981).

61. One study indicated that only three of eighteen resource regions in the United States would face water shortages by the year 2000: the Lower Colorado Region below Lee's Ferry in Arizona; the Great Basin Region located in Nevada and western Utah; and the Rio Grande Region in southern Colorado, central New Mexico, and western Texas (U.S. Water Resources Council, *The Nation's Water Resources 1975–2000: Second National Water Assessment*, Vol. 4, *Missouri Region* (Washington, D.C., December 1978).

CHAPTER FIVE: NATIONALIZATION OF THE MISSOURI RIVER

1. John Ferrell, "Missouri Basin Institutions" (June 1990), unpublished outline.

2. Statement of Gov. M. Q. Sharpe (S.D.), "Proceedings of the Missouri River States Committee" 2–3 (May 21, 1943).

3. Marian Ridgeway, *The Missouri Basin's Pick-Sloan Plan: A Case in Congressional Policy Determination* (Urbana: University of Illinois Press, 1955), 173.

4. Council of State Governments, *Missouri River Basin Compact*, 1952 draft and revised draft (Chicago, January 1953). See Chapter 6 for a discussion of this proposed interstate compact.

5. Ridgeway, *Missouri Basin's Pick-Sloan Plan*, 281.

6. Missouri River Inter-Agency Commission, "The Role of the Missouri Basin Inter-Agency Committee in the Missouri Basin Resources Development" (1950).

7. Frank Trelease, "A Federal-State Compact for Missouri Basin Development," *Wyoming Law Review* 7 (1953): 161.

8. Trelease identified the following principal water resource activities: land reclamation, aid to navigation, flood control, hydroelectric power development, soil conservation, and watershed treatment. Secondary activities included municipal and industrial water supply, control of pollution, fish and wildlife resources, public lands, national forests, national parks, mineral resources, rural electrification, research and investigation, public education, "rehabilitation" of Indians, and water data collection (ibid., 162, 164).

9. Section 1 of the act requires the Corps of Engineers to submit its reports to the Department of Interior if they relate to waters arising west of the ninety-seventh meridian. Similarly, bureau reports must be submitted to the secretary of the army.

10. Trelease, "A Federal-State Compact," 164. He adds, "Under present procedures the separate agencies present their separate programs to different committees, and no all-agency multiple purpose plan is presented to guide Congress in making its selection of the projects best designed and most urgently needed for optimum use and control of the resources" (166).

11. Ibid., 177.

12. C. McKinley, "The Valley Authority and Its Alternatives," *American Political Science Review* 44 (September 1950): 629.

13. Ridgeway, *Missouri Basin's Pick-Sloan Plan*, 282.

14. For an evaluation of the Missouri River Basin Commission, see S. Miller, "Multi-State River Basin Organizations: The Relationship of Structure, Function and Decision Process" (Master's thesis, University of Nebraska, 1985), 28–35.

15. A proposal had been made in 1944 to create a Missouri River Commission (S. 1812, 78th Cong., 2d sess. [1944] [Sen. Clark]). Patterned after the old Mississippi River Commission, the bill would have given to the corps "virtually complete control over dam and reservoir management for the whole nation and would [have] remove[d] from the Bureau of Reclamation any authority whatsoever over the Missouri River Basin except, presumably, over irrigation" (Ridgeway, *Missouri Basin's Pick-Sloan Plan*, 89).

16. Executive Order no. 11658; reprinted in 1972 U.S. Code, Congressional and Administrative News 5524 (1972).

17. Act of July 22, 1965, 79 Stat. 244 (codified in scattered sections of 42 U.S.C.).

18. Ibid., § 201(b).

19. Ibid.

20. Missouri River Basin Commission, *Fiscal Year 1981 Annual and Final Report* (Omaha, 1981), 32.

21. Ibid., 34–35.

22. Mark D. O'Keefe et al., *Boundaries Carved in Water: An Analysis of River and Water Management in the Upper Missouri Basin* (Missoula, Mont.: Northern Lights Institute, 1986), 18.

23. Miller, "Multi-State River Basin Organizations," 34.

24. Executive Order no. 12319, 46 Federal Reg. 45,591 (1981).

25. *Omaha Morning World Herald*, October 24, 1981.

26. Missouri Basin States Association, *Annual Report, Fiscal Year 1982* (Omaha, 1982), 3.

27. Letter of Gov. John Carlin (July 15, 1985).

28. Ibid.

29. Ibid. This carefully worded sentence barely contained the governor's apparent sympathy for an interim allocation to each state. In a separate letter to Governor Janklow of South Dakota, Carlin was even more explicit: "I am of the belief that each state has a clear right to manage the river within reasonable limits to achieve what it considers development in its own best interest" (letter of Gov. Carlin to Gov. Janklow [July 15, 1985]).

30. Letter of Gov. Carlin to Gov. Janklow (November 25, 1985).

31. "Although the statement of principle contains room for interpretation, it acknowledges a basic right to permit the use of reasonable amounts of Missouri River water in accordance with state law" (letter of Gov. Janklow to Gov. Carlin [January 6, 1986]).

32. Ibid.

33. Letter of governors Carlin, Branstad, Ashcroft, and Kerrey to Gov. Janklow (January 15, 1986).

34. The actual dates of the 1986 negotiating sessions were April 24 and 25 (St. Paul); May 22 and 23 (Minneapolis); June 12 and 13 (Denver); July 31 and August 1 (Denver); September 18 and 19 (Denver); November 13 (Billings); and December 17 (Denver). The minutes of these meetings have been used for the analysis presented in the text.

35. "Statement of Principles for Management of Missouri River Basin Water Resources," draft of November 20, 1986; see Appendix 5.

36. For other analyses of the reasons for the failure of these negotiations, see Larry Morandi, *Missouri Basin Water: Negotiating an Allocation Accord* (Denver: National Conference of State Legislatures, June 1987); M. Salkoff and F. Blechman, *Mediation among States in the Missouri River Basin 1984–87* (St. Louis: Conflict Clinic, 1988).

37. See Missouri Basin States Association, *A Review of the Missouri River Main Stem System Operations* (Omaha, 1988).

38. Daniel J. Elazar, "The Shaping of Intergovernmental Relations in the Twentieth Century," *Annals of the American Academy of Political and Social Science* 359 (May 1965): 10.

39. Ibid., 16.

40. Ibid., 18.

41. Ibid., 18–19.

42. *Annals of the American Academy of Political and Social Science* 270 (1940): 1.

43. David Fellman, "The Future of Grants-in-Aid," *Annals of the American Academy of Political and Social Science* 207 (1940): 27.

44. James W. Fesler, "Federal Use of Administrative Areas," *Annals of the American Academy of Political and Social Science* 207 (1940): 111; "Relation of Federal Regional Authorities to State and Local Units," *ibid.* (1940): 130.

45. Elazar, "Shaping of Intergovernmental Relations," 21.

46. Daniel J. Elazar, "Opening the Third Century of American Federalism: Issues and Prospects," *Annals of the American Academy of Political and Social Science* 509 (May 1990): 11, 12.

47. Ibid.

48. Ibid.

49. T. Eastland, "Keeping the Federal Government in Its Place," *Wall Street Journal*, August 19, 1987, A-15.

CHAPTER SIX: TRADITIONAL PATTERNS OF
FEDERALISM

1. For example, "layer cake federalism" and "marble cake federalism," two concepts developed by Morton Grodzins, describe the American federal system in terms of federal agencies, states, and local governments. "Layer cake federalism" portrays these governments as layers, one on top of the other. "Marble cake federalism" sees the structure and functions of these governments as intertwined. These concepts do not lend themselves well to hydrologic regions and do not include tribal governments as ingredients in the cake (see Grodzins, *The American System* [Chicago: Rand McNally, 1966]).

2. Felix Frankfurter and James Landis, "The Compact Clause of the Constitution—A Study in Interstate Adjustment," *Yale Law Review* 34 (1925): 685, 692; Bernard Schwartz, *A Commentary on the Constitution of the United States, Part I: The Powers of the Government* (New York: Macmillan, 1963), 84.

3. The nine agreements are the Connecticut and New Netherlands Boundary Agreements of 1656, the Rhode Island and Connecticut Boundary Agreement of 1663, the New York and Connecticut Boundary Agreement of 1664, the New York and Connecticut Boundary Agreement of 1683, the Connecticut and Rhode Island Boundary Agreement of 1703, the Massachusetts and Rhode Island Boundary Agreements of 1710 and 1719, the New York and Connecticut Boundary Agreement of 1725, the North Carolina and South Carolina Boundary Agreement of 1735, and the New York and Massachusetts Boundary Agreement of 1773 (Frankfurter and Landis, "The Compact Clause," 730–32).

4. Articles of Confederation.

5. Frankfurter and Landis, "The Compact Clause," 693.

6. Article 6 of the Articles of Confederation provided that "no two or more states shall enter into any treaty, confederation or alliance whatsoever between them, without the consent of the united states in congress assembled, specifying accurately the purpose for which the same is to be entered into, and how long it shall continue."

7. Articles of Confederation, Art. 9.

8. William F. Swindler, "Our First Constitution: The Articles of Confederation," *American Bar Association Journal* 67 (1981): 166, 169.

9. "In the wide field of Western territory, therefore, we perceive an ample theater for hostile pretensions, without any umpire or common judge to interpose between the contending parties. To reason from the past to the future, we shall have good ground to apprehend that the sword would sometimes be appealed to as the arbiter of their common differences" (*Federalist*, No. 7, A. Hamilton).

10. One contemporary observer has summarized the defects as follows: "Drafted by a bickering Congress in 1781, the articles provided for no centralized government. The loose Confederation had no power to collect taxes, could not effectively defend the country and was unable to promote foreign and domestic commerce. Each state minted its own currency and taxed each other's goods. Some states even refused to pay the debts they had assumed while fighting the Revolutionary War. There were border skirmishes between states, and

threats of secession" (Stephen F. Rohde, "The Other Founding Fathers," *California Lawyer* [May 1987]: 51, 52).

11. David F. Epstein, *The Political Theory of the Federalist* (Chicago: University of Chicago Press, 1984), 27; emphasis in original.

12. Senators began to be popularly elected after ratification of the seventeenth amendment in 1913.

13. *Rhode Island v. Massachusetts,* 37 U.S. (12 Pet.) 657 (1838).

14. "The judicial Power shall extend . . . to Controversies between two or more States; . . . and in those in which a State shall be a Party, the supreme court shall have original Jurisdiction" (U.S. Constitution, Art. 3, § 2). In disputes concerning the division of interstate waters, these cases are known as equitable apportionment suits. For the procedural aspects of original actions before the Supreme Court, see Charles Wright, *The Law of Federal Courts* (St. Paul, Minn.: West Publishing Company, 1983), §§ 109–10; E. Gressman and R. Stern, *Supreme Court Rules—The 1980 Revisions* (Washington, D.C.: Bureau of National Affairs, 1980); E. Gressman and R. Stern, *Supreme Court Practice, 5th ed.* (Washington, D.C.: Bureau of National Affairs, 1978), §§ 10.1 to -.14; "The Original Jurisdiction of the United States Supreme Court," *Stanford Law Review* 11 (1959): 665. For the substantive law of equitable apportionment, see A. Tarlock, "The Law of Equitable Apportionment Revisited, Updated, and Restated," *University of Colorado Law Review* 56 (1985): 381; Select Committee on Water Marketing, *Report* (Helena: Montana Legislature, 1985), III-8 to -11.

15. Congress still has authority to resolve these conflicts. In interstate water disputes, Congress can legislate an equitable apportionment of the quantity or quality of the water among the contesting states (see *Arizona v. California,* 373 U.S. 546 [1963], and *Illinois v. Milwaukee,* 406 U.S. 91 [1972]).

16. "Even more so than is the case between states and nations, cooperation must be the guiding principle in the relations between the states. Where those concerned are equals, with none possessing an overriding power such as that derived by the Federal Government from the Supremacy Clause, comity alone can prevent the discordances that might otherwise characterize interstate relations" (B. Schwartz, *A Commentary on the Constitution of the United States, Part I: The Powers of the Government* [New York: Macmillan, 1963], 83).

17. David E. Engdahl, *Constitutional Federalism,* 2d ed. (St. Paul, Minn.: West Publishing Company, 1987).

18. "No state shall, without the consent of Congress . . . enter into any agreement or compact with another state or with a foreign power."

19. In a famous article on the compact clause, Felix Frankfurter and Harvard Law School Dean James Landis argued that interstate compacts could make a positive contribution to the solution of regional problems: "The overwhelming difficulties confronting modern society must not be at the mercy of the false antithesis embodied in the shibboleths 'States-Rights' and 'National Supremacy.' We must not deny ourselves new or unfamiliar modes of realizing national ideals. Our regions are realities. Political thinkers must respond to these realities. Instead of leading to parochialism, it will bring a fresh ferment of political thought whereby national aims may be achieved through various forms of political adjustments" (Frankfurter and Landis, "The Compact Clause," 729).

20. 14 Pet. (39 U.S.) 540 (1840). See David Engdahl, "Characterization of Interstate Arrangements: When Is a Compact not a Compact?" *Michigan Law Review* 64 (1965): 63.

21. 48 U.S. 503 (1893).

22. Ibid., 518.

23. *New Hampshire v. Maine,* 426 U.S. 363 (1976).

24. *United States Steel Corporation v. Multistate Tax Commission,* 434 U.S. 452 (1978).

25. *Cuyler v. Adams,* 449 U.S. 433 (1981). See also *Northeast Bancorp v. Board of Governors of Federal Reserve System,* 472 U.S. 159 (1985).

26. Engdahl, *Constitutional Federalism,* 399.

27. Jerome C. Muys, "Allocation and Management of Interstate Water Resources: The Emergence of the Federal-Interstate Compact," *Denver Journal of International Law and Policy* 6 (1976): 307. See also Muys, *Interstate Water Compacts: The Interstate Compact and the Federal-Interstate Compact* (Arlington, Va.: National Water Commission, 1971), and Muys, "Interstate Compacts and Regional Water Resources Planning and Management," *Natural Resources Lawyer* 6 (1973): 153.

28. 33 U.S.C. §§ 1251–1387 (1988).

29. Approximately ten compacts address interstate water pollution. The older compacts have limited purposes while the more recent agreements provide more comprehensive approaches to water quality. Some of the compacts provide only for the study and recommendation of remedial actions. Other compacts authorize standard setting and enforcement. All of these compacts provide for an administrative entity to implement the agreement (U.S. General Accounting Office, *Federal-Interstate Compact Commissions: Useful Mechanisms for Planning and Managing River Basin Operations* [February 21, 1981]). See generally, Paul T. Chambers, "Water Pollution Control through Interstate Agreement," *University of California, Davis Law Review* 1 (1969): 43; James W. Curlin, "The Interstate Water Pollution Compact—Paper Tiger or Effective Regulatory Device," *Ecological Law Quarterly* 2 (1972): 333.

The 1910 International Boundary Waters Treaty, 36 Stat. 2448 (Treaty Series no. 548), though only a bilateral effort between Canada and the United States, is a useful example of international law to mitigate water pollution. The treaty constitutes an important effort to address transboundary water pollution, as well as the apportionment of some of the waters of the Missouri River basin. The treaty provides that, except as therein authorized, the natural flow of boundary waters is to be preserved. The treaty is most famous for the establishment of the International Joint Commission, composed of six commissioners, which has had a constructive role in the resolution of many water-related conflicts between the United States and Canada. The commission is given jurisdiction to "pass upon all cases involving the use or obstruction or diversion" of boundary waters. Other disputes between the countries can also be referred to the commission for investigations and recommendations. Both the U.S. and Canadian sections of the commission have permanent staffs.

30. Muys, *Interstate Water Compacts,* 95.

31. For the definitive treatment of the law and formulation of interstate compacts, see F. L. Zimmermann and M. Wendell, *The Law and Use of Interstate Compacts* (Lexington, Ky.: Council of State Governments, 1976).

32. Ibid., 312.

33. See Wright Water Engineers, *A Water Protection Strategy for Montana: Missouri River Basin* (Helena: Montana Department of Natural Resources and Conservation, 1982); Andrew Dana, "An Evaluation of the Yellowstone River Compact: A Solution to Interstate Water Conflict" (Master's thesis, University of Washington, 1984).

34. See Norris Hundley, Jr., "The West Against Itself: The Colorado River—An Institutional History," in *New Courses for the Colorado River* (Albuquerque: University of New Mexico Press, 1986), 9; Hundley, *Dividing the Waters: A Century*

of Controversy between the United States and Mexico (Berkeley: University of California Press, 1966); Hundley, *The Colorado River Compact and the Politics of Water in the American West* (Berkeley: University of California Press, 1975); and Charles Meyers, "The Colorado River," *Stanford Law Review* 19 (1966): 1.

35. Colorado Revised Statutes Annotated § 37-61-101.1 (1990). Approved by Congress in Public Law no. 70-642, § 13, 45 Stat. 1057, 1059 (1928).

36. Public Law no. 81-37, 63 Stat. 31 (1949). See generally, G. D. Weatherford, "Some Musings about a Compact for the Missouri River Basin," in Montana Environmental Quality Council, *Annual Report Ninth Edition: Montana's Water* (Helena: Montana Environmental Quality Council, December 31, 1985), 54.

37. 259 U.S. 419 (1922).

38. Art. 3(d), Colorado Revised Statutes Annotated § 37-61-101 (1990).

39. 43 U.S.C. §§ 617–619b (1988).

40. 373 U.S. 546 (1963).

41. Act of February 3, 1944, 59 Stat. 1219.

42. 43 U.S.C. §§ 620–620o (1984).

43. 373 U.S. 546 (1963); 376 U.S. 340 (1964) (decree).

44. Colorado River Basin Salinity Control Act of 1974, Public Law no. 93-320, 88 Stat. 266 (codified in scattered sections of 43 U.S.C.); see Taylor O. Miller et al., *The Salty Colorado* (Washington, D.C.: Conservation Foundation, 1986).

45. For the definitive history of the Rio Grande from antiquity to the twentieth century, see Paul Horan, *Great River: The Rio Grande in North American History* (Austin: Texas Monthly Press, 1984).

46. Public Law no. 76-96, 53 Stat. 785 (1939).

47. See generally, Paul Elliott, "Texas' Interstate Water Compacts," *St. Mary's Law Journal* 17 (1986): 1241, 1245–52; Raymond A. Hill, "Development of the Rio Grande Compact of 1938," *Natural Resources Journal* 14:2 (April 1974): 163; Gilmer, "Interstate Compacts" (Presentation to Arkansas-White-Red Basin Inter-Agency Committee, May 1986).

48. 1929 New Mexico Laws ch. 42, 61.

49. *Texas v. New Mexico*, 296 U.S. 547 (1935)(motion for leave to file bill of complaint granted).

50. Hill, "Development of the Rio Grande Compact of 1938," 167–68.

51. Convention-Mexico, May 21, 1906, United States–Mexico, art. 1, 34 Stat. 2953 (1906).

52. See *Texas v. New Mexico*, 308 U.S. 510 (1939)(special master's report confirmed).

53. *Texas v. New Mexico*, 343 U.S. 932 (1952)(motion for leave to file complaint granted).

54. *Texas v. New Mexico*, 352 U.S. 991 (1957).

55. *Texas v. Colorado*, 389 U.S. 1000 (1967)(motion for leave to file complaint granted).

56. *Texas v. Colorado*, 391 U.S. 901 (1968).

57. *Texas v. Colorado*, 474 U.S. 1017 (1985).

58. Public Law no. 82-231, 65 Stat. 663 (1951), also codified in Montana Code Ann. § 85-20-101 (1993; hereafter cited as Yellowstone Compact).

59. Yellowstone Compact, art. 6: "Nothing contained in this compact shall be so construed or interpreted as to affect adversely any rights to the use of the waters of the Yellowstone River and its tributaries owned by or for Indians, Indian tribes, and their reservations." A 1975 study by the U.S. Department of Interior indicated that water withdrawals by the year 2020 could reach 2.1 million

ac-ft/yr for the Crows, 0.5 million ac-ft for the Northern Cheyenne, and 2.2 million ac-ft for the Wind River Indians.

60. See generally, Dana, "An Evaluation of the Yellowstone River Compact"; Dana, "The Yellowstone River Compact: An Overview," *Public Land Law Review* 3 (1983): 179; Constance M. Boris and John V. Krutilla, *Water Rights and Energy Development in the Yellowstone River Basin* (Baltimore: Resources for the Future/Johns Hopkins University Press, 1980); Henry Loble, "Interstate Water Compacts and Mineral Development (with Emphasis on the Yellowstone River Compact)," *Rocky Mountain Mineral Law Institute* 21 (1976): 777.

61. Yellowstone Compact, art. 3(G).

62. Ibid., art. 16(a).

63. Ibid., art. 3(E).

64. Dana, "An Evaluation of the Yellowstone River Compact."

65. Ibid., 154–55.

66. Ibid., 166.

67. Ibid., 173.

68. Ibid.

69. Ibid., 170.

70. Ibid.

71. Wright Water Engineers, *Water Protection Strategy*, VII-20–21.

72. At the time of the compact's ratification, Secretary of Interior Oscar Chapman was concerned about "the spirit of localism" behind that limitation.

73. *Intake Water Company v. Yellowstone Compact Commission*, 769 F.2d 568 (9th Cir. 1985).

74. Act of August 11, 1955, ch. 784, 69 Stat. 654.

75. Red River Compact, Act of December 22, 1980, Public Law no. 96-564, 94 Stat. 3305 (1980). For the definitive treatment of the negotiation of the compact, see Marguerite Ann Chapman, "Where East Meets West in Water Law: The Formulation of an Interstate Compact to Address the Diverse Problems of the Red River Basin," *Oklahoma Law Review* 38 (1985): 1.

76. Chapman, "Where East Meets West in Water Law," 111–12.

77. Ibid., 109–110.

78. Ibid., 109.

79. In addition to its water pollution features, the 1910 International Boundary Waters Treaty (see note 29) also constitutes an apportionment of the waters of the St. Mary River and the Milk River (a tributary of the Missouri), both of which originate in Montana and flow into Canada. The treaty considers the two rivers to be "one stream for the purposes of irrigation and power." The waters of this combined stream are divided equally between the two countries, although one country can take more from one river and less from the other. During the irrigation season, the United States is entitled to a prior appropriation of 500 cfs or three-quarters of the flow of the Milk River, whichever is less. Likewise, Canada is entitled to a prior appropriation of 500 cfs or three-quarters of the flow of the St. Mary River, whichever is less. Because the United States diverts water from the St. Mary to the Milk for downstream uses when the Milk again crosses into Montana, the treaty allows the diverted water to be carried in the Canadian portion of the Milk River.

80. See generally, Bruce Godwin, "Canadian Regional Basin Management," in *Border Waters: Proceedings of a Conference on U.S./Canada Transboundary Management* (Bozeman, Mont.: 49th Parallel Institute, October 1987), 80; Barry Barton, "The Prairie Provinces Water Board as a Model for the Mackenzie Basin,"

in *Institutional Arrangements for Water Management in the Mackenzie River Basin* (Banff, Alta.: Banff Centre, 1984), 37.

81. See generally, Harvey R. Doerksen, *Columbia River Interstate Compact, Politics of Negotiation* (Pullman: State of Washington Water Research Center, 1972).

82. Ibid., 25.

83. Ibid., 33.

84. Ibid., 37.

85. Ibid., 60–61.

86. Columbia Interstate Compact (Draft of October 3, 1960).

87. Council of State Governments, *Missouri River Basin Compact*, revised draft (January 1953), 1.

88. Ibid.

89. Ibid., 5; art. 5, para. 2.

90. Ibid., 3.

91. Ibid., art. 7.

92. Ibid., art. 11.

93. Although not included in the commission organization, the proposal did provide that "nothing contained in this compact shall be construed so as to: (1) Affect any obligation of the United States to the Indian tribes" (ibid., 9; art. 8).

94. See note 27.

95. Muys, *Interstate Water Compacts*, 313.

96. Ibid., 314.

97. Ibid.

98. This is not just the concern of states having their primacy over water resources disrupted: "Federal agencies also contend that such regional entities should not be allowed to preempt federal agency responsibilities for national water programs allegedly requiring uniform, functional implementation throughout the Nation" (ibid., 315).

99. Ibid., 314.

100. Ibid. Over the years, this consequence has been noted many times in the Missouri River basin—most recently in the efforts of the Corps of Engineers to develop a "surplus water marketing" policy for the basin.

101. See generally, Engdahl, *Constitutional Federalism*, 393–403.

102. Muys, *Interstate Water Compacts*, 317. Muys notes that the Bureau of Reclamation and Corps of Engineers took sixteen months to conclude a one-page power marketing agreement on the Missouri River. It also took more than thirty years for Arizona to get its case on the Colorado River accepted and decided by the U.S. Supreme Court. The National Water Commission in 1972 also made recommendations (which have gone unheeded by Congress) to speed compact negotiations: (1) an explicit statement of congressional policy on water compacts; (2) more constructive federal participation in compact negotiations; and (3) liberalization of state and federal ratification processes.

103. Ibid., 319.

104. Ibid., 318.

105. 13 How. (54 U.S.) 518, 565–66 (1851).

106. *West Virginia v. Sims*, 341 U.S. 22 (1951).

107. Engdahl, *Constitutional Federalism*, 401–2. See, e.g., *Texas v. New Mexico*, 462 U.S. 554 (1983) (Law of the Union doctrine applied); *Hinderlider v. La Plata River and Cherry Creek Ditch Company*, 304 U.S. 92 (1938) (Law of Union doctrine repudiated).

108. 449 U.S. 433 (1981).

109. Engdahl, *Constitutional Federalism,* 402.

110. *Lake Country Estates, Inc., v. Tahoe Regional Planning Agency,* 440 U.S. 391 (1979).

111. Engdahl, *Constitutional Federalism,* 403. See also Engdahl, "Construction of Interstate Compacts: A Questionable Federal Question," *Virginia Law Review* 51 (1965): 987.

112. John Guhin, "The Law of the Missouri," *South Dakota Law Review* 30 (1985): 346, 476; see also Frank Trelease, "A Federal-State Compact for Missouri Basin Development," *Wyoming Law Journal* 7 (1953): 161.

113. Guhin, Law of the Missouri," 477.

CHAPTER SEVEN: NEW PATTERNS OF FEDERALISM

1. See, e.g., Ludwik Teclaff, *The River Basin in History and Law* (The Hague: Martinus Nijhoff, 1967).

2. Public Law no. 87-328, 75 Stat. 688 (1961). See generally, R. Timothy Weston, "The Delaware River Basin: Courts, Compacts, and Commissions," in *Boundaries and Water: Allocation and Use of a Shared Resource* (Boulder: University of Colorado Natural Resource Law Center, 1989); Richard C. Albert, *Damming the Delaware* (University Park: Pennsylvania State University Press, 1987).

3. Public Law no. 91-575, 84 Stat. 1509 (1968).

4. For instance, the purpose stated by the Delaware River Basin Compact is to "adopt and promote uniform and coordinated policies for water conservation, control, use, and management in the basin [and to] encourage the planning, development, and financing of water resource projects according to such plans and policies."

5. U.S. General Accounting Office, *Federal-Interstate Compact Commissions: Useful Mechanisms for Planning and Managing River Basin Operations* (February 21, 1981).

6. *New Jersey v. New York,* 283 U.S. 336 (1931).

7. *New Jersey v. New York,* 347 U.S. 995 (1954).

8. Presentation of Gerald Hansler, executive director, Delaware River Basin Commission, Missouri River Assembly (June 4, 1990).

9. Ibid.

10. U.S. General Accounting Office, *Federal-Interstate Compact Commissions,* 7.

11. Hansler presentation to Missouri River Assembly. In other cases, unanimous voting requirements led to impasse.

12. Delaware River Basin Compact, § 3.8 (hereafter cited as DRBC); Public Law no. 87-328 75 Stat. 688 (1961).

13. DRBC, § 15.1(s)(1).

14. Level-B studies were undertaken under the auspices of the federal Water Resources Council to develop plans "for managing the water resources of a river basin by identifying policies, programs, and projects in certain areas" (U.S. General Accounting Office, *Federal-Interstate Compact Commissions,* 9 n.1). These plans were criticized because they failed "to produce implementable plans or recommendations to guide future water resource decisions" (ibid., 9).

15. DRBC, § 3.6(a).

16. DRBC, §§ 3.3(a), 3.4, 3.5.

17. Interstate Water Management Recommendations of the Parties to the U.S. Supreme Court Decree to the Delaware River Basin Commission Pursuant to Commission Resolution 78-20 (November 1982).

18. Jerome C. Muys, "Allocation and Management of Interstate Water Resources: The Emergence of the Federal-Interstate Compact," *Denver Journal of International Law and Policy* 6 (1976): 307.

19. Ibid., 322–23.

20. U.S. General Accounting Office, *Federal-Interstate Compact Commissions*, 10–14.

21. Delaware River Basin Commission, Delaware River Basin Water Code (January 1992).

22. U.S. General Accounting Office, *Federal-Interstate Compact Commissions*, 10–14.

23. "New York as the headwaters State is not interested in having any Commission actually managing the water resources in New York" (letter dated January 19, 1981, from then-Governor Hugh L. Carey, ibid., 41).

24. Ibid., 17.

25. Hansler presentation to Missouri River Assembly.

26. Muys concludes that the earlier, traditional compacts in the West grossly underestimated the water needed by individual states to satisfy reserved water rights claims (Muys, "Allocation and Management of Interstate Water Resources," 324).

27. Ibid., 323–25.

28. Montana Code Annotated § 85-20-201 (1993).

29. Portions of this discussion have appeared in John E. Thorson, "Resolving Conflicts through Intergovernmental Agreements," in *Indian Water 1985* (Oakland, Calif.: American Indian Lawyer Training Program/American Indian Resources Institute, 1986), 25.

30. 1973 Montana Laws ch. 452 (codified in various sections of Montana Code Annotated tit. 85 [1993]).

31. Ibid.

32. *United States v. Tongue River Water Users Association*, no. CV-75-20-BLG (D. Mont. filed August 1, 1975); *United States v. Bighorn Lowline Canal*, no. CV-75-34-BGL (D. Mont. filed August 29, 1975); see also *Northern Cheyenne v. Tongue River Water Users Association*, no. CV-75-6-BLG (D. Mont. August 14, 1975).

33. 424 U.S. 800 (1976).

34. Montana Code Annotated §§ 85-2-211 to -243 (1993).

35. Ibid., § 2-15-212.

36. 463 U.S. 545 (1983).

37. States in which jurisdiction over tribes is disclaimed in the state constitution.

38. See generally, address by T. Wapato, chairman, U.S.-Canada Pacific Salmon Commission, Symposium on the Future of the Missouri River, May 2, 1988; C. Wilkinson and D. Conner, "The Law of the Pacific Salmon Fishery: Conservation and Allocation of a Transboundary Common Property Resource," *University of Kansas Law Review* 32 (1983): 17.

39. 520 F.2d 676 (9th Cir. 1975), cert. denied, 423 U.S. 1086 (1976).

40. 16 U.S.C. §§ 839–39h (Supp. V 1981).

41. 99 Stat. 7, Public Law no. 99-5 (1985).

42. 16 U.S.C. §§ 839–39h (Supp V 1981).

43. See generally, Wilkinson and Conner, "Law of the Pacific Salmon Fishery," 53–56; R. Cavanagh, "The Pacific Northwest Electric Power Planning and

Conservation (and Thermal Power Plant Relief) Act," *University of Puget Sound Law Review* 4 (1980): 27; Gerald Mueller, "The Northwest Power Planning Council: A Model for Cooperative Planning in the Missouri River Basin?" in *Boundaries and Water: Allocation and Use of a Shared Resource* (Boulder: University of Colorado Natural Resource Law Center, 1989); John Volkman and K. Lee, "Within the Hundredth Meridian: Western States and Their River Basins in a Time of Transition," *University of Colorado Law Review* 59 (1988): 551; D. Lee and A. Kneese, "Fish and Hydropower Vie for Columbia River Waters," *Resources* 94 (1989): 1.

44. Lee and Kneese, "Fish and Hydropower," 1.

45. Northwest Power Planning Council, *Northwest Conservation and Electric Power Plan* (Portland, Ore.: Northwest Power Planning Council, 1991).

46. Northwest Power Planning Council, *Columbia River Basin Fish and Wildlife Program* (Portland, Ore.: Northwest Power Planning Council, 1987).

47. 16 U.S.C. §§ 1531 to 1544 (1988).

48. J. Harrison, "Head Start for Salmon Recovery," *Northwest Energy News* (July/August 1992): 25.

49. See Peter V. MacAvoy, "The Great Lakes Charter: Toward a Basinwide Strategy for Managing the Great Lakes," *Case Western Reserve Journal of International Law* 18 (1986): 49. The text of the charter is set forth in Appendix 6.

50. Minnesota, Wisconsin, Michigan, Illinois, Indiana, Ohio, Pennsylvania, and New York.

51. Great Lakes Charter, Principle I (see Appendix 6). One observer says that the charter utilizes "a watershed management approach that respects the hydrologic unity of the Great Lakes" (Jack Ditmore, "Great Lakes Charter," presentation before the Annual Conference of the National Association of Environmental Professionals, April 28, 1987).

52. See generally, T. Kuchenberg, "Great Lakes Need Wise Dispute Resolutions," *Conservation Foundation Letter* (Washington, D.C., November 1983), and Kuchenberg, "Two Centuries of Abuse Transform the Great Lakes," *Conservation Foundation Letter* (Washington, D.C., October 1983).

53. See generally, Center for Great Lakes, *Summary Proceedings, Legislative Conference on Great Lakes Natural Resource Management Issues* (Chicago, 1984).

54. 458 U.S. 941 (1982).

55. Ditmore, "Great Lakes Charter." See also Great Lakes Governors' Task Force on Water Diversion and Great Lakes Institutions, *Final Report and Recommendations* (January 1985).

56. Ibid.

57. R. Halstead, *Wisconsin Coastal Management Program: The Proposed Powder River–Midwest Coal Slurry Pipeline* (N.p., 1985).

CHAPTER EIGHT: FEDERALISM AND NEW POLICIES

1. The Missouri River Management Project was supported by the Ford Foundation, the Rockefeller Family Fund, the William H. Donner Foundation, the Bitterroot Fund, the General Services Foundation, the Jesse Smith Noyes Foundation, the Northwest Area Foundation, and individual donors.

2. In *Getting to Yes* (Boston: Houghton Mifflin Company, 1981), the authors, Roger Fisher and William Ury, emphasize the relational aspects of the dispute resolution process. They indicate that in a negotiating setting, each disputant has an interest in securing a substantive result and an interest in maintaining a working relationship—at least one good enough to produce an acceptable agree-

ment. Traditional negotiating and bargaining techniques tend to put relationship and substance in conflict. Fisher and Ury stress the importance of separating the relationship from the substance. The relational "people" problem in negotiations can be addressed through better perception of the other party's position, recognition of and appropriate response to emotions and outbursts, and improved efforts at communication. Fisher and Ury also stress the importance of negotiating the underlying interest of the parties rather than their stated position. They contend that negotiating techniques should allow the parties to brainstorm and develop options for mutual gain. Finally, they note the importance of utilizing objective criteria in reaching final results in negotiated settings.

3. Lawrence Susskind and Jeffrey Cruikshank, in *Breaking the Impasse* (New York: Basic Books, 1987), focus their attention on the characteristics of good negotiated settlements. They identify disputes such as those involved in the Missouri River as distributional disputes. In concentrating on attaining "win-win" results in distributional disputes, they criticize compromise as a method of dispute resolution in that it often produces minimally acceptable results or no results at all. In particular, the authors identify four characteristics of well-negotiated settlements: fairness, efficiency, wisdom, and stability. Settlements are usually considered fair when all the stakeholders have been given a chance to participate, when the result has been reached without any party feeling victimized, and when, "in the eyes of the community," a good precedent was set. Settlements are efficient if they are reached without the expenditure of an inordinate amount of time or money. A wise settlement is usually the one that is based on the most information. A settlement is stable if it can adjust to changing circumstances or the changing needs of the parties.

4. John Wesley Powell, *Report on Lands of the Arid Region* (facsimile of 1879 ed; Cambridge, Mass.: Harvard Common Press, 1983).

5. Charles Wilkinson, "Aldo Leopold and Western Water Law: Thinking Perpendicular to the Prior Appropriation Doctrine," *Land and Water Law Review* 24 (1989): 22.

6. Charles H. W. Foster, "Bioregionalism," *Renewable Resources Journal* 4:3 (Summer 1986): 12–14; Foster, *The Cape Cod National Seashore: A Landmark Alliance* (Hanover, N.H.: University Press of New England, 1985); Foster, *Experiments in Bioregionalism: The New England River Basins Story* (Hanover, N.H.: University Press of New England, 1984).

7. Mark D. O'Keefe et al., *Boundaries Carved in Water: An Analysis of River and Water Management in the Upper Missouri Basin* (Missoula, Mont.: Northern Lights Institute, 1986).

8. Titles in the series were "The Missouri: River of Promise or River of Peril?" by John E. Thorson, "Toward an Ethic of Place" by Charles E. Wilkinson, "A Dream of Water" by Donald Worster, "High Noon in the Missouri River Basin" by Gov. William Janklow, "Learning from the Colorado River Basin Experience" by David Getches, "A Watershed Vision of the Future" by Daniel Kemmis, "Water in the West" by Karen Lewotsky, "Indian Water Rights" by Karen Lewotsky, "Tribal Sovereignty" by Karen Lewotsky, "Pick-Sloan and the Tribes" by M. Lawson, "Indian Reservations and Tribes of the Missouri River Basin" by Bob Anderson, "A Downstream Perspective" by Bill Crews, "Missouri River Hydropower and Revenues" by Gerald Mueller, "Symposium on the Future of the Missouri River" by John E. Thorson, "Toward an Upper Basin Perspective" by Gene Krentz, and "The Missouri River: The Great Plains' Thread of Life" by Larry W. Hesse and James C. Schmulbach.

9. John E. Thorson, "Symposium on the Future of the Missouri River," in

Boundaries Carved in Water: The Missouri River Brief Series, no. 14 (Missoula, Mont.: Northern Lights Institute, February 1989), 10.

10. Ibid.

11. The objectives for the assembly were: "1. Through dialogue and listening, gain an understanding of the interests and concerns of the other participants and meet them as individuals; 2. Create a sense of belonging to a river system rather than simply to individual sovereign entities; and 3. Develop a consensus list of basin water-related issues, resolve to address them, and agree on a process for doing so." The entire work plan of the Missouri River Assembly is set forth as Appendix 7.

12. Small Group Questionnaire, Missouri River Assembly (June 5, 1990).

13. "A Proposal to Establish a Missouri River Council" (draft, February 1991).

14. Ibid. § 6.

15. *Missouri River Report* (May 1991), 2.

16. *Missouri River Report* (January 1992), 1.

17. *Missouri River Report* (April 1993), 1.

18. *Missouri River Report* (July 1992), 6.

19. By-Laws of Mni Sose, Inc. (October 5, 1992).

20. Charter of the Mni Sose Water Rights Coalition art. V (undated).

21. *Indian Country Today*, June 23, 1993, A6.

22. *Western States Water*, no. 1013 (October 15, 1993).

23. *Indian Country Today*, October 14, 1993, A3.

24. Letter from Senator Quentin Burdick to President George Bush, October 25, 1993; emphasis in original.

25. U.S. Army Engineer Division, Missouri River, *Master Manual* (Omaha, 1979), I-1.

26. Ibid., V-2.

27. U.S. Army Corps of Engineers, Missouri River Division, "Draft Phase 1 Report for the Review and Update of the Missouri River Main Stem Master Water Control Manual" (May 1990); the corps did not finalize this report but moved directly into the second phase of the review process.

28. *Missouri River Report* (1991), 3.

29. Ibid.

30. *South Dakota et al. v. Bornhoft*, no. Cv. 91-26-JDS-BLG (D. Mont.).

31. *Missouri River Report* (April 1992), 9.

32. *Missouri River Report* (April 1993), 4–5.

33. Letter to President Clinton, February 17, 1993: "In its study, the Corps has considered over 250 scenarios for managing the Missouri River system, nearly all of which assume higher reservoir levels than prescribed in the current Master Manual. Many of those alternatives threaten to lower water levels in the Missouri to a point where navigation would be imperiled. This would have serious consequences for the entire Mississippi River system. . . . In June of 1988, when the Upper Mississippi experienced serious drought conditions, the Missouri provided as much as 65 percent of the water in the Mississippi. During that drought, about 180 blockages occurred over a span of 900 miles. The economic toll was disastrous as barge rates tripled and remained at inflated rates. If it weren't for strong flows from the Missouri, conditions would have been dramatically worse."

34. U.S. Army Corps of Engineers, Missouri River Division, "Preliminary Draft Environmental Impact Statement, Missouri River Master Water Control Manual Review and Update," *Missouri River Report* (September 1993), 7.

35. *Missouri River Report* (November 1993), 1.

CHAPTER NINE: OF RIVERS, FISH, AND MEN

1. Stephen Fox, *John Muir and His Legacy: The American Conservation Movement* (Boston: Little Brown, 1981), 291.

2. The refusal of the corps to approve an ETSI-like project brought to it by a state could also precipitate litigation.

3. One commentator, the former Missouri River coordinator for the state of Iowa, has outlined the considerations he believes are important for the cooperation of lower basin states: "Continued insistence that downstream interests are taken into account during the decision-making processes of the federal agencies; continued efforts to better understand the effects of various water levels on the full range of manmade and natural water systems; an acknowledgment of the past and a desire to learn from the mistakes of homocentrism; an insistence on sharing shortages" (Bill Crews, "A Downstream Perspective," in *Boundaries Carved in Water: The Missouri River Brief Series*, no. 12 [June 1988], 8).

4. Philip Selznick, *Leadership in Administration* (New York: Harper and Row, 1957), 5.

5. Sarah F. Bates et al., *Searching Out the Headwaters: Change and Rediscovery in Western Water Policy* (Washington, D.C.: Island Press, 1993), ix.

6. Ibid., 178-92.

7. Presentation of E. Kim Nelson to Missouri River Assembly, June 5, 1990.

8. M. Esman, "The Elements of Institution Building," in John W. Easton, ed. *Institution Building and Development* (Beverly Hills, Calif.: Sage Publications, 1972), 25.

9. Ibid., 22-23.

10. Ibid., 23.

11. Ibid.

12. Ibid.

13. Charles H. W. Foster, "Bioregionalism," *Renewable Resources Journal* (Summer 1986), emphasis in original.

14. Charles H. W. Foster, "Regionalism and the Missouri River Basin: A New England Perspective" (Paper presented at second meeting of Missouri River Assembly, Bismarck, N.D., June 1990), 7: "In general, [the regional organization] must supply something that its member jurisdictions cannot produce by or for themselves. . . . A clear definition of mission will usually help. . . . Within this broad statement of objectives, the organization should deliberately select activities that are visible, tangible, and doable. . . . The actions must be large enough to be significant, but small enough to be accomplished within a reasonable time frame." Also see Foster, "What Makes Regional Organizations Succeed or Fail?" (Unpublished paper, n.d.), 5.

15. Foster, "Regionalism and the Missouri River Basin," 8.

16. The basin states and tribes should have the opportunity to express and pursue their distinctive interests and to search for common ground between themselves. Thus, the states need an organization, such as the Missouri Basin States Association, to address their unique water interests. The Indian tribes also need their own caucus, and efforts of the Sioux tribes to form such a "tribal commission" are encouraging. The federal agencies also need to fashion an interagency process for coordinating their Missouri River interests. Although the

three sovereigns have their separate interests, they share an interest in candidly addressing the distribution of Missouri River benefits; fashioning a new set of public policies for the river; ensuring that those policies are implemented; and resolving disputes short of expensive, divisive litigation.

17. See John E. Thorson, "Symposium on the Future of the Missouri River," in *Boundaries Carved in Water: The Missouri River Brief Series,* no. 14 (Missoula, Mont.: Northern Lights Institute, February 1989).

18. G. W. F. Hegel, *The Philosophy of History,* trans. J. Sibree (New York: Willey Book Company, 1944), 84–85; see also Daniel Kemmis, *Community and the Politics of Place* (Norman: University of Oklahoma Press, 1990), 23.

19. Amitai Etzioni, *The Spirit of Community* (New York: Crown Publishers, 1993), 3.

20. Ibid., 15; emphasis in original.

21. *Tikkun* 8 (September/October 1993): 97.

22. Kemmis, *Community and the Politics of Place,* 6.

23. Ibid., 71.

APPENDIX FOUR

1. The 1936 and 1938 legislation is set forth at 33 U.S.C. § 701c (1986).

2. Now codified at 16 U.S.C. § 460d (1989).

3. This section is referenced in the notes to 33 U.S.C. § 701f (1986), which is a consolidated authorization for these and similar projects authorized since 1936.

4. Act of June 28, 1938, ch. 795, 52 Stat. 1215 (now codified in scattered sections of 33 U.S.C.).

5. 33 U.S.C. § 701b-1 (1989).

BIBLIOGRAPHY

GENERAL WORKS

Albert, Richard C. *Damming the Delaware*. University Park: Pennsylvania State University Press, 1987.

American Indian Lawyer Training Program. *Indian Tribes as Sovereign Governments*. Oakland, Calif., 1988.

Anderson, Bob. "Indian Reservations and Tribes of the Missouri River Basin." In *Boundaries Carved in Water: The Missouri River Brief Series*, no. 11. Missoula, Mont: Northern Lights Institute, June 1988.

Andrews, Barbara T., and Marie Sansone. *Who Runs the Rivers? Dams and Decisions in the New West*. Stanford, Calif: Stanford Environmental Society, 1983.

Arkansas-White-Red Basin Inter-Agency Committee. *Activities Report*. March 1982.

———. *Planning Process Study*. 1981.

Athearn, Robert G. *Forts of the Upper Missouri*. Englewood Cliffs, N.J.: Prentice-Hall, 1967.

Banks, H. O. "Future Water Demands in the United States." In *The Interbasin Transfer of Water . . . The Great Lakes Connection*. Milwaukee: Wisconsin Coastal Management Council, 1982.

Bartlett, Richard A., ed. *Rolling Rivers: An Encyclopedia of America's Rivers*. New York: McGraw-Hill, 1984.

Barton, Barry. "The Prairie Provinces Water Board as a Model for the Mackenzie Basin." In *Institutional Arrangements for Water Management in the Mackenzie River Basin*. Banff, Alta.: Banff Centre, 1984.

Barton, Weldon V. *Interstate Compacts in the Political Process*. Chapel Hill: University of North Carolina Press, 1965.

Bates, Sarah F., et al. *Searching Out the Headwaters: Change and Rediscovery in Western Water Policy*. Washington, D.C.: Island Press, 1993.

Baumhoff, Richard G. *The Dammed Missouri River Valley: One-Sixth of Our Nation*. New York: Knopf, 1951.

Beck, Robert E., ed. *Water and Water Rights*. Charlottesville, Va.: Michie Company, 1991.

Berman, David. *Interstate Compact Water Commissions: Selected Case Studies*. Washington, D.C.: Washington Center for Metropolitan Studies, 1962.

The Big Missouri: Hope of Our West. Washington, D.C.: Public Affairs Institute, 1948.

Bingham, Gail. *Resolving Environmental Disputes: A Decade of Experience*. Washington, D.C.: Conservation Foundation, 1986.

Bittiner and Associates, Inc. *Management and Administration of Ground Water in Interstate and International Aquifers*. Fort Collins, Colo., 1970.

Blackman, Susan. "Resisting Water Diversions: The Great Lakes Charter." *Resources* 17 (Winter 1987): 3.

Boris, Constance M., and John V. Krutilla. *Water Rights and Energy Development in the Yellowstone River Basin.* Baltimore: Resources for the Future/Johns Hopkins University Press, 1980.

Brackenridge, Henry Marie. "Brackenridge's Journal of a Voyage up the River Missouri in 1811." In Reuben G. Thwaites, ed., *Early Western Travels 1748–1846,* 6:19–66. Cleveland: A. H. Clark, 1904.

Bradbury, John. *Travels in the Interior of America (1817).* Ann Arbor, Mich.: University Microfilms, 1966.

Brandon, William. *The Last Americans: The Indian in American Culture.* New York: McGraw-Hill, 1974.

Briggs, Harold Edward. *Frontiers of the Northwest: A History of the Upper Missouri Valley.* New York: Appleton-Century, 1940.

Brower, J. V. *The Missouri River and Its Utmost Source.* St. Paul, Minn.: Pioneer Press, 1897.

Burdick, Quentin. Letter to President George Bush. October 25, 1990.

Burt, Struthers. *Powder River: Let'er Buck.* New York: Farrar and Rinehart, 1938.

Canby, William C., Jr. *American Indian Law.* St. Paul, Minn.: West Publishing Company, 1981.

Carey, Hugh L. Letter of January 19, 1981, to the Delaware River Basin Compact Commission.

Cargo, David N., and Bob F. Mallory. *Man and His Geologic Environment.* 2d ed. Reading, Mass.: Addison-Wesley, 1977.

Carlin, John. Letter of July 15, 1985, to the Missouri River Basin governors.

_____. Letter to Governor Janklow. October 25, 1985.

_____. Letter to Governor Janklow. November 25, 1985.

_____. Letter to Governor Janklow. January 6, 1986.

Carlin, John, and Governors Branstad, Ashcroft, and Kerrey. Letter to Governor Janklow. January 15, 1986.

Carmer, Carl Lamson, ed. *Songs of the Rivers of America.* New York: Farrar and Rinehart, 1942.

Cavanagh, R. "The Pacific Northwest Electric Power Planning and Conservation (and Thermal Power Plant Relief) Act." *University of Puget Sound Law Review* 4 (1980): 27.

Center for Great Lakes. "Summary Proceedings, Legislative Conference on Great Lakes Natural Resource Management Issues." Chicago, 1984.

Chambers, Paul T. "Water Pollution Control through Interstate Agreement." *University of California Davis Law Review* 1 (1969): 43.

Chapman, Marguerite Ann. "Where East Meets West in Water Law: The Formulation of an Interstate Compact to Address the Diverse Problems of the Red River Basin." *Oklahoma Law Review* 38 (1985): 1.

Chittenden, Hiram Martin. *History of Early Steamboat Navigation on the Missouri River: Life and Adventures of Joseph La Barge.* 2 vols. New York: F. P. Harper, 1903.

Clark, Robert E. *Water and Water Rights.* Indianapolis: Allen Smith, 1967.

Columbia Interstate Compact. Draft of October 3, 1960.

Council of State Governments. *Book of the States.* Vol. 14. Chicago, 1982–1983.

_____. *Interstate Compacts and Agencies.* Lexington, Ky, 1983.

_____. *Missouri River Basin Compact.* Revised draft. Chicago, January 1953.

Crews, Bill. "A Downstream Perspective." In *Boundaries Carved in Water: Missouri River Briefs,* no. 12. Missoula, Mont.: Northern Lights Institute, June 1988.

Culbertson, Thaddeus A. "Journal of an Expedition to the Mauvaises Terres and the Upper Missouri in 1850." In Smithsonian Institution, *Fifth Annual Report,* 84–145. Washington, D.C., 1851.

Cummings, Robert. "Memorandum for the Fort Berthold Tribes." Albuquerque, N.Mex., 1986.

Curlin, James W. "The Interstate Water Pollution Compact—Paper Tiger or Effective Regulatory Device." *Ecological Law Quarterly* 2 (1972): 333.

Dana, Andrew C. "An Evaluation of the Yellowstone River Compact: A Solution to Interstate Water Conflict." Master's thesis, University of Washington, 1984.

———. "The Yellowstone River Compact: An Overview." *Public Land Law Review* 3 (1983): 179.

Davies, J. "The Missouri Basin Account: Accounting, Repayment, and Financial Status of the Pick-Sloan Missouri Basin Program and Integrated Projects." In *The Pick-Sloan Missouri Basin Plan*, 47, 1983.

Debo, Angie. *A History of the Indians of the United States.* Norman: University of Oklahoma Press, 1970.

Delaware River Basin Commission. *Delaware River Basin Water Code.* West Trenton, N.J., January 1992.

Deloria, Vine. *Custer Died for Your Sins.* New York: Macmillian, 1969.

Ditmore, Jack. "Great Lakes Charter." Presentation before the Annual Conference of the National Association of Environmental Professionals. April 28, 1987.

Doerksen, Harvey R. *Columbia River Interstate Compact, Politics of Negotiation.* Pullman: State of Washington Water Research Center, 1972.

Dunne, Thomas, and Luna B. Leopold. *Water in Environmental Planning.* San Francisco: W. H. Freeman, 1978.

Easton, John W., ed. *Institution Building and Development.* Beverly Hills, Calif.: Sage Publications, 1972.

Elazar, Daniel J. "Opening the Third Century of American Federalism: Issues and Prospects." *Annals of the American Academy of Political and Social Science* 509 (May 1990): 11.

———. "The Shaping of Intergovernmental Relations in the Twentieth Century." *Annals of the American Academy of Political and Social Science* 359 (May 1965): 10.

Elliot, Paul. "Texas' Interstate Water Compacts." *St. Mary's Law Journal* 17 (1986): 1241.

Engdahl, David E. "Characterization of Interstate Arrangements: When Is a Compact Not a Compact?" *Michigan Law Review* 64 (1965): 63.

———. *Constitutional Federalism.* 2d ed. St. Paul, Minn.: West Publishing Company, 1987.

———. "Construction of Interstate Compacts: A Questionable Federal Question." *Virginia Law Review* 51 (1965): 987.

Epstein, David F. *The Political Theory of the Federalist.* Chicago: University of Chicago Press, 1984.

Etzioni, Amitai. *The Spirit of Community.* New York: Crown Publishers, 1993.

Federalist Papers. Ed. Benjamin F. Wright. Cambridge, Mass.: Belknap Press of Harvard University Press, 1961.

Fellman, David. "The Future of Grants-in-Aid." *Annals of the American Academy of Political and Social Science* 207 (January 1940): 27.

Ferejohn, John A. *Pork Barrel Politics: Rivers and Harbor Legislation, 1947–1968.* Stanford: Stanford University Press, 1974.

Ferrell, John. "Corps Assesses Flood Damage." Unpublished paper. Omaha, n.d.

———. "Missouri River Institutions." Unpublished outline. June 1990.

Fesler, James W. "Federal Use of Administrative Areas." *Annals of the American Academy of Political and Social Science* 207 (January 1940): 111.

Fisher, Roger, and William Ury. *Getting to Yes.* Boston: Houghton Mifflin, 1981.

Florence, M. Taylor. "Using the Interstate Compact to Control Acid Deposition." *Journal of Energy Law and Policy* 6 (1985): 413–46.

Floyd, Charles. "The New Found Journal of Charles Floyd, A Sergeant under Captains Lewis and Clark, by John Davie Butler." *Proceedings of the American Antiquarian Society* 9 (1895): 225–52.

Folk-Williams, John A. *What Indian Water Means to the West.* Santa Fe: Western Network, 1982.

Foster, Charles H. W. "Bioregionalism." *Renewable Resources Journal* 4:3 (Summer 1986): 12–14.

———. *The Cape Cod National Seashore: A Landmark Alliance.* Hanover, N.H.: University Press of New England, 1985.

———. *Experiments in Bioregionalism: The New England River Basins Story.* Hanover, N.H.: University Press of New England, 1984.

———. "Regionalism and the Missouri River Basin: A New England Perspective." Paper presented at second meeting of Missouri River Assembly, Bismarck, N.D., June 1990.

———. "What Makes Regional Organizations Succeed or Fail?" Unpublished paper, Cambridge, Mass., n.d.

Fox, Stephen. *John Muir and His Legacy: The American Conservation Movement.* Boston: Little, Brown, 1981.

Frankfurter, Felix, and James Landis. "The Compact Clause of the Constitution—A Study in Interstate Adjustments." *Yale Law Journal* 34 (1925): 685.

Freeman, Lewis Ransome. *Waterways of Westward Wandering: Small Boat Voyages Down the Ohio, Missouri, and Mississippi Rivers.* New York: Dodd, Mead, 1927.

Gass, Patrick. *A Journal of the Voyages and Travels of a Corps of Discovery.* Minneapolis: Ross and Harris, 1958.

Getches, David. *Water Law in a Nutshell.* St. Paul, Minn.: West Publishing Company, 1984.

Gibson, A. M. *The American Indian.* Lexington, Mass.: D. C. Heath, 1980.

Gildart, R. C. *Montana's Missouri River.* Montana Geographic Series. Helena: Montana Magazine, n.d.

Godwin, Bruce. "Canadian Regional Basin Management." *Border Waters: Proceedings of a Conference on U.S./Canada Transboundary Management.* Bozeman, Mont.: 49th Parallel Institute, October 1987.

Grant, Bruce. *American Indians: Yesterday and Today.* Rev. ed. New York: E. P. Dutton, 1960.

Great Lakes Governors' Task Force on Water Diversion and Great Lakes Institutions. *Final Report and Recommendations.* Chicago, January 1985.

Gressman, E., and R. Stern. *Supreme Court Practice.* 6th ed. Washington, D.C.: Bureau of National Affairs, 1986.

———. *Supreme Court Rules—The 1980 Revisions.* Washington, D.C.: Bureau of National Affairs, 1980.

Gresswell, R. Kay, ed. *Standard Encyclopedia of the World's Rivers and Lakes.* New York: Putman, 1965.

Grodzins, Morton. *The American System.* Chicago: Rand McNally, 1966.

Guhin, John. "The Law of the Missouri." *South Dakota Law Review* 30 (1985): 346.

Harris, Edward. *Up the Missouri with Audubon: The Journal of Edward Harris.* Ed. John Francis McDermott. Norman: University of Oklahoma Press, 1951.

Harrison, J. "Head Start for Salmon Recovery." *Northwest Energy News* (July/August 1992): 25.

Hart, Henry Cowles. *The Dark Missouri.* Madison: University of Wisconsin Press, 1957.

Hays, Samuel P. *Conservation and the Gospel of Efficiency: The Progressive Conservation Movement.* Cambridge, Mass.: Harvard University Press, 1959.

Hegel, Georg Wilhelm Friedrich. *The Philosophy of History.* Trans. J. Sibree. New York: Willey Book Company, 1944.

Helfman, Elizabeth S. *Rivers and Watersheds in America's Future.* New York: D. McKay Company, 1965.

Hensler, Gerald. Presentation to Missouri River Assembly. June 4, 1990.

Hesse, Larry W. *The Middle Missouri: A Collection of Papers on the Biology with Special Reference to Power Station Effects.* Norfolk, Nebr.: Missouri River Study Group, 1982.

Hesse, Larry W., and J. Schmulbach. "The Missouri River: The Great Plains' Thread of Life." In *Boundaries Carved in Water: The Missouri River Brief Series,* no. 16. Missoula, Mont.: Northern Lights Institute, April 1991.

High Plains Associates. *Six-State High Plains–Ogallala Aquifer Regional Resources Study.* Austin, Tex.: March 1982.

Hill, Raymond A. "Development of the Rio Grande Compact of 1938." *Natural Resources Journal* 14 (1974): 163.

Horan, Paul. *Great River: The Rio Grande in North American History.* Austin: Texas Monthly Press, 1984.

Hundley, Norris, Jr. *The Colorado River Compact and the Politics of Water in the American West.* Berkeley: University of California Press, 1975.

———. *Dividing the Waters: A Century of Controversy between the United States and Mexico.* Berkeley: University of California Press, 1966.

———. "The West against Itself: The Colorado River—An Institutional History." In *New Courses for the Colorado River,* ed. Gary D. Weatherford and F. Lee Brown, 9–49. Albuquerque: University of New Mexico Press, 1986.

Hutchins, Wells A. *Water Rights Laws in the Nineteen Western States.* Washington, D.C.: U.S. Department of Agriculture, 1977.

Hyde, George E. *Indians of the High Plains: From the Prehistoric Period to the Coming of the Europeans.* Norman: University of Oklahoma Press, 1959.

Information Guide, Resources & Services. Nebraska Natural Resource Commission Data Book. Lincoln, Nebr., July 1985.

Interstate Commission on the Delaware River Basin. INCODEL: *A Report on Its Activities and Accomplishments.* Philadelphia, n.d.

Iowa Department of Water, Air and Water Management. *Iowa State Water Plan.* January 1985.

Kemmis, Daniel. *Building on Common Ground: A Community Workbook.* Missoula, Mont.: Northern Lights Research and Education Institute, 1987.

———. *Community and the Politics of Place.* Norman: University of Oklahoma Press, 1990.

Krutilla, John V., and Otto Eckstein. *Multiple Purpose River Development: Studies in Applied Economic Analysis.* Baltimore: Johns Hopkins University Press, 1958.

Kuchenberg, T. "Great Lakes Need Wise Dispute Resolutions." *Conservation Foundation Letter.* Washington, D.C., 1983.

———. "Two Centuries of Abuse Transform the Great Lakes." *Conservation Foundation Letter.* Washington, D.C., 1983.

Lawson, M. *Dammed Indians.* Norman: University of Oklahoma Press, 1982.

———. "Pick-Sloan and the Tribes." *Boundaries Carved in Water: The Missouri*

River Brief Series. no. 10. Missoula, Mont.: Northern Lights Institute, April 1988.

Leach, R., and R. Suggs, Jr. *The Administration of Interstate Compacts.* Baton Rouge: Louisiana State University, 1958.

Lee, D., and A. Kneese. "Fish and Hydropower Vie for Columbia River Waters." *Resources* 94 (1989): 1.

Leopold, Aldo. *A Sand County Almanac.* New York: Oxford University Press, 1987.

Lewotsky, Karen. "Tribal Sovereignty." *Boundaries Carved in Water: The Missouri River Brief Series,* no. 9. Missoula, Mont.: Northern Lights Institute, April 1988.

Library of Congress, Legislative Reference Service. *Missouri Valley Authority: Background and Analysis of Proposal, S. 555, 79th Cong.* Washington, D.C., 1946.

Litterer, Oscar F. *The Missouri Basin Development Program.* Minneapolis: Federal Reserve Bank, 1958.

Loble, Henry. "Interstate Water Compacts and Mineral Development (With Emphasis on the Yellowstone River Compact)." *Rocky Mountain Mineral Law Institute* 21 (1976): 777.

Maass, Arthur. *Muddy Waters: The Army Engineers and the Nation's Rivers.* First printed 1951. Reprinted, New York: De Capo Press, 1974.

MacAvoy, Peter V. "The Great Lakes Charter: Toward a Basinwide Strategy for Managing the Great Lakes." *Case Western Resource Journal of International Law* 18 (1986): 49.

McGovern, Francis E. "Toward a Functional Approach for Managing Complex Litigation." *University of Chicago Law Review* 53 (1986): 440.

McKinley, C. "The Valley Authority and Its Alternatives." *American Political Science Review* 44 (September 1950): 629.

Magedanz. "Historical Perspectives on the Pick-Sloan Plan." *Public Affairs* 97 (April 1988): 5.

Mann, Roy. *Rivers in the City.* New York: Praeger, 1973.

Martin, Roscoe Coleman. *River Basin Administration and the Delaware.* Syracuse, N.Y.: Syracuse University Press, 1960.

Meeks, G., Jr. *Managing Environmental and Public Policy Conflicts: A Legislator's Guide.* Denver: National Conference of State Legislatures, 1985.

Meyers, Charles. "The Colorado River." *Stanford Law Review* 19 (1966): 1.

Miller, S. "Multi-State River Basin Organizations: The Relationship of Structure, Function, and Decision Process." Master's thesis, University of Nebraska, 1985.

Miller, Taylor O., et al. *The Salty Colorado.* Washington, D.C.: Conservation Foundation, 1986.

Minnesota Environmental Quality Board. *Protecting Minnesota's Waters: An Agenda for Action in the 1987–1989 Biennium.* Prepared by the Minnesota State Planning Agency. February 1987.

Mississippi River Basin Commission. *Final Report—The Upper Mississippi River Main Stem Level B Study.* 1981.

Missouri Basin Inter-Agency Committee. *Comprehensive Framework Study: Missouri River Basin.* Vol. 2. Washington, D.C.: Government Printing Office, 1969.

Missouri Basin States Association. *Agricultural Water Use Including Identification of Irrigated Lands.* Omaha, September 1982.

———. *Alternative Institutional Arrangements for Interstate River Basin Management.* Omaha, February 1984.

———. *Annual Report, Fiscal Year 1982.* Omaha, 1982.

———. *Basin Bulletin.* Irregular.

_____. *Biennial Report*. Fiscal years 1985–1986.

_____. *Coordination Directory of State and Federal Water Resource Officials*. Omaha, May 1985.

_____. *Directors' News Bulletin*. Biweekly.

_____. *Ground Water Depletions*. "Appendix I." Omaha, February 1982.

_____. *Ground Water Depletions*. "Appendix II: Transmissivity and Stream Depletion Factor Maps, Platte and Kansas River Basins, Colorado-Kansas-Nebraska-Wyoming." Omaha, February 1982.

_____. *Interstate Cooperation in Ground Water Management*. Omaha, November 1985.

_____. "Issue Analysis of Missouri Basin States Association, An Issue Analysis of Placing a Surcharge on Pick-Sloan Hydropower Generation." Draft of October 1985.

_____. *Issue Analysis on Out-of-Basin Water Transfer*. Omaha, May 1983.

_____. *Issue of Indian Reserved Water Rights*. Omaha, November 1984.

_____. *Missouri River Basin Hydrological Study Report and Technical Papers*. Omaha, May 1983.

_____. *Missouri River Basin Hydrology Final Report*. Omaha, May 1983.

_____. *Missouri River Basin Water Accounting System*. Omaha, September 1981.

_____. *Missouri River Floodplain Atlas*. Omaha, 1981.

_____. *Missouri River Flood Plain Final Report*. Omaha, May 1983.

_____. *Missouri River Flood Plain River Stage and Levee Inventory Study*. Omaha, October 1981.

_____. *Municipal, Industrial, Energy, and Rural Domestic Water Use*. Omaha, February 1982.

_____. *Pick-Sloan Missouri Basin Program Analysis Summary Report*. Summary of eight interim reports on functional components of Pick-Sloan Missouri Basin Program. Omaha, September 1986.

_____. "Proceedings: Missouri River Basin State Water Resources Planning Seminar." Omaha, January 1983.

_____. "Proceedings: Missouri River Basin State Water Resources Planning Seminar." Omaha, June 1984.

_____. "Proceedings: Pick-Sloan Missouri Basin Plan Conference." Omaha, August 1983.

_____. *A Review of the Missouri River Main Stem System Operations*. Omaha, 1988.

_____. *Selected Missouri River Basin Water Use and Transfer Proposals*. Reprinted Omaha, May 1982.

_____. *Summaries of Existing Interstate Compacts, U.S. Supreme Court Decrees, and International Treaties Affecting Interstate and International Waters of the Missouri River Basin*. Omaha, May 1986.

_____. "Summary Proceedings: Conference on Missouri River Streambed Degradation, Aggradation, and Bank Erosion." Omaha, May 1986.

_____. *Surface Water Supply Including Instream Water Use*. Omaha, February 1982.

_____. *System Methods and Operation*. Omaha, April 1983.

_____. *Ultimate Development Concept in Power Repayment Studies by Power Marketing Administrations*. Omaha, May 1984.

_____. *User Guide: Missouri River Basin Water Accounting System*. Omaha, November 1983.

Missouri Department of Natural Resources. *Missouri Atlas of Water Resources*. Jefferson City, Mo., 1982.

Missouri River Basin Commission. *Fiscal Year 1981 Annual and Final Report*. Omaha, 1981.

_____. *Fiscal Year 1982 Water Project and Program Priorities.* Omaha, February 1981.

_____. *Missouri River Basin Water Resources Management Plan.* Omaha, May 1980.

Missouri River Inter-Agency Commission. "The Role of the Missouri Basin Inter-Agency Committee in the Missouri Basin Resources Development." 1950. Mimeo.

Missouri Valley Regional Planning Commission. *Report for 1942 on the Missouri Valley.* N.p., 1942.

Montana Agricultural Statistics Service. *Montana Agricultural Statistics.* Helena, Mont., 1942, 1952, 1962, 1972, 1982.

Montana Department of Natural Resources and Conservation. *Water Development Program Summary Report.* Helena, Mont., January 1987.

Montana Environmental Quality Council. *Annual Report: Montana's Water.* Helena, Mont., 1985.

Montana Select Committee on Water Marketing. *Report of the Select Committee on Water Marketing.* Helena, Mont., 1985.

Morandi, Larry. *The Great Lakes Charter: A Guide for Managing the Missouri?* Denver: National Conference of State Legislatures, June 1987.

_____. *Management Authority.* Denver: National Conference of State Legislatures, 1986.

_____. *The Missouri Basin Negotiation Process.* Denver: National Conference of State Legislatures, 1987.

_____. *Missouri Basin Water: Negotiating an Allocation Accord.* Denver: National Conference of State Legislatures, June 1987.

_____. *Water Allocation Capacity: A Description of State Planning and Management Authority.* Denver: National Conference of State Legislatures, 1986.

Mueller, Gerald. "Missouri River Hydropower and Revenues." In *Boundaries Carved in Water: The Missouri River Brief Series,* no. 13. Missoula, Mont.: Northern Lights Institute, February 1988.

_____. "The Northwest Power Planning Council: A Model for Cooperative Planning in the Missouri River Basin?" In *Boundaries and Water: Allocation and Use of a Shared Resource.* Boulder: University of Colorado Natural Resource Law Center, 1989.

Muys, Jerome C. "Allocation and Management of Interstate Water Resources: The Emergence of the Federal-Interstate Compact." *Denver Journal of International Law and Policy* 6 (1976): 307.

_____. "Interstate Compacts and Regional Water Resources Planning and Management." *Natural Resources Lawyer* 6 (1973): 153.

_____. *Interstate Water Compacts: The Interstate Compact and Federal-Interstate Compact.* Arlington, Va.: National Water Commission, 1971.

Nasatir, Abraham Phineas. *Before Lewis and Clark: Documents Illustrating the History of the Missouri, 1785–1804.* St. Louis: St. Louis Historical Documents Foundation, 1952.

Neihardt, John Gneisenau. *The River and I.* New York: G. P. Putnam's Sons, 1910.

Nelson, Bruce Opie. *Land of the Dacotahs.* Minneapolis: University of Minnesota Press, 1946.

Nelson, E. Kim. Presentation to Missouri River Assembly. June 5, 1990.

Northwest Power Planning Council. *Columbia River Basin Fish and Wildlife Program.* Portland, Ore.: Northwest Power Planning Council, 1987.

_____. *1987 Annual Report.* Portland, Ore.: Northwest Power Planning Council, 1987.

_____. *Northwest Conservation and Electric Power Plan*. 2 vols. Portland, Ore.: Northwest Power Planning Council, 1986–1991.

_____. *Northwest Energy News*. Portland, Ore.: Northwest Power Planning Council. Monthly.

O'Keefe, Mark D., et al. *Boundaries Carved in Water: An Analysis of River and Water Management in the Upper Missouri Basin*. Missoula, Mont.: Northern Lights Institute, 1986.

Onuf, Peter S. "Constitutional Politics: States, Sections, and the National Interest." In N. L. York, ed., *Toward a More Perfect Union: Six Essays on the Constitution*, 29–58. Provo, Utah: Brigham Young University Press, 1988.

"Original Jurisdiction of the United States Supreme Court." *Stanford Law Review* 11 (1959): 665.

Osterberg, David. *The Cost to Iowa of Diverting Water from the Missouri River*. Iowa City: Institute of Urban and Regional Research, University of Iowa, January 1982.

Peirce, Neal R., and Jerry Hagstrom. *The Book of America: Inside Fifty States Today*. New York: Warner Books, 1984.

Powell, John Wesley. *Report on the Lands of the Arid Region of the United States, with a More Detailed Account of the Lands of Utah*. 1879 facsimile edition; Cambridge, Mass.: Harvard Common Press, 1983.

Powers, William K. *Indians of the Northern Plains*. New York: G. P. Putnam's Sons, 1969.

President's Water Resources Policy Commission. *Ten Rivers in America's Future*. Washington, D.C.: U.S. Government Printing Office, 1950.

Reisner, Marc, *Cadillac Desert*. New York: Penguin Books, 1986.

Ridgeway, Marian E. *The Missouri Basin's Pick-Sloan Plan: A Case Study in Congressional Policy Determination*. Urbana: University of Illinois Press, 1955.

Rohde, Stephen F. "The Other Founding Fathers." *California Lawyer* 7 (May 1987): 51.

Rosenberg, Norman. "Climate Change: A Primer; Part 2." *Resources* 87 (Spring 1987): 8, 13.

Rosenman, S., ed. *The Public Papers and Addresses of Franklin D. Roosevelt*. New York: Random House, 1938.

Salkoff, M., and F. Blechman. *Mediation among States in the Missouri River Basin 1984–87*. St. Louis: Conflict Clinic, 1988.

Schramm, Gunter. "Integrated River Basin Management in a Holistic Universe." *Natural Resources Journal* 20 (1980): 787.

Schwartz, Bernard. *A Commentary on the Constitution of the United States, Part I: The Powers of the Government*. New York: Macmillan, 1963.

Selznick, Philip. *Leadership in Administration*. New York: Harper and Row, 1957.

Sharpe, M. Q. "Proceedings of the Missouri River States Committee." May 21, 1943.

Sheer, D. Presentation at the Symposium on the Future of the Missouri. May 1988.

Snow, Don, et al. "The Wet and Wild Missouri." *Northern Lights* 6:1 (November/December 1985): 7.

Solomon, Richard A. *Additional Alternative Arrangements for River Basins and Other Regions: The Federal-State Regional Government Corporation*. Washington, D.C.: Wilner, Scheiner and Greeley, 1971.

"Statement of Principles for Management of Missouri River Basin Water Resources." Draft of November 11, 1986.

Stone, Albert W. "Are There Any Adjudicated Streams in Montana?" *Montana Law Review* 19 (1957): 19.

_____. "The Long Count on Dempsey: No Final Decision in Water Right Adjudication." *Montana Law Review* 31 (1969): 1.

_____. "Montana Water Rights—A New Opportunity." *Montana Law Review* 34 (1973): 57.

Stuart, Granville. *Diary and Sketchbook of a Journey to "America" in 1888, and Return Trip Up the Missouri River to Fort Benton, Montana.* Los Angeles: Dawson's Book Shop, 1963.

Susskind, Lawrence, and Jeffrey Cruikshank. *Breaking the Impasse: Consensual Approaches for Resolving Public Disputes.* New York: Basic Books, 1987.

Swindler, William F. "Our First Constitution: The Articles of Confederation." *American Bar Association Journal* 67 (1981): 166.

Tabeau, Pierre Antoine. *Tabeau's Narrative of Loisel's Expedition to the Upper Missouri.* Ed. Annie Heloise Abel. Norman: University of Oklahoma Press, 1939.

Tarlock, A. "The Law of Equitable Apportionment Revisited, Updated, and Restated." *University of Colorado Law Review* 56 (1985): 381.

Teclaff, Ludwik. *The River Basin in History and Law.* The Hague: Martinus Nijhoff, 1967.

Terral, Rufus. *The Missouri Valley, Land of Drought, Flood, and Promise.* New Haven: Yale University Press, 1947.

Thomas, Bill. *America's Rivers: A Natural History.* New York: Norton, 1978.

Thorson, John E. "The Missouri: River of Promise or River of Peril?" In *Boundaries Carved in Water: The Missouri River Brief Series,* no. 1. Missoula, Mont.: Northern Lights Institute, February 1988.

_____. "Resolving Conflicts through Intergovernmental Agreements: The Pros and Cons of Negotiated Settlements." In *Indian Water 1985,* 25–47. Oakland, Calif.: American Indian Lawyer Training Program/American Indian Resources Institute, 1986.

_____. "Symposium on the Future of the Missouri River." In *Boundaries Carved in Water: The Missouri River Brief Series,* no. 14. Missoula, Mont.: Northern Lights Institute, February 1989.

Trelease, Frank. "A Federal-State Compact for Missouri Basin Development." *Wyoming Law Journal* 7 (1953): 161.

Underhill, Ruth Mary. *Red Man's America: A History of Indians in the United States.* Chicago: University of Chicago Press, 1953.

United Nations. Department of Economic and Social Affairs. *Integrated River Development: A Report of a Panel of Experts.* New York, 1958.

U.S. Army Corps of Engineers, Missouri River Division. "Draft Phase 1 Report for the Review and Update of the Missouri River Mainstem Master Water Control Manual." Omaha, May 1990.

_____. *Missouri River Floodplain River Stage Trends and Levee Inventory Study.* Omaha, 1981.

_____. *1987–1988 Annual Operating Plan.* Omaha, January 1988.

_____. *1992–1993 Annual Operating Plan.* Omaha, December 1993.

_____. *Preliminary Draft Environmental Impact Statement, Missouri River Master Water Control Manual Review and Update.* Omaha, 1993.

U.S. Army Engineer Division, Missouri River Corps of Engineers, Omaha, Nebraska. *Missouri River Mainstem Reservoir System, Reservoir Regulation Manual, Master Manual.* Omaha, 1979.

U.S. Congress. Letter to President Clinton. February 17, 1993.

U.S. Congress. Senate. *Missouri River Basin: Conservation, Control, and Use of Wa-*

ter Resources of the Missouri River Basin . . . (Report of the Secretary of Interior). S. Doc. 191, 78th Cong., 2d sess., April 12, 1994.

U.S. Congress. Senate. Committee on Interior and Insular Affairs. "Upper Missouri Basin Water Rights. Memorandum of the Chairman to the Committee . . . Transmitting a Legal Opinion on Upper Basin Water Rights under the O'Mahoney-Milliken Amendment." 86th Cong., 2d sess., May 1960.

U.S. Department of Commerce. Bureau of the Census. *County and City Data Book*. Washington, D.C.: Government Printing Office, 1952, 1962, 1972, 1982.

_____. *Historical Abstract of the United States*. 1942, 1952, 1962, 1972, 1982.

_____. *1987 Census of Agriculture*.

_____. *Statistical Abstract of the United States*. 1992.

U.S. Department of Interior. Bureau of Reclamation. *The Colorado River*. 1946.

_____. *Documents on the Use and Control of the Waters of Interstate and International Streams: Compacts, Treaties, and Adjudications*. Compiled and edited by T. Richard Witmer. 1956.

_____. Pick-Sloan Missouri Basin Program. Undated.

U.S. General Accounting Office. *Federal-Interstate Compact Commissions: Useful Mechanisms for Planning and Managing River Basin Operations*. 1981.

_____. *River Basin Commissions Have Been Helpful, but Changes Are Needed*. 1981.

_____. *Water Issues Facing the Nation: An Overview*. 1982.

U.S. Geological Survey. *National Water Summary 1985*. 1986.

U.S. National Resources Planning Board. *Development of Resources and Stabilization of Employment in the United States*. H.R. Doc. 142, 77th Cong., 1st sess. 1941.

U.S. President's Committee on Water Flow. *Development of the Rivers of the United States*. Washington, D.C.: Government Printing Office, 1934.

U.S. Water Resources Council. *The Nation's Water Resources 1975–2000: Second National Water Assessment*. Vol. 4, *Missouri Region*. Washington, D.C., December 1978.

Vestal, Stanley. *The Missouri*. New York: Farrar and Rinehart, 1945.

Vineyard, Jerry. "Water Planning in Missouri." State Water Resources Planning Seminar Proceedings, sponsored by Upper Missouri River Basin Association. November 1, 1983.

Volkman, John, and K. Lee. "Within the Hundreth Meridian: Western States and Their River Basins in a Time of Transition." *University of Colorado Law Review* 59 (1988): 551.

Wapato, Tim. "U.S.-Canada Pacific Salmon Commission." Address to Symposium on the Future of the Missouri River. May 2, 1988.

Warne, William E. *The Bureau of Reclamation*. New York: Praeger, 1973.

Weatherford, G. D. "Some Musing about a Compact for the Missouri River Basin." In *Annual Report Ninth Edition: Montana's Water*, 54–61. Helena: Montana Environmental Quality Council, December 31, 1985.

Weatherford, G. D., and F. Brown, eds. *New Courses for the Colorado*. Albuquerque: University of New Mexico Press, 1986.

Weatherford, G. D., and G. Jacoby. "Impact of Energy Development on the Law of the Colorado River." *Natural Resources Journal* 15 (1975): 171.

Webb, Walter Prescott. *The Great Plains*. New York: Grosset and Dunlap, 1931.

Weinberg, Edward. Remarks at "Water Forum '84: Water Issues Facing Montana." December 6, 1984.

Western Area Power Administration. *1986 Annual Report*. Golden, Colo., 1986.

_____. *1992 Annual Report*. Golden, Colo., 1992.

_____. *Pick-Sloan Missouri Basin Program Power Rate Adjustment Customer Brochure*. Golden, Colo., July 1987.

_____. *Power Repayment Study for Fiscal Year 1986: Pick-Sloan Missouri Basin Program*. Golden, Colo., n.d.

_____. *Proposed Power Rate Adjustment*. Golden, Colo., 1987.

Western Governors' Association. *Staff Report to the Governors Providing Information on the Federal Hydroelectric System in the West*. Denver, August 13, 1984.

_____. *The Western Hydro System*. Denver, October 1985.

Western States Water Council. *Indian Water Rights in the West*. Study prepared for the Western Governors' Association. Denver, 1984.

Weston, R. Timothy. "The Delaware River Basin: Courts, Compacts, and Commissions." In *Boundaries and Water: Allocation and Use of a Shared Resource*. Boulder: University of Colorado Natural Resource Law Center, 1989.

White, Gilbert, ed. *Environmental Effects of Complex River Development*. Boulder, Colo.: Westview Press, 1977.

Wiel, Samuel. "Fifty Years of Water Law." *Harvard Law Review* 50 (1936): 252.

_____. *Water Rights in the Western States*. 3d ed. San Francisco: Bancroft-Whitney, 1911.

Wilkinson, C., and E. Biggs. "The Evolution of the Termination Policy." *American Indian Law Review* 5 (1977): 139.

Wilkinson, C., and D. Conner. "The Law of the Pacific Salmon Fishery: Conservation and Allocation of a Transboundary Common Property Resource." *University of Kansas Law Review* 32 (1983): 17.

Wilkinson, Charles. "Aldo Leopold and Western Water Law: Thinking Perpendicular to the Prior Appropriation Doctrine." *Land and Water Law Review* 24 (1989): 22.

_____. *American Indians, Time and the Law*. New Haven: Yale University Press, 1987.

Williams, Albert Nathaniel. *The Water and the Power: Development of the Five Great Rivers of the West*. New York: Duell, Sloan and Pearce, 1951.

Wise and Potamkin [Committee]. *Upper Missouri Basin Water Rights. Memo of Chairman to Senate Interior Committee Transmitting Legal Opinion on Upper Missouri Water Rights under O'Mahoney-Milliken; Legal Opinion Prepared for South Dakota Water Resources Commission*. Washington, D.C.: Government Printing Office, 1960.

Witmer, T. Richard. *Documents on the Use and Control of Waters of Interstate and International Streams*. Washington, D.C.: Government Printing Office, 1956.

Wright, Charles. *The Law of Federal Courts*. St. Paul, Minn.: West Publishing Company, 1983.

Wright Water Engineers, Inc. *A Water Protection Strategy for Montana: Missouri River Basin*. Helena: Montana Department of Natural Resources and Conservation, 1982.

Wyoming Water Resources Research Institute. *Compacts, Treaties, and Court Decrees*. Compiled by P. A. Rechard and Ragsdale for series on Documents on the Use and Control of Wyoming's Interstate Streams. Laramie, Wyo., 1971.

Zimmerman, F. L., and M. Wendell. *The Interstate Compact since 1925*. Chicago: Council of State Governments, 1951.

_____. *The Law and Use of Interstate Compacts*. Lexington, Ky.: Council of State Governments, 1976.

LEGISLATION AND RELATED MATERIALS

Act of August 11, 1955, ch. 784, 69 Stat. 654.

Act of August 14, 1964, 78 Stat. 446.

Act of August 4, 1977, Public Law no. 95-91, § 302, 91 Stat. 578.

Act of January 21, 1927, ch. 47, 44 Stat. 1010, 1013, adopting H.R. Doc. no. 1120, 60th Cong. 2d sess. 1908.

Articles of Confederation. Ed. Samuel A. Pleasants. Columbus, Ohio: Merrill, 1968.

Bashore, Harry. Statement. Flood-Control Plans and New Projects: Hearings on H.R. 4485 before the Committee on Flood Control, House of Representatives. 78th Cong., 1st sess., 1943.

Boulder Canyon Project Act, 43 U.S.C. §§ 617 to 619b. 1989.

Case, Francis. House Debate on H.R. 4485, *Congressional Record,* 78th Cong., 2d sess., 1943.

Clean Water Act, 33 U.S.C. §§ 1251 to 1387. 1988.

Clean Water Act Amendments § 518, 33 U.S.C. § 1377. 1987.

Colorado River Basin Salinity Control Act of 1974, Public Law no. 93-320, 88 Stat. 266, codified in scattered sections of 43 U.S.C.

Colorado River Compact. Colorado Revised Statutes Annotated § 37-61-101. 1990. Approved by Congress in Public Law no. 70-642, § 13, 45 Stat. 1057, 1059. 1928.

Colorado River Storage Project Act of 1956, 43 U.S.C. §§ 620–620o. 1988.

Committee on Flood Control, H.R. Rep. no. 1309, 78th Cong., 2d sess., March 29, 1944, reported in 1944 U.S. Code Congressional Service, 1349. 1944.

Convention-Mexico, United States–Mexico, Art. 1, 34 Stat. 2953. 1906.

Delaware River Basin Compact, Public Law no. 87-328, 75 Stat. 688. 1961.

Department of Energy Organization Act of August 4, 1977, Public Law 95-91, § 302, 91 Stat. 565, 578. 1977.

Desert Lands Act of March 3, 1877, ch. 107, 19 Stat. 377. 1877.

Endangered Species Act, 16 U.S.C. §§ 1531 to 1544. 1988.

Executive Order no. 11658, reprinted in 1972 U.S. Code Congressional and Administrative News, 5524. 1972.

Executive Order no. 12319, 46 Federal Register 45,591. 1981.

Federal Advisory Committee Act of October 6, 1972, Public Law no. 92-463, 86 Stat. 770. 1972.

Federal Power Act of June 10, 1920, ch. 285, 41 Stat. 1063, codified at 16 U.S.C. §§ 791a–828c. 1988.

Flood Control Act of June 28, 1938, ch. 795, 52 Stat. 1215, now codified in scattered sections of 33 U.S.C.

Flood Control Act of 1944, Public Law no. 78-534, 58 Stat. 887, codified in scattered sections of 16 U.S.C., 33 U.S.C. and 43 U.S.C.

General Allotment Act (Dawes Act), 24 Stat. 388. 1887.

Great Lakes Charter. Chicago: Center for the Great Lakes, February 11, 1985.

Homestead Act of May 20, 1862, ch. 75, 12 Stat. 392.

House Debate on H.R. 3961, *Congressional Record,* 78th Cong., 2d sess., 1943.

H.R. 11958, 74th Cong., 2d sess., 1936.

H.R. 3961, 78th Cong., 2d sess., 1944.

H.R. 2203, 79th Cong., 1st sess., 1945.

H.R. 1010, H.R. 3849, H.R. 3857, H.R. 1749, H.R. 2516, S. 267, 98th Cong., 1983–1984.

H.R. Concurrent Resolution 108, 83d Cong., 1st sess, 67 Stat. B132. 1953.

H.R. Doc. No. 308, 69th Cong., 1st sess., as enacted into law by the Rivers and Harbors Act of January 21, 1927, and the Flood Control Act of May 15, 1928.

H.R. Doc. No. 238, 73d Cong., 2d sess., 1934.

H.R. Doc. No. 214, 78th Cong., 2d sess., 1944.

Indian Reorganization Act, 25 U.S.C. §§ 461 to 479. 1988.

International Boundary Waters Treaty, 36 Stat. 2448. Treaty Series no. 548. 1910.
Iowa Acts.
Kansas Statutes Annotated.
McCarran Amendment, 43 U.S.C. § 666. 1988.
Mni Sose Water Rights Coalition. By-Laws. October 5, 1992.
_____. Charter. Undated.
Minnesota Statutes Annotated.
Missouri Revised Statutes.
Montana Code Annotated.
Nebraska Revised Statutes.
New Mexico Statutes Annotated.
Northwest Ordinance, Art. 4, 1 Stat. 52. 1789.
Pacific Northwest Electric Power Planning and Conservation Act, 16 U.S.C. §§
    839–839h. 1988.
Pacific Salmon Treaty, Public Law 99-5, 99 Stat. 7. 1985.
Potomac River Compact, Public Law no. 76-93, 54 Stat. 748. 1940.
Potomac River Compact, Public Law no. 91-407, 84 Stat. 856. 1970.
Reclamation Act of June 17, 1902, ch. 1093, 32 Stat. 388, codified in scattered por-
    tions of 43 U.S.C.
Reclamation Project Act of August 4, 1939, ch. 418, § 9, 53 Stat. 1187, codified as
    amended at 43 U.S.C. § 485h. 1988.
Red River Compact, Act of December 22, 1980, Public Law no. 96-564, 94 Stat.
    3305. 1980.
Rio Grande Compact, Public Law no. 76-96, 53 Stat. 785. 1939.
Rivers and Harbors Act of March 2, 1945, ch. 19, 59 Stat. 10, codified at 33 U.S.C.
    §§ 544b, 603a. 1988.
S. Doc. 247, 78th Cong., 2d sess., 1944.
S. 1812, 78th Cong., 2d sess., 1944.
S. 2089, 78th Cong., 2d sess., 1944.
S. 555, 79th Cong., 1st sess., 1945.
Senate Committee on Interior and Insular Affairs. *Upper Missouri Basin Water
    Rights, Memorandum of the Chairman.* 85th Cong., 2d sess., May 1960.
Susquehanna River Basin Compact, Public Law no. 91-575, 84 Stat. 1509. 1968.
Tennessee Valley Authority Act of May 18, 1933, ch. 32, 48 Stat. 58, codified at 16
    U.S.C. §§ 831–831dd. 1988.
Treaty on the Utilization of the Waters of the Colorado and Tijuana Rivers and of
    the Rio Grande, 59 Stat. 1219. 1945.
Upper Colorado River Basin Compact, Public Law no. 81-37, 63 Stat. 31. 1949.
Veto message, H.R. 15444, 60th Cong., 1st sess., *Congressional Record,* 4698, April
    13, 1906.
Water Resources Planning Act of July 22, 1965, 79 Stat. 244, codified in scattered
    sections of 42 U.S.C.
Water Use Act. 1973 Montana Laws ch. 452. 1973.
Yellowstone River Compact, Public Law no. 82-231, 65 Stat. 663. 1951.

CASES

Arizona v. California. 373 U.S. 546. 1963.
Arizona v. California. 376 U.S. 340. 1964.
Arizona v. San Carlos Apache Tribe. 463 U.S. 545. 1983.
Cherokee Nation v. Georgia. 30 U.S. 1. 1831.

Colorado River Conservation District v. United States (Akin). 424 U.S. 800. 1976.
Colorado v. New Mexico. 459 U.S. 176. 1982.
Colorado v. New Mexico. 467 U.S. 310. 1984.
Connecticut v. Massachusetts. 282 U.S. 660. 1931.
Cuyler v. Adams. 449 U.S. 433. 1981.
ETSI *Pipeline Project v. Burlington Northern, Inc.* No. B-84-979CA, E. D. Tex.
ETSI *Pipeline Project v. Missouri.* 484 U.S. 495. 1988.
Hinderlider v. La Plata River and Cherry Creek Ditch Co. 304 U.S. 92. 1938.
Holmes v. Jennison. 14 Pet. (39 U.S.) 540. 1840.
Illinois v. Milwaukee. 406 U.S. 91. 1972.
Illinois v. Milwaukee. 451 U.S. 304. 1981.
In re General Adjudication of All Rights to Use Water in the Big Horn System and All Other Sources. 753 P.2d 76, Wyoming 1988.
Intake Water Co. v. Yellowstone River Compact Commission. 590 F. Supp. 293, D. Mont. 1983, aff., 769 F.2d 568, 9th Cir. 1985, cert. denied, 476 U.S. 1163. 1986.
Johnson v. M'Intosh. 21 U.S. 543. 1823.
Kansas v. Colorado. 206 U.S. 46. 1907.
Lake Country Estates, Inc. v. Tahoe Regional Planning Agency. 440 U.S. 391. 1979.
McClanahan v. Arizona Tax Commission. 411 U.S. 164. 1973.
Missouri v. Andrews. 586 F. Supp. 1268, D. Neb. 1984.
Missouri v. Andrews. 787 F.2d 270, 8th Cir. 1986.
Montana Coalition for Stream Access v. Curran. 682 P.2d 163. Montana 1984.
Montana Coalition for Stream Access v. Hildreth. 684 P.2d 1088. Montana 1984.
Nebraska v. Wyoming. 325 U.S. 589. 1945.
Nevada v. United States. 463 U.S. 110. 1983.
New Hampshire v. Maine. 426 U.S. 363. 1976.
New Jersey v. New York. 283 U.S. 336. 1931.
New Jersey v. New York. 347 U.S. 995. 1954.
Northeast Bancorp. v. Board of Governors of Federal Reserve System. 472 U.S. 159. 1985.
Northern Cheyenne Tribe v. Tongue River Water Users Association. 484 F. Supp. 31, D. Montana 1979, rev. 668 F.2d 1080, 9th Cir. 1982.
Oahe Conservancy Sub-Dist. v. Alexander. 493 F. Supp. 1294. D.S.D. 1980.
Pennsylvania v. Wheeling & Belmont Bridge Company. 54 U.S. (13 How.) 518. 1851.
Rhode Island v. Massachusetts. 37 U.S. (12 Pet.) 657. 1838.
Santa Clara v. Andrus. 572 F.2d 660. 9th Cir. 1978, cert. denied, 439 U.S. 859. 1979.
South Dakota v. Bornhoft. no. Cv 91-26-JDS-BLG. February 3, 1993.
South Dakota v. Hazen. CIV. no. A1-90-097. D.N.D. 1990.
South Dakota v. Hazen. 914 F.2d 147. 8th Cir. 1990.
South Dakota v. Kansas City Southern Industries. 880 F.2d 40. 8th Cir. 1989, cert. denied, 493 U.S. 1023. 1990.
South Dakota v. Nebraska. No. 103 Original, filed August 16, 1985.
Sporhase v. Nebraska. 458 U.S. 941. 1982.
Tennessee Valley Authority v. Hill. 437 U.S. 153. 1978.
Texas v. Colorado. 389 U.S. 1000. 1967.
Texas v. Colorado. 391 U.S. 901. 1968.
Texas v. Colorado. 474 U.S. 1017. 1985.
Texas v. New Mexico. 296 U.S. 547. 1935.
Texas v. New Mexico. 308 U.S. 510. 1939.
Texas v. New Mexico. 343 U.S. 932. 1952.
Texas v. New Mexico. 352 U.S. 991. 1957.
Texas v. New Mexico. 462 U.S. 554. 1983.

United States v. Bighorn Lowline Canal. no. CV-75-34-BGL. D. Mont., filed August 29, 1975.

United States v. Northeast Texas Elec. Co-op, Inc. 693 F.2d 392. 5th Cir. 1982.

United States v. Oregon. 295 U.S. 1. 1935.

United States v. Rio Grande Dam & Irrigation Company. 174 U.S. 690. 1899.

United States v. Tongue River Water Users Association. no. CV-75-20-BLG. D. Mont. filed August 1, 1975.

United States v. Washington. 520 F.2d 676. 9th Cir. 1975, cert. denied, 423 U.S. 1086. 1976.

United States Steel Corp. v. Multistate Tax Commission. 434 U.S. 452. 1978.

Virginia v. Tennessee. 148 U.S. 503. 1893.

West Virginia v. Sims. 341 U.S. 22. 1951.

Williams v. Lee. 358 U.S. 217. 1959.

Winters v. United States. 207 U.S. 564. 1908.

Worcester v. Georgia. 31 U.S. 515. 1832.

Wyoming v. Colorado. 259 U.S. 419. 1922.

Wyoming v. United States. 492 U.S. 406. 1989.

INDEX

269